With best wishes

Ed Walton 29/9/95.

The Bridgend - Cowbridge Union
Workhouse and Guardians

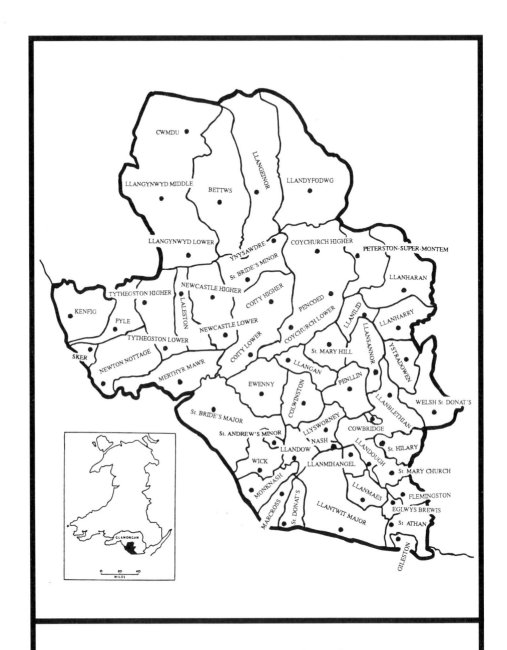

The Bridgend-Cowbridge Union
1836-1886

The Bridgend - Cowbridge Union Workhouse and Guardians

by

J. H. THOMAS
W. E. WILKINS

1995
D. BROWN & SONS LIMITED
COWBRIDGE

ISBN 1 872808 35 2

Printed in Wales by:
D. Brown & Sons Ltd., Cowbridge & Bridgend, Glamorgan

Contents

Preface

When the Bridgend – Cowbridge Union Workhouse was sold in 1985 we were encouraged by our colleagues to write its history because it had been an integral part of Bridgend General Hospital. This involved inquiring into the role of the Board of Guardians in its building and staffing, and we soon learnt that the Guardians had been more important in the social development of the community than we had realized. But although Boards survived until 1929, and Overseers of the Poor until 1925, we limited our enquiry to the first fifty years because by then the Workhouse was becoming an Infirmary. Special subjects have been dealt with separately and we hope that this will help the average reader to understand what was happening; similarly the chapter on the background.

We are grateful to many people for their co-operation, particularly Mrs. Patricia Moore and her staff in the Mid Glamorgan Records Department, Cardiff and Mr. J. Iorwerth Davies, the Chief County Librarian. The Chief Superintendent of Bridgend gave us copies of relevant photographs from the South Wales Police Museum and Mr. Geoffrey Davenport, Librarian of the Royal College of Physicians, London, supplied information about the doctors. The Archivist in Burlington House, London and the Archivist in Hobart, Tasmania, gave us the data about Mr. Bicheno who was Chairman of the Board when the Workhouse was built. Mr. Gwyn Petty produced the map of the Union's Parishes, and Mrs. Lyn Page and Mrs. Eirwen Morgan did the typing. Mr. R. D. Whitaker and the staff of D. Brown & Sons Limited were most helpful.

We hope the book will serve a useful purpose.

J. H. Thomas
W. E. Wilkins

Chapter 1

The Background

Poverty has bedevilled society throughout the ages. The term implies insufficient means to cope with the needs of daily living, but it has no fixed definition because expectation varies. Poverty to one person can be affluence to another. Housing, nutrition and clothing are the main points of reference, but there is no agreed measurement that can be universally applied to any of them because the ill, the handicapped, the young and the old need special consideration.

The peasants of ancient times were serfs to the lords, but gradually over centuries they were replaced with labourers and hired servants. When the Black Death in the 14th century drastically reduced the workforce much of the land could not be cultivated and as a result large tracts were taken over by aristocrats and Monasteries. But there still remained the landless labourers struggling for existence.

Poverty in those days was equated with destitution, and although it was accepted that support was necessary it was believed that it had to be minimal and just enough to avoid starvation. Too much was not to be given too quickly.

Monks gave alms and succour to the needy, but those living too far away had to rely on their own initiative. When the Monasteries were closed around 1539 the support ceased, and after the associated farms were sold many of the servants became Vagrants.

In an effort to control their number and behaviour the Suppression of Vagrancy Act was passed in 1597. Despite modifications it was still operative in the 19 C (Chapter 17) although public flogging had been made illegal in 1792 and no female had been whipped in Cowbridge since 1758.

This was the age of the Reformation and there were debates and counter debates on how the poor should be dealt with. Evangelists defended the unity of the family and believed that schools, hospitals and houses of correction would be beneficial. An occasional parish collected money for the poor, and the advantage of having a Poorhouse was discussed.

The view held generally was that the giving of money was an evil practice that, unfortunately, could not always be avoided. Consequently religious affairs were transferred entirely to the Church and secular affairs to the civil authorities. The conscience of kindly individuals, however, did not disappear.

Parishes increased in importance. They had existed since the 12 C as geographical units near Churches utilized solely for Church affairs, but it was now realized that they formed convenient divisions for general administration, and gradually the ancient Hundreds diminished in importance though they survived well into the 19 C. There also came the understanding that society as a whole had a responsibility for the destitute and the disabled and as a result Parliament, in 1601, passed the Poor Law Act.

By its terms Wardens collected money and distributed it among the needy. Until then they had been chosen by parishioners for the exclusive purpose of attending to the Church and its requirements, while the Clerk dealt with the Priest and the flock. Special agents assessed and reassessed the rateable value of properties, and Justices decided the rate in the pound that applied. The money thus collected was available for dispersal and naturally varied from parish to parish. Overseers of the Poor were appointed annually by each parish committee with the special duty of assuring that the sick, the 'worthy' poor and the aged were helped financially when necessary, and, together with the Wardens, they were expected to find work for the able-bodied poor and to apprentice pauper children. The relief could be in money or in kind and the recipients were known as paupers during the period they were helped. Distribution took place in the Vestry of the Church, or some other convenient centre, and a record of it was kept in the Parish Vestry Book. As the Vestry was the usual site of meetings the parish council that met there became itself known as the Vestry.

Justices of the Peace had taken over most of the duties of the sheriffs and the deputy Lieutenants who had come into being with the Acts of Union of 1536 and 1543. They were invariably members of the landed Gentry, and, as such, had considerable influence over the Lord Lieutenant who appointed them. Through their officers they supervised the state of the roads, the licensing of taverns, the maintenance of order and the pricing of agricultural produce. They interpreted and applied the law in Petty Sessions and attended to administrative matters in the Quarter Sessions. Some were members of Parliament. Their control over the social life of the parishioners was extensive.

Parliament attempted to limit claims on the parishes in 1662 by directing Overseers to return to their place of birth those incomers who were likely to become a burden on the poor rate. This restricted the movement of people to such an extent that it limited initiative. So in 1691 they replaced it with another Act which stipulated that persons had to claim relief before the law could be enacted. Six years later it was decreed that a special badge be worn by those receiving relief so that they could be recognized wherever they went – and places such as Lampeter, Aberavon, Cowbridge and Newcastle Higher eventually complied. An Act of 1781 excused them from wearing it if they could prove that their behaviour was decent and orderly and in 1810 it was repealed.

Taxation had very little effect on these unfortunates. They did not pay the Hearth Tax, but when it was replaced with the Poll Tax in 1689 labourers and farmers were not exempt if they earned over £1 a year. The Window Tax was levied around the same time and was not discontinued until 1851. Consequently many houses were built without windows – particularly in industrial areas.

Officers were unable to find work for all the unemployed in their parish so

Knatchbull's Act was passed in 1722. This allowed them to purchase buildings to be used as Workhouses by able-bodied paupers. Should they refuse to enter them no relief was to be given. Co-operation of the parishes was so poor that it was followed by Gilbert's Act in 1782. This consolidated an idea he had voiced in Parliament twenty years previously, namely, that it would be reasonable for a small group of parishes to unite and build a Workhouse if the majority of the ratepayers thought it desirable. The intention was that the buildings would become receptacles for the paupers of the parish. The remunerative tasks that would be undertaken by able-bodied inmates would be less pleasant than those obtained outside. Competition with ordinary labour would thereby be avoided and entry made uninviting. Only a few parishes co-operated, though in 1783 Llantrisant built a Workhouse that was governed by a Board of Trustees. No relief was given to non-residents and families were disrupted. There was considerable hostility in the community and Overseers of the Poor and Wardens frequently resigned.

Gilbert's Act allowed the wages of labourers to be supplemented from parish funds, and the Speenhamland agreement of 1795 indicated that the relief should be on a scale governed by the price of corn and the number of dependents. No such scale was adopted in Wales with the result that the out-door relief was either withheld or at best haphazard.

Small Poorhouses or almshouses (sometimes called Old Workhouses) were built or taken over by some parishes and used for the housing of decrepit old people, orphans, invalids and single mothers who could not, or would not, look after their children. (In 1830 the one in Coity contained two youngish families each consisting of husband, wife and several children – one of the husbands was 'mentally strange').

The religious revival of the mid eighteenth century had a great effect on the social life of the inhabitants of Glamorgan, but it did not improve the lot of paupers or limit their number.

The 'settlement' of paupers was a persistent problem and many efforts were made to clarify the position. The Act of 1732 dealt with 'bastard children'. It allowed the mother to attend a Magistrates' Court and give evidence on oath so that a Filiation Order could be issued against the putative father in order for him to support the child or contribute towards the upbringing. If the father did not comply he could be arrested and compelled.

The Settlement Act of 1794, on the other hand, dealt directly with the pauper. 'Settlement' was usually in the parish where he had been born, and a 'Settlement Certificate' could be supplied by the Vestry there, binding them to maintain him or receive him back if he became a burden on the rates elsewhere. Women, with or without children, were 'settled' in the parish of their birth or that of the husband. 'Settlement' in another parish was possible under certain conditions (Chapter 17). When the criteria did not apply the pauper was 'removed' to his last known place of 'legal settlement'. He had no right of appeal but the parish deputed to receive him could take proceedings against the Removal Order, and when this happened – which was fairly often – the legal cost to the parishes concerned was considerable.

There was no legal 'settlement' in Irish law, so people from there who applied for parish relief were 'returned' as quickly as possible to Ireland under the terms of the Vagrancy Act. The parish constable took them to the nearest seaport and a shipmaster was found to convey them home. Both were paid. (People from Scotland were similarly dealt with).

Another item of consequence contained in the Act was that the kith and kin could be made totally responsible for the pauper, or to contribute towards his support.

Inflation and depression were ever recurring problems. Both increased the number of paupers, because the dividing line between them and general labourers was narrow and rising prices or falling wages removed it. A shortage of corn in the late 18 C had a catastrophic effect because it became so expensive that buying it took half their earnings. Potato growing had not yet become popular. A 'bread riot' occurred in Bridgend which local constables, recruited by the Magistrates, were unable to quell with the result that it spread to neighbouring villages.

Income Tax was introduced in 1799. It had no direct impact on the poor, but indirectly it limited wages and increased their rent, because employers and landlords became more heavily taxed as the years went by. It was abolished in 1817 but re-introduced in 1842 by Robert Peel.

Servicing farms was the main work that was available before the full development of industry and the popularizing of shops, though many were employed in the mansions, such as the one built by Sir John Nicholl in Merthyr Mawr in 1809. He employed a butler, under-butler, housekeeper, cook, lady's maid, housemaid, kitchen maid, still room maid, laundry maid, coachman, second coachman, groom, footman, governess and a nurse. Other mansions were similarly staffed, and, furthermore, nearly every middle class family had a maid or two.

Village cottages had small gardens that were used for growing vegetables and fruit. Hens were sometimes kept but the eggs were sold rather than eaten. Salted bacon was the main protein and so most families, even in towns, reared a pig. Poaching was popular with the daring and desperate despite the rigours of the law and the presence of game keepers. Man traps were legal until 1827. The cruel gaming laws, introduced in 1671, remained in force until 1831.

Wives and children did all they could to supplement the family income. Home crafts of various kinds were practised. These ranged from knitting woollen socks to sewing flannel shirts. Women usually had one dress and men a Sunday suit that lasted a lifetime. The children – and there were usually many of them – wore ill-assorted clothes that were handed down as necessary. When opportunity arose lodgers were kept and the overcrowding that often resulted was extreme. Furniture was scarce and the most revered item that the family possessed was the Bible. Childhood mortality was high mainly because of the ravages of infectious fevers and the weakening effect of malnutrition.

Acquiring accommodation was not difficult if a cottage or a room in a lodging house was available as the rent was paid by the parish should the tenant default.

The cottages were usually owned by wealthy landlords whose money made up most of the parish funds.

The laws of the land were strict. People who owed money were sent to jail, hunting and selling game could lead to transportation for five to seven years and out-door relief could not be received until their worthwhile possessions had been sold to swell the Vestry coffers.

Industrialization was spreading in the Welsh valleys, but was slow to affect the hinterland of Bridgend. Although coal was mined in Caerau in the sixteenth century and iron ore in Cefn Cribbwr around 1780 there was no real development until the zinc spelter works were opened in Caerau in 1820. From then on there was progressive involvement of the Llynfi Valley. This attracted workers from elsewhere, mainly from the neighbourhood, but many came from West Wales or Ireland. When they became ill, had an accident, or went on strike they had to seek parish relief because they had no reserve. Most of them were 'non-settled' and therefore liable to be sent home. The terraced houses that they lived in were shabbily built and poorly ventilated. Sanitation was virtually nonexistent and the water supply grossly defective (Chapter 15).

Rents increased three fold between 1801 and 1814, and farm leases were shortened. Earnings did not keep pace with the inflation. Laws were passed to stabilize the price of corn, but unemployment soared and, to make matters worse, the weather was appalling. Production fell to such a low level that wages were reduced. Rioting took place in Merthyr Tydfil in 1816 and Henry Knight of Tythegston Court, Deputy Lieutenant of the County, was complimented by the Prince Regent on the way he handled the militia in coping with it. Local Magistrates holding their Quarter Sessions at Pyle Inn decided that lowering wages was a dangerous practice.

Industrial development led to overcrowding and disharmony between employers and workmen. Another serious riot occurred in Merthyr Tydfil in 1831 following which Richard Lewis (Dic Penderyn) – a native of Pyle – was hanged in Cardiff and then buried in Aberavon. When the cortége passed through Bridgend thousands lined the road and their mood was ugly.

The Chartist and Scotch Cattle movements hardly affected the Vale and Bridgend though a troublesome Chartist meeting was held in Cefn Cribbwr in 1839 and hayricks were put on fire in Dyffryn, St Nicholas – near which was a letter containing the words: "It is my full intention to see your house burnt to the ground, take this hint." The Gentry were so alarmed that a 'Society for the dissemination of useful knowledge among the poor' was formed in Cowbridge in an effort to allay their discontent. Education, machinery and the control of wages by market forces were discussed. Pamphlets containing the information were sent to the rural labourers but it is unlikely that they were read and understood because at best the labourers were only semiliterate. The society had about sixty members. The Marquess of Bute was its patron and Charles Redwood its secretary, but it only lasted a few months.

Some people left money in their will for distribution among the poor of their family or of the neighbourhood, and interest from such endowments continued for many years. Denominational chapels frequently contained collection boxes so that money could be given to poverty stricken members. Ministers of religion and poor Clerics organized provident societies to assist their widows and dependents, and themselves in old age, but success was limited though the Glamorgan Clergy Charity amounted to £3,521 by 1837.

Members of the public were determined to avoid 'going on the parish' if at all possible. The earlier Charities and Guilds had become largely ineffective and so they formed Provident Societies and Friendly Societies, dozens of which sprouted throughout the country. Some of the Friendly Societies were general while others were local and specific. Most were confined to men though a few were exclusive to women. By 1815 Glamorgan alone had 14,601 registered members, which amounted to about half of the adult males, but some belonged to more than one.

The population of Britain increased from eleven million in 1801 to sixteen million in 1831, of whom 80% or so were labourers, with about a fifth being paupers at any given time. Too much was expected of the Reform Bill of 1832. A separate Member of Parliament for Merthyr Tydfil and an additional member for the County were unlikely to benefit the ordinary man. Administrative changes had to come whereby central measures for improving their lot could be applied peripherally.

Consequently the New Poor Law Amendment Act was passed in 1834. By its terms three Government Commissioners were appointed centrally to supervise peripheral Boards of Guardians composed of elected representatives of all ratepayers, together with a limited number of prominent local people. Magistrates were ex-officio members. An appropriate number of parishes were to amalgamate into a Union, and a Union Workhouse was to be built. The Commissioners were to supervise its accounts, the standard of accommodation, the diet and dress of inmates and the salary of staff. Only when the Commissioners' rules were followed could relief be given to able-bodied non-resident personnel. Justices could order relief in kind, but not in money, when there was severe illness or an accident, and so could the Overseers of the Poor and the new Relieving Officers. Otherwise judgement was to be left to the Board. New instructions or orders were frequently issued by the central body.

There was considerable objections from Dissenters as shown by the contents of the numerous Welsh periodicals that were published at the time. Nevertheless the measures could be introduced because the Anglican Church, with its powerful Clerics and landowning Magistrates and Gents, were in favour.

The populace hoped that the moral, intellectual and material standards of life would be improved, and the county newspapers – the Cambrian and the Merthyr Guardian – contained repeated notices of meetings dealing with education, religion, temperance, payment of tithes, abolition of slavery and the prevention of juvenile prostitution.

Uniting the parishes and hamlets of Bridgend with those of Cowbridge was an interesting experiment. Both towns had a long history going back beyond Norman times, and both had markets and were centres of trade and commerce:

but they differed in many respects. Cowbridge was manorial, Bridgend was not. Cowbridge's hinterland was agricultural, while Bridgend's was becoming industrial.

The people in both areas were mainly Welsh-speaking and religious. When Nonconformity spread in the eighteenth and early nineteenth centuries the inhabitants of Mid Glamorgan participated enthusiastically and there were still famous authors, ministers of religion and hymn writers in the parishes. Consequently, the questions that arose were: Would Anglican dominance within the Union and its Workhouse be accepted? Would the Bible be taught to pauper children in English or in Welsh? Would denominational ministers hold religious services if requested by inmates to do so? and would it be allowed? These were important questions at the time but it is unlikely that members of the Board were disturbed by any of them.

Minor boundary changes were necessary west of Bridgend involving the separation of Pyle, Cornelly, Tythegston and Kenfig from the parish of Margam and inclusion within the Bridgend-Cowbridge Union.

The major immediate task, however, was to agree on the location of the Workhouse. Several parishes had a claim, and being largely ecclesiastic republics dominated by Squarsons (landed proprietors in Holy Orders), their claim had to be considered, but it was reasonably certain from the beginning that the centre had to be either in Bridgend or in Cowbridge. The question was which one?

Bridgend was eventually chosen presumably because the population there was increasing more rapidly than in Cowbridge due to the industrialization of Maesteg, Tondu, Kenfig and adjacent localities. There were also other reasons. One of them was that the new main road from Cardiff to Swansea went through the town and not as hitherto via Corntown and Ewenny Bridge. This was already giving a fillip to the growth of Bridgend as the main urban centre and market in Mid Glamorgan. It was also improving the facilities for communication and correspondence. Another reason was that the South Wales Railway line was going to traverse the town of Bridgend, whereas it had been rejected by the authorities in Cowbridge.

Furthermore, the leading inhabitants of that town had voiced their disapproval of the New Poor Law when it was introduced and naturally did not wish to appear to have changed their minds. Cowbridge was a County town and emporium of the Vale, and in the early 1830s was still in its heyday. Those living there hoped that its genteel tranquillity would continue undisturbed.

There were also other matters to attend to. One of them was the accurate recording of Births, Marriages and Deaths. Since 1538 Vicars and Wardens had entered such data about Anglicans in the Parish Vestry Book, but some were lax in doing so and the entries did not always tally with those in the Bishop's Transcript. Besides, emphasis was placed on Baptism rather than on Birth. Rose's Bill (1812) established a definite pattern, but even then the facts concerning Dissenters were either absent or based on hearsay. Ministers filled the gap by keeping records of their own but these were sometimes difficult to locate as several chapels could be involved. Marriages solemnized in church had been recorded since Hardwicke's Act (1753) but as very few Dissenters were married by Parsons there was a void which was overcome when Peel in 1836 permitted the service to be performed in certain chapels (Chapter 3) and in order to have a complete picture of what was taking place Registrars of Births, Marriages and Deaths were appointed (Chapter 14).

The medical treatment of paupers and poor people was, to say the least, inadequate. They relied mainly on home remedies and when these were unsuccessful obtained free medicine from a dispensary or were given money by the Vestry to pay a doctor – though some did not charge. The matter was put on a sounder footing when Poor Law Doctors were appointed (Chapter 11).

The education of poor children was another problem that had to be solved (Chapter 13) as was the care of psychiatric paupers (Chapter 16).

Administrative developments occurred centrally over the years. The Poor Law Commissioners were replaced by the Poor Law Board in 1847 under the Presidency of a Member of Parliament, with Hugh Owen, a well known Welsh Educationalist, as Chief Clerk. Then in 1871 it was amalgamated with the Local Government Act Office (part of the Home Office) and the Medical Department of the Privy Council to form the Local Government Board.

Chapter 2

The Guardians (1836)

The Board of Guardians, Clerk, Treasurer, Districts,
Acquisition of Land for the Workhouse. Relief in the Community,
"Out-door Relief", Burials.

The Bridgend-Cowbridge Union was formed in 1834, but did not function until 1836. The first meeting was at the Town Hall on 10th October of that year. There were fifty-two parishes and a representative was returned from each. They were mainly farmers, some of whom were Gentry. (The title Gentry implied ownership of a home farm or manor house and an estate containing tenants).

Prominent persons, such as Justices of the Peace and Clerics, attended when they wished. Their wide experience in local administration was invaluable. Several of them had participated in the development of the Dyffryn Llynfi Porthcawl Railway and the growth of industry in Maesteg and the neighbouring hamlets. All were landowners. Few, if any, could speak Welsh, despite its being the everyday language of the populace, and, with the possible exception of Bicheno (referred to later), were leading members of the Established Anglican Church. Most of the elected representatives on the other hand were Welsh-speaking, but it is unlikely that any of them were known Dissenters. There was certainly no objection to their being members of the Board, and it is well known that Dissenters in the early years were unacceptable to the Gentry. In Bala the Guardians threatened to resign when a Methodist was elected to the Board and there is no reason to suppose that their counterparts in the Bridgend-Cowbridge Union were more tolerant than they were. The proceedings were in English and denominational matters were not discussed.

The Chairman and Vice-Chairman were invariably Gents, and, as expected, Gents were dominant in all discussions and presented all the resolutions.

In later years the composition of the Board gradually changed as the middle class proliferated but even when craftsmen, business men, solicitors, doctors and publicans were elected to the Board, the Gentry still had the greater say. The only Minister of Religion to be elected was in 1854 and he was an Unitarian – a very small, though influential, sect at the time.

Thirteen unelected Gents were present at the first meeting. They were: the Reverend Robert Knight, John Wick Bennett, Robert Savours, the Reverend William Williams, D.D., Hugh Entwhistle, the Reverend Robert Nicholl, The Reverend Thomas Hancombe, John Nicholl M.P., R.T. Turberville, Llewelyn Traherne, Richard Franklen, David Jones and the Reverend Thomas Edmondes.

They were all well known, and their forebears had been prominent for generations – and sometimes centuries.

It is unnecessary to outline their careers because most of them have been described in local history books, but brief comments about some of those who took a leading role in the affairs of the Board may be of interest.

The REVEREND ROBERT KNIGHT, aged 47 years, was Rector of Newton Nottage and lived in Tythegston Court. He was the father-in-law of William Llewelyn of Court Colman. He had been on the committee of the Dyffryn-Llynfi Railway and had shares in the company. Apparently he had a long acrimonious argument with its clerk, because in his view the clerk was trying to wield too much power. There is also evidence that he, and Morgan P. Smith – another shareholder and later a Guardian – regularly disagreed with each other. While on the Board he was accused of having a bias against Dr. Price Jacob – the first Medical Officer for Bridgend – this was probably unjustified. Perhaps his direct manner and meticulous attention to detail irritated colleagues. Nevertheless, he was a pillar of society. When the formation of the Glamorgan Police Force was discussed at the Quarter Session in 1841 he supported the idea together with Lord Adare, J. E. Bicheno, Lewis Weston Dillwyn, Richard Franklen, John Nicholl, M.P. and C.R.M. Talbot M.P. He remained active in local affairs till his death in 1854.

JAMES EBENEZER BICHENO was a remarkable man. He was born in Newbury, Berkshire, in 1785, the son of a Baptist Minister and in 1822 was called to the Bar, serving on the Oxford circuit. He had a life-long interest in botany and was secretary of the Linnaean Society from 1825 to 1832. He then resigned and came to live in Tymaen, Cornelly. By then he was a Fellow of the Royal Society, and naturally when he came to the area he soon became friendly with local Fellows of the Society - such as L.W. Dillwyn and De la Beche.

But there was another side to his nature. He had a consuming passion to improve the lot of the unfortunates in society. When in London he had investigated the treatment of criminals in jails, and later he surveyed the poverty that existed in Ireland. In particular, he had strong views about the transportation of wrongdoers and thought the sentencing was much too harsh. In 1817 he had written a book about the Poor Laws, questioning the morality of their administration. A second and expanded edition was published in 1824.

It is not surprising that he became a Magistrate, a Guardian, and a participant in the industrial development of Cwmdu. He represented Cwmdu as well as Pyle on the Board of Guardians. He also chaired nearly every weekly meeting of the Board during the first six years of its existence.

When the Guardians met in 1836, the intended Chairman, Colonel Morgan, was absent and Bicheno, the elected Vice-Chairman at the time deputized for him. A General Purpose Sub-committee was formed, consisting of Robert Knight, William Freeman, Hugh Entwhistle, Edward Bradley, John Wick Bennett, Thomas Lewis, Richard Franklen, John Howells, William Wood, David Lewis, Christopher Wilkins, David James, Morgan P. Smith, Richard Llewelyn and Edward Perkins.

Its first assignment was to advise the Board on how many Relieving Officers were necessary and what their salary should be, bearing in mind the extent of the territory, the population involved, and the amount of out-door relief (this was defined as support to paupers living in the community rather than in an institution) that would be paid to paupers. It was also to consider whether it was expedient to appoint one surgeon for the whole area, who would give up all private practice and be resident thereafter in the Workhouse; or three surgeons, each one attending to a district co-extensive with that of the Relieving Officer. The salary that would be paid had also to be evaluated.

The Guardians met weekly and at the next meeting with John Nicholl M.P. in the chair it was decided to place a notice in the Merthyr Guardian informing the public that the Union area would be divided into three districts with a Relieving Officer and a Medical Officer for each. It was also agreed that some attention had to be given to the Welsh language.

J.E. Bicheno chaired the remaining meetings that year, apart from two, when the Reverend Robert Knight and Morgan P. Smith deputized.

The Clerk

The Clerk was the most important member of the Board's administrative staff. He received all the correspondence and, when replying, conveyed the views of the Guardians. He wrote regularly to the Poor Law Commissioners and received their instructions. All problems were referred to them for solution. Their advice and guidance were invaluable even when they did not accord with the desires of the Board.

But corresponding with local individuals and central bodies was only one aspect of his work, he also checked the accounts of the Workhouse after initial preparation by the Master and the Treasurer. He authenticated the expense accounts of the Relieving Officers, and although it was the Chairman of the Board who signed cheques to cover the running costs of the Workhouse every week, he was the person responsible for their accuracy.

He interpreted the law as it applied to paupers and sent 'Calls' to the Parish Officers informing them what their contribution should be.

When Births, Marriages and Deaths became registrable in 1837 he was made the Superintendent Registrar, and, in this capacity informed the Registrar General of all marriages in Church and Chapel as well as births and deaths in the three districts of the Union. Accurate records had to be kept because it was an important development affecting the Public Health of the country. It is then that Epidemiology, as understood today, really began.

The Clerk's organizing skill was exercised annually when he arranged the election of the Guardians in each of the fifty-two parishes.

The first Clerk, William Edmondes, was appointed at the first meeting of the Board. He was a member of a well-known and illustrious family in Cowbridge and in 1852 was Town Clerk of the Borough and Clerk to the Magistrates. His salary was £80 a year with additional money for arranging the annual election of the Guardians and for being Superintendent Registrar.

The Treasurer

Mr. William Llewelyn, agent to the National Provincial Bank, Bridgend was appointed in November 1836 with sureties of £500 each from William Morris Nicholson of Clapham Common and Philip Warren Courtney of the Inner Temple. It was decided that a bank balance of £300 would be kept in hand to cover eventualities. Contributions from Parishes were received by him and he kept the details in a book which was checked by the Auditor and Clerk.

One of the tasks given to the Clerk at the first meeting was to ask the Overseers to inform all non-resident paupers in their respective parishes, that from the 25th November out-door relief would cease, unless personal application was made to the Board on a certificate signed by the Clergyman or Overseer of the parish and one respectable householder. The 'infirmity' was to be indicated.

The Guardians then passed a resolution that it was expedient to erect a Workhouse and a sub-committee was formed to look into the way it could be expedited.

At the next meeting, on 17th October with fifty-two members present, it was agreed that there should be three districts and that the Relieving Officer of each should be between twenty-five and fifty years of age, resident in the district concerned and fluent in both Welsh and English. The three districts were to be called Eastern, Western and Northern, but the Commissioners, while approving of the divisions thought they should have specific names, so the Eastern became Cowbridge; Western, Bridgend and Northern, Maesteg - despite the fact that the latter was not a distinct parish at the time being covered by Llangynwyd Middle and Lower, and Cwmdu.

The Poorhouses of Coity Lower, St. Bride's Major, Newton Nottage, Llantwit Major, Cowbridge and St. Athan were allowed £50 each, exclusive of furniture.

The number of Medical Officers that was necessary was discussed and it was decided that there should be one for each district, but there was also a view that one doctor could attend to all the paupers, including those in the Workhouse if he relinquished his private practice. The Commissioners did not consider this to be practicable and insisted that there had to be three with the one in Bridgend attending the Workhouse inmates in addition to the district work.

Within a month the Relieving Officers, Medical Officers, Auditor and Treasurer had been appointed and the Union was a workable unit. This was no mean achievement.

On 24th October, the Clerk wrote to Lord Dunraven requesting him to sell land: "To accommodate the Workhouse and two acres, part of a field on the Wyndham Arms Farm on which the barn stands, and adjoining the turnpike road from Bridgend to Cowbridge". If Lord Dunraven refused they were going to approach other landowners, in which event they would consider a wider scope of land, on either side of the proposed site, within half a mile of the town of Bridgend.

On 21st November, having not heard from Lord Dunraven, a letter was sent to Colonel Mackworth requesting him to sell to them 'a piece of land to the north of Bridgend in the occupancy of Mr. William Thomas, Chandler, for the purpose of building a Workhouse'. If refused they would approach others.

No names were mentioned but they could have approached Turberville (Ewenny Priory) who owned about 3,300 acres, Traherne (Coytrahen) with about 3,600 acres, Nicholl (Merthyr Mawr) with 4,900 acres, Nicholl (Ham Manor, Llantwit Major) with over 3,000 acres, and possibly C.R.M. Talbot who had about 34,000 acres in all, some of them in Maesteg. The Mackworth estate was over 3,000 acres and Lord Dunraven had about 24,000 acres, but in both instances the bulk was outside the Union area.

There was no reply from Sir Digby Mackworth for over two months and in January 1837 the Guardians wondered whether the development should be on the Cowbridge Poorhouse site. Indeed, the Clerk was asked to convey a resolution to that effect to the Church Wardens and Overseers concerned. However, such a move was not necessary because agreement was reached soon afterwards and an abstract of the title of Sir Digby and Lt. Col. Mackworth to the land site of the proposed Workhouse was sent to the Commissioners for inspection on 20th February 1837.

This meant that the building would be near the Ogmore river, separated from it by the horse-drawn tram railway which had been opened in 1830 as a branch of the one leading from Maesteg to Porthcawl. The site was about half a mile long and about ten yards wide. It terminated at the coal depot, opposite which the gasworks were built a year later. When the Bridgend line opened there was great rejoicing and the company sent twenty tons of coal for distribution among the poor. Beyond the Workhouse site was the quarry owned by William Franklen and Evan Jenkins and further north, Wild Mill (Felin Wyllt Mills) and Wild Mill farm of 48 acres in which William Morgan and his family lived. There were four houses at the lower end of Quarella Road but otherwise the area was undeveloped and consisted of open fields. Before the tram railway came there was only a path along the river bank.

The Board appointed Mr. Wilkinson as Architect, Mr. Thomas Lewis as Clerk of Works, and Mr. Roberts from Chepstow as Builder.

Administrative division of the Union area into Registrar districts of Births, Marriages and Deaths now became necessary and it was accepted that they would be co-terminus with the districts already formed. As a result each Relieving Officer took over the post in his own district. Two hundred copies of the information were given to the Guardians for 'fixing on doors of different churches and chapels in their respective hamlets'.

The Clerk issued a 'Call' to the parishes and hamlets in March '37 indicating how much each was to pay. It amounted to a fifth of their annual expenditure.

The general administration was tightened. Each Medical Officer was to keep a Book in which visits and treatments were to be entered, and the Book was to be presented to the Clerk every week or 'at least monthly with a weekly abstract'. If the Medical Officer could not attend a pauper in his district he was 'to provide another Medical Officer to do so at his own expense provided such a Medical Officer was satisfactory to the Board'.

Each Relieving Officer had also to keep a special Book in which expenditure was entered, and these Books had to be authenticated weekly by the Clerk. The amount averaged £30 a week for each Officer. Comparable sums of money were then given them to cope with the following week's requests.

The money given to paupers as 'out-door relief' varied from person to person. Sometimes an accident or illness made the need an emergency as illustrated by a report in the Cambrian (5th February 1836): 'Thomas Thomas, an industrious labourer living in the neighbourhood of Cowbridge has recently been visited by a series of afflictions. His son aged 10 years died after a short illness and was buried in Cowbridge on 24th, his daughter aged 12 years was buried three days later, and another daughter aged 2 years three days after that. Though at all times heart rending to a feeling mind, sorrow when visiting a peasant's hearth has a double claim on our sympathy; poverty too often wings the venomous barb and adds a deeper poignancy to its sting'. A week later another labourer in the same village lost five children from scarlet fever leaving only one, and the reporter adds: "Latterly the hand of charity has been extended to them, not, we are sorry to say, before they much required it."

When Relieving Officers were appointed the Guardians agreed to support them as much as possible. New, non-emergency requests for relief were considered by the Board and also that given the previous week by the Officers themselves at their own discretion. This universal supervision or support was supplied during the first ten months of the Board's existence, but afterwards they limited their deliberation to the requests that were unusual.

Illustrative examples of the usual type are listed below:-

M.D.　male 71y, Penlline – continue allowance of 2/0 per week
C.W.　female, Penlline, resident in Merthyr, 2 sons (19y, 17y) – 1/0 per week.
W.D.　male, 56y, living in Clifton, wife, son 13y, daughter 21y, – no relief.
M.J.　widow, 66y, Ewenny – 2/0 per week
E.R.　female, 34y, St Bride's, 3 children (12y, 11y, 4y) – 1/0 per week.
C.J.　female, 49y, St. Bride's, 3 children (idiot 11y, 7y, 4y) – 6/0 per week.
M.O.　female, 71y, Newton Nottage, – 6d per week.
E.T.　female, Newton Nottage – burial £1.5.10d
A.R.　spinster, St. Bride's, – 2/0 per week plus pair of shoes
M.J.　female, 82y, Newton Nottage now in Morriston – 10/0 for Rev. Knight of Neath to buy clothing.
J.S.　male, 93y and wife 90y, Tythegston – 6/0 per week
L.N.　female, 83y, Colwinston now Bryncethin – pair of shoes and bedgown.
H.T.　female, 98y, Newton Nottage – 4/0 and pair of blankets
A.D.　female, 71y, Newcastle, very infirm – 1/6 per week
Bastard child of M.T. Newcastle – 1/3 per week.

The 'out-door relief' could be in money and/or kind. No particular rules were followed, but the Relieving Officers supplied the Guardians with a limited social history. It should be realized that a shilling (1/0) then would be worth about eight pounds today.

The burial expense of a pauper was the responsibility of the parish where he or she had died, but if a person who was not a pauper died without leaving enough money for the funeral, the Board paid. The name was entered in the Relieving Officer's book as if the person had claimed benefit when alive. In some Unions the Clergy were not always willing to undertake the burial ceremony. The Clerk of one of them complained to the Home Secretary about three such cases and a précis of his reply was published in the Cambrian: "A Clergyman cannot legally refuse to allow a grave to be made in the churchyard for the burial of a pauper residing in his parish at the time of death; or refuse to perform the burial ceremony until he has received a fee. He could be suspended because the 68th clause prohibits it. He has discretionary power regarding the admission of the body into the church".

The services were so brief that they were virtually non-existent. One Parson wrote many years later that four Workhouse patients could be buried in ten minutes, while an ordinary Welsh funeral took four hours.

Why a Parson was not paid a fee for the service is difficult to understand. When the Reverend William Thomas of Llangynwyd charged five shillings for burying a pauper it was unceremoniously refused, as was a similar request a few weeks later for the burial of another. On that occasion the representative on the Board was requested 'to examine the Parish Books of Llangynwyd respecting the custom of a fee being paid to the Clergyman of the parish for burials of paupers belonging to the parish'. His findings were not divulged.

Some kind of order had to be introduced so that people would know how much the Board was prepared to pay for a pauper's funeral. The costs were fixed:

Coffin – a grown up pauper	–	15/0d
Coffin – child below 10 years	–	10/0d
Shroud	–	1/0d
Dressing the corpse	–	2/0d
Digging the grave	–	3/0d
Total for a grown up person	–	21/0d
Total for a child under 10 years	–	16/0d

There was no mention of a Clergyman's fee and so it is reasonable to assume that none was intended.

Many of the paupers must have been Nonconformists but until the Burial Act of 1880 only the Anglican form of service was allowed in the parish churchyard. Permission had to be obtained from the relevant Parson before the body could be buried there. The subject was not discussed by the Guardians, presumably because such burials were not objected to.

Furthermore, the Anatomy Act which had become law in August 1832 – two months after the Reform Bill – was not applicable to the Workhouse paupers in

Bridgend as no Medical School existed in the vicinity. By that Act inmates who died alone were to be referred for dissection instead of the executed murderers that had hitherto been the case.

A list of the Guardians who attended the first meeting of the Board is appended.

List of Guardians 10th October 1836

Rev. Robert Knight, John Wick Bennet, Robert Savours, Rev. William Williams D.D., Hugh Entwistle, Rev. Robert Nicholl, Rev. Thomas Hancombe, John Nicholl, R. T. Turberville, Llewelyn Traherne, Richard Franklen, Thomas Edmondes, David Jones.

Llanharan	Thomas Rees	Marcross	Rev. John Williams
St. Mary Church	William Spencer	Newton Nottage	Watkin Bevan
Ystradowen	William Wood	Landow	Richard Sant
St. Donatts	William Evans	Langan	no return
Newcastle Higher	Jenkin Powell	Laleston	William Howells
Newcastle Lower	William Lewis	Coity Higher	Richard Llewelyn
Llantwit Major	Christopher Wilkins	Coity Lower	William Truman
	Phillip Price		Morgan Jones
Lanmaes	Richard Price	Langonwyd Middle	William Major
Colwinstone	Edward Bowen	Langonwyd Lower	Morgan P. Smith
Monknash	Edward Perkins	Cwmdu	no return
Pennline	Jonathan Howells	Coychurch Higher	Thomas Thomas
St. Athan	Llewelyn Williams	Coychurch Lower	Thomas Mathew
Llansanor	David Lewis	Landefodwg	Thomas William
St. Hilary	Henry George	St. Brides Major	Rev. J. P. Jenkins
Wick	Evan Preece	Ynysawdre	David Thomas
Llysworney	John Barnes	Bettws	Davied James
Tythegstone Higher	William Morgan	Llanharry	William Hopkin
Tythegstone Lower	Thomas Jones	Ewenny	William Jones
Llanmihangle	William Thomas	Flemingstone	John Spencer
Pyle	J. E. Bicheno	Llandough	John Sands
Llangeinor	Thomas Thomas	St. Hary Hill	Edmund Jenkins
Peterston Super Montem	Robert Morgan	Eglwsbrewis	John Davies
Pencoed Lanilid	John Howell	Llanbleddian	David Davies
St. Brides Major	Thomas David	Cowbridge	Edward Bradley
			Thomas Lewis
Merthyr Mawr	Cadogan Thomas	Kenfig	Rev. Richard Williams
Gilestone	no return		

*N.B. The original spelling has been retained.

Chapter 3

The Guardians (1837 and 1838)

Building of the Workhouse, Auditor, Out-door Relief, Overseers,
Endowments. Payment of Rent, Parish Property, Job Training,
Marriages, Bastard Children, Alterations in Workhouse up to 1861.

The yearly Elections were held in March and the names announced in April. There were very few changes in '37. Watkin Bevan was returned for Newton Nottage, John Howell for Pencoed, Bicheno for Pyle (though he also represented Cwmdu), Hopkin Williams for Tythegston Higher and Griffith Evans for Tythegston Lower. These two were new members, as was John Howell for Marcross. J.E. Bicheno was again elected Vice-Chairman.

The General Purposes Committee was reduced to thirteen members. To Robert Knight, Richard Franklen, William Wood (Ystradowen), David Lewis (Llansannor), Morgan P. Smith (Llangynwyd Lower), Richard Llewelyn (Coity Higher) and Edward Perkins (Monknash) were added William Truman (Coity Lower), John Howells (Pencoed and Llanilid), Richard Price (Llanmaes), Captain Davy (Sarn) the Reverend Watkin Edwards and the Reverend Thomas Edmondes.

This committee later became the Building Sub-committee to supervise the erection of the Workhouse, while still performing its previous function. Other problems to be considered were: how and from whom was money to be borrowed, how much should it be, how was contribution from the parishes to be arranged, and what was the best means of introducing the Registration of Births, Marriages and Deaths.

The enthusiasm and enterprise of Bicheno in the work of the Board was remarkable. He chaired forty-eight meetings in the absence of the Chairman, John Nicholl M.P. The Reverend Robert Knight, the Reverend Richard Williams, Morgan P. Smith and Richard Llewelyn chaired the remaining four.

Mr. Elias Bassett, a solicitor in Llantwit Major, was appointed Auditor in March 1837 at a salary of £16 per annum payable quarterly. He resigned a year later and Thomas Stockwood of Cowbridge was approached. He accepted the post, but resigned in May 1845 to become Clerk to the Bridgend Magistrates while continuing as Church Warden in Cowbridge. John Stockwood replaced him.

There was also a Union District Auditor. The Commissioners insisted that such a person was necessary. In fact they suggested in 1837 that one person could audit not only the accounts of the Bridgend Union District but also those of Cardiff and Merthyr Union Districts as well. The idea was not acceptable to the

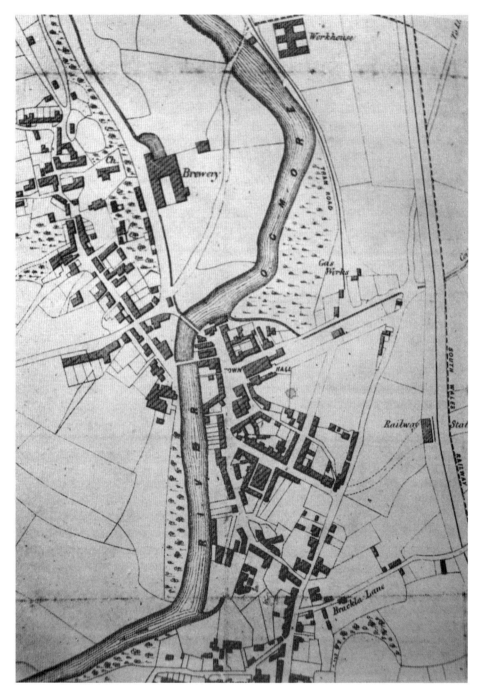

2. *Board of Health Plan of Bridgend 1848 with schematic location of Workhouse in right upper quadrant.*

Guardians and they had a combined meeting of representatives of the three Unions to discuss it. By then the Bridgend-Cowbridge Union had its own Auditor. The scheme was temporarily withdrawn, but was revived in April 1845 when a South Wales Audit District was formed and a Major Bowen appointed. He died suddenly from apoplexy in December 1853. His accounts were up to date. The Poor Law Board replaced him temporarily with Mr. Murrell, who was Auditor for the Gloucester and Monmouth Districts. He came in February of the following year, and then a Mr. Jones was appointed. His task was to oversee the accounts of the whole Union District – the Workhouse as well as the parishes. Nothing is known about him as a person, not even his Christian name. He was referred to bluntly as Mr. Jones. Perhaps the Guardians still had reservations about the post that he held. They certainly had no part in his appointment. That had been carried out by the Poor Law Board itself. He was a member of **their** staff, not of the Board of Guardians.

Provisional agreement was reached with Mr. Roberts, the Workhouse builder, at the end of April '37 and the contract was signed in July. The Planning Sub-committee had already met on the site to discuss the layout – the land having cost five hundred pounds.

The Clerk wrote to the Commissioners requesting their advice on the best way of obtaining a loan and whether it should be in a lump sum or in quarterly amounts. An application form was supplied for referral to the Royal Exchange Assurance Company, London. A loan of £4,100 at 5% interest was obtained with repayment by instalments over ten years. This was later extended to twenty years. No stamp duty was paid because it was confidently expected that an Act would be passed in the next session of Parliament declaring such deeds exempt.

Meanwhile there was a slight complication. Mr William Lewis, a solicitor at Bridgend, informed them that Colonel Mackworth was complaining that the Board had possessed the land without his tenant William Thomas' permission. He also made it clear that the Colonel expected to be paid before any further proceedings took place, and what was more, he expected the adjoining unsold land to be drained and a wall built between the two plots. Furthermore, a pool had to be constructed on the North side to replace the lower one that would be destroyed. What this pool was for is a matter for conjecture, but it could have been used, perhaps, for sheep dipping. The Board offered £20 in lieu of the pool. It was refused initially though accepted later. A dividing wall would be built in due course, so there was no disagreement on that issue. The request regarding drainage was ignored. Neither was any comment passed on the complaint of the tenant. Presumably the Guardians thought that the Colonel's agent or solicitor should have informed him.

The Workhouse building was insured with the same company, the Royal Exchange Assurance, for £2,500 with an additional £500 for the contents.

Financial arrangements with the parishes and hamlets were complicated. Not only did they have to pay a general rate to maintain the pauper service – which equalled their usual expenditure with 25% added for exigencies – but also their appropriate portion of the interest on the loan, as well as its repayment. There was also the occasional endowment to attend to. Each one had its own characteristics. In September '37 the Overseer of the Poor in Newcastle Lower referred for clarification the case of William Jones and his wife Mary, whose children had been chargeable to the parish since July 1832. It appeared that Mary had been left an annual life annuity of £10 on trust in the will of the late Father Thomas Leyshon. She had died in 1835 and the Overseer had received the money not only during her lifetime, but since. The children had not lately been chargeable to the hamlet, but relief had been given for five years. The parishioners had thereby overpaid a sum of £20 and the Overseer wished to indemnify them. Permission was granted.

The poor had no difficulty in obtaining a rented house because if they failed to pay the rent the Guardians did it for them.The accommodation was usually provided by the Gentry. Failure to provide such support would have resulted in a considerable increase in the number of homeless paupers. The first reference to the practice was in May '37 when the Overseer of Newcastle was directed 'to pay Richard Llewelyn the sum of £3 being two years' rent of a home for Evan David a pauper of that parish.' The next was for the Overseer of Pyle to pay C.R.M. Talbot £5.14.0 for two years' rent, and Thomas Porter £2 for one year 'being due November last.'

Then came a number of requests in rapid succession: four in April, fifteen in May, forty-one in June, eleven in July and three in August. By then there was consternation and the Board gave notice: 'That they would not in future afford any relief to the poor in the form of rent because the Commissioners expected them to conform with the order they had given. In future the Relieving Officers would distribute same among the landlords of the several paupers in the Union.'

In September ten rents were paid:- £4.15.0 to John Nicholl MP for three cottages in Merthyr Mawr, £3.3.0 to the Marquess of Bute for two in Llanmaes, £4 to William Williams for one in Cowbridge, £3.10.0 to John Wick Bennet for three in Laleston and £2 to the Reverend Evan Jones for one in St Mary Hill.

In October the Guardians stated that when the Workhouse was functioning 'no out-door relief would be afforded by the Board to any able-bodied person between sixteen and sixty years of age except during sickness and in cases of sudden and urgent necessity – widows with children dependent on them to form an exception to the rule'. Regarding rents they added: 'Those cases of the aged and destitute, where they have been used to have their rents paid for them, an additional allowance will be made to enable them to pay themselves.' This meant in essence that the responsibility was being transferred from the Overseers of the Poor to the Board itself.

It was not only individuals who owned such cottages, some of the parishes did as well and the Guardians were equally helpful to them. In March '38 the Overseers of Tythegston were paid £3 for the rent of two paupers, and Llansannor £3.11.0 for the two they were accommodating. Newton Nottage was given £5 in January '39 to repair two cottages in which paupers lived, while in July Llanbleddian was requested to dispose of the two pauper cottages that they owned.

When parish property was sold the money was kept by the Board in a special fund. Sales were initiated by the Commissioners, the Board, or the parish, but it was always the Board that was the focal point. In May '37 there was a request from the Officers of Coychurch Lower for the Guardians to apply to the Commissioners for permission to sell a cottage with a garden. Permission was granted. A year later it transpired that £31 had been received from the sale and that the Officers were retaining the money for the parish's use. This could not be allowed. The Board was ordered by the Commissioners to write to the Overseer of the Poor and the Church Warden of the parish to have the money transferred to the Union funds.

In the same month the Commissioners instructed the Board to sell within thirty days a 'certain property belonging to the parish of Cowbridge'. This they did by arranging for Mr John Aubrey to do so at the Bear Inn on the sixth of June between two and four in the afternoon – after advertising twice in the Cambrian and the Merthyr Guardian. A Mr Nathaniel Young bought the property and the Chairman of the Board affixed the seal on the Deed of Conveyance. The following December they were directed to pay the expenses which amounted to £5.3.0.

Only sparse attention was being given to job training of young paupers, but occasionally special efforts were made. A tailor in Llantwit Major was given a premium of £1 towards the apprenticing of a pauper for four years, and a similar sum was granted for the same period to a shoemaker. There were other instances where this was done, but in the main boys became labourers of some sort and girls maids. It took several years for them to realize that training for a job was essential if future pauperization was to be reduced, and it has to be admitted that the Guardians were somewhat tardy in accepting this reasoning.

Religion, as always, played an important part. Calvinistic Methodists had separated from the Anglican Church in 1811 and by now around seventy to eighty per cent of the populace were Nonconformists. A large number of independent chapels were built – especially between 1821 and 1838. In Bridgend alone they numbered five and in four of them the services were entirely in Welsh. The Church authorities could not ignore these developments and gradually Clerics had to accept the right of Ministers to perform secular functions. Consequently, in 1836 when Peel's Marriage Act was passed Nonconformist Ministers were allowed to solemnize marriages provided the Superintendent Registrar was informed.

The first such notice of marriage they received was on December 30th. 1837. It was entered thus in the minutes: 'A notice of marriage to be solemnized at the Ruhamah Baptist Chapel, Bridgend, under the hand of Abraham Lewis having been delivered by the Superintendent Registrar and having been entered by him in the Marriage Notice Book was read by him for the first time.' The other two readings followed at weekly intervals. (The Superintendent Registrar was the Clerk of the Board). The next notice was in the following April when a marriage was to be solemnized at Treoes, Llangan. These notices continued to be received over the years, and occasionally there were four or five together. Most chapels in the Union area were referred to and some further afield, such as the Catholic Church, Swansea, and Rock Chapel, Trelech, Carmarthenshire.

The Comptroller of Her Majesty's Stationery Office was paid £10.13.7 for the register books of the Superintendent Registrar: but the bill of £31.3.3 for the books of the District Registrars and the Clergymen of the Established Church was debited to the several parishes of the Union at the rate of 17/9 each.

At the Election in '38 Robert Bassett was returned for Llangan. It had not hitherto been represented. The Reverend Thomas Edmondes and James Reynolds were chosen by the inhabitants of Cowbridge instead of Edward Bradley and Thomas Lewis, but otherwise there was no significant change. John Nicholl M.P., who had been the automatic Chairman when present, resigned the office because of illhealth and Bicheno's Chairmanship was regularized. He thanked Mr Nicholl on behalf of the Board for the valuable assistance he had given. William Truman became the Vice-Chairman.

At the next meeting, with Bicheno in the Chair, John Nicholl was among the eleven who were present, and he occasionally attended afterwards. During the year the Guardians dealt with the building and financing of the Workhouse, the appointment and payment of its Officers, the assessment of out-door relief for paupers and payment of their rents, the collection of funds from the parishes, the supervision of Parish Overseers and the careful balancing of the Board's accounts.

William Truman chaired two Board meetings and Richard Llewelyn and the Reverend Robert Knight one each, but all the others were chaired by Bicheno. It was a strenuous, though satisfying, year. The building of the Workhouse was progressing satisfactorily and by the end of the year it was almost ready to accept admissions. A Master and a Matron had been appointed and so had the three District Relieving Officers and the three District Medical Officers.

In April '38 there was an unusual request: the Parish Officers of Cowbridge applied for repayment of ninepence which had been given to George Williams 'in conformity with a pass from the House of Correction for the City and liberties of Westminster.' The House of Correction of Cowbridge, which had been built for the housing, training and disciplining of offenders had ceased in 1829 when its function was transferred to the County Goal of Swansea. The building was then modernized to become the Town Hall though it still contained a few cells for passing Vagrants and the emergency sheltering of Paupers.

A circular was sent in July '38 to the Wardens and Overseer of all the parishes and hamlets indicating that the number of paupers on the list had increased over the year, and suggesting that they should meet the relevant Relieving Officer to see whether it could be reduced. The object was: "To explore whether any able-bodied or partially able young person, not now a child, ought to be omitted: Did any pauper have new means of subsistence by moving elsewhere? Could any children support or assist in supporting themselves? In many such case relief could be reduced or discontinued."

Revised lists for the three districts were then produced by the Relieving Officers and accepted by the Board. Similar exercises were repeated when thought necessary.

In November a claim was made on behalf of the widows of the Lower Hamlet of Coity for an annual payment of 15/0 each 'out of the funds.' The Guardians were nonplussed, so Mr Nicholl MP was asked to investigate. It appeared that three legacies had been left for distribution among the poor widows of the hamlet who were not receiving alms. One of £5.5.0 had been left by Owen Williams in July 1782; another of £5 by David Jones in August 1790; and the third, also of £5, by Thomas Redwood in May 1792. At a public Vestry meeting in January 1793 the Overseer was asked to reduce the £40 mortgage received from Charles Llewelyn for repair of the Poorhouse, and to grant fifteen per cent interest on the remainder. The money accruing had been distributed as directed by the testators. It had amounted to 17/0 each. Fifteen widows received the money in December 1793 and a similar sum had been paid almost every year since. Isaac Nicholas, the present Overseer of the Poor, had paid it in 1836. The principal was still being held by the parish.

Mr Nicholl recommended application to the Poor Law Commissioners to allow, 'with the consent of the parish in Vestry assembled' a sum of £15.5.0 from the sale of the Poorhouse to be deposited in the building fund of the Union at 15% interest, the money accruing from it to be paid to the Minister, the Warden, and the Overseer of the parish for distribution as before. If the Commissioners and Vestry sanctioned his proposal 'a memorandum of the transaction was to be signed by the Chairman of the Board, the Minister and the Church Warden of the hamlet, and a copy deposited in the parish chest, and another among the archives of the Board'. Needless to say he had seen the relevant records in the Vestry books and had studied copies of the Wills. The suggestions he made were accepted.

Soon afterwards the Board requested the Overseers to enquire in their respective division 'as to the mutual ability of parents and children to support each other.' Following receipt of the replies the Overseer of Llantwit Major was asked to apply to the Magistrates for orders of maintenance on three sons and one daughter to support their parents who were receiving out-door relief. The sum of money they were expected to contribute was indicated. It amounted to 2/0 a week for an able-bodied son, a shilling for a daughter and sixpence for a younger working person, the total being approximately equal to what the Guardians would have allowed.

The Master was instructed to go to Neath to 'procure material for twenty suits of women's clothing, and twenty suits for children, of cotton and yarn' and to arrange for 'twelve suits of each to be made up immediately with red cotton.' Shoes were obtained from Daniel Thomas, crockery from Robert Roberts and tubs from Thomas Thomas - all of Bridgend. The general fittings were fixed by William Edwards. Combs, brushes, spoons, kitchen utensils, buckets and fire tongs were also bought. The list was substantial and comprehensive.

A strange alteration was now made to the inside of the Workhouse. It seems that the room originally earmarked as the chapel had become the dining room, but it still contained the pulpit and the word 'chapel' was still present on its door. To avoid confusion they decided to move the pulpit to the schoolroom and to transfer the word chapel' to the door that was there. The schoolroom was thereby eliminated and became the Chapel. They did not consider loss of the schoolroom important because the residential teaching of pauper children was low on their priority list.

When the outside yard was paved in February '39 the Workhouse was ready, but the Board decided that it was necessary to appoint a Porter before paupers could be admitted. They evidently thought that they would be inundated with requests for admission as soon as the House opened (Chapter 13).

Bedgowns of 'cotton and yarn - manufacture of the country - and not more than a quarter being cotton' were ready for the women, but it is not clear when the first pauper was admitted. Certainly by March there were sufficient inmates for Dr. Price Jacob to be asked to attend to them.

The Board had already adopted the dietary of the Carmarthen Union Workhouse, a copy of which is attached. Analysis shows that able-bodied men had a calorie intake of 2,442 and women, 2,290, with sufficient protein, fat, carbohydrate, fibre and minerals but the vitamin content of the diet was inadequate. There was no mention of poultry, bacon, eggs, fish or fruit.

Another item deserves to be included. It is quoted verbatim from the minutes. 'Each pauper on entering the Workhouse do invariably have his or her hair cut close to the head, the head and the whole body washed with soap and water and the clothes in which they enter the House boiled. That each morning before meals each able-bodied pauper shall be duly washed from head to foot and that the hands and face of each be again washed previous to meals.'

This curt command caused annoyance, and a month later the Guardians explained that what they intended by the regulation was to have the hair cut and the bathing done in such a way as to ensure cleanliness.

Although the Workhouse had been completed to the satisfaction of the Board, and was large enough to accommodate two hundred inmates if need be, various alterations were carried out from time to time. Some of them were modifications of usage, but a few were structural. A list of them is given:-

February '39   : Separate room provided for the disorderly in which their food was to be limited to one ounce of bread at each meal.
April '39   : Bell pulls obtained.
February '40   : Privy built in Vagrants' yard.
December '41   : The pathway that had been made from the town to the Workhouse was considered by Mr John Randall, agent to the Dunraven estate, to have taken up more land than had been agreed.
April '42   : Walls around yard wired to prevent inmates scaling them so easily.
May '44   : Men's workshop partitioned to make room for 'task bones' to be stored. Part of the Probationary ward divided so as to provide a general store room.
September   : Laundry attended to and flue repaired.
October   : Old infirm male paupers to occupy empty boys' ward (open to south and airy), Female able-bodied paupers to occupy girls' yard. Old women allowed to use the garden door for transit.

October '45	: Base of chimney in boys' bedroom leaded because of 'smokiness.' Stove from kitchen taken outside and then repaired.
March '49	: Pipes laid to water closet.
September'50	: Pump and water cocks repaired. Two privies moved to a more suitable place with a cesspool for each privy 8 feet long, 3½, feet wide and 5 feet deep.
December	: Pigsties tiled.
March '51	: Chimneys in sick ward repaired.
January '52	: Casual Ward divided.
December '53	: Chimney in board room opened and repaired. Drains opened for inspection.
April '54	: Schoolroom to be used as a day room.
September'54	: Fifteen chimneys swept (6d each).
November '54	: Girls' bedroom divided to provide schoolroom.
July '57	: Locks bought for doors of store room and outer door of Workhouse padlocked with key left in custody of Matron (she was deputizing for the Master at the time).
September	: Women's sleeping room plastered.
October	: Drains and tanks cleaned (by John Davies for £2.10.0d.).
November	: Reception ward for paupers constructed within the building - and fireplace provided. Part of store room to be used for clothes, and adjoining room converted into a bathroom. Room next to the Porter's lodge became store-room. Small dining room for children provided by separation from main dining room. Smaller seats for children's privies provided. Door made in the wall of the women's yard.
January '58	: Outer wall of front yard raised three feet and iron spikes and glass placed on it. Aged women's ward converted into aged men's sick ward by changing door leading to garden into a window, and by making two windows in the opposite wall, while closing those facing garden. Store-room divided into two, 'ceiled' and plastered, and a fire place provided in order to use it as the aged women's ward. Door leading from women's yard to the garden closed, and placed on the other wall.
March '58	: New stack of chimneys built for £10.
May '58	: Steam boiler 'fixed.'
July '58	: Doors, woodwork and windows painted. Porter's room repaired. Men's bedroom and passage plastered.
March '59	: Drainage of pigsties improved.
September '59	: Men's yard covered with asphalt. Taps provided so as to have water supply in each yard. Sick wards 'ceiled' and plastered.
October '59	: New boiler bought and also new appliances for cooking apparatus.
March '60	: Drains attended to: the one passing under women's yard closed, and a new pipe drain placed in men's yard leading to grating

with men's lavatories draining into it. New barrel drain placed in boys' yard leading to tank. All pipes, drains, cisterns and chutes attended to.

Call to Parishes (5th January 1839)
Instalment towards Building fund and Interest excluded

	£ s d		£ s d
St. Athan	32.18. 6	Coychurch Higher	16.17. 7
Colwinstone	14.17.10	Coychurch Lower	12.17.10
Cowbridge	64.10.10	Cwmdu	25. 0. 0
St. Donats	11.11. 9	Llandyfodwg	9.13. 2
Eglwys Brewis	4.16. 6	Llangeinor	28. 3.10
Flemingstone	5.17. 4	Llangonwyd Lower	4.17. 6
Gilestone	1. 2. 2	Llangonwyd Middle	24.13. 0
St. Hilary	17. 6. 6	Llanharan	15.10. 0
Llanbleddian	38. 6. 4	Llanilid	19. 6. 5
Llandough	6.13.10	Pencoed	26.13. 6
Llandow	6.17.11	Peterstone	16. 5.10
Llangan	21.10. 6	Ynysawdre	7.16. 0
Llanharry	15.19. 2	St. Brides Major	95. 7. 6
Llanmaes	27. 8. 6	Coity Higher	30.14. 6
Llanmihangle	9. 3. 5	Coity Lower	57. 8. 4
Llansanan	15. 5. 7	Ewenny	29. 7. 5
Llantwit Major	49. 2. 2	Kenfig	17. 6. 6
Llysworney	14.15. 2	Laleston	12.14.10
Marcross	14.15. 2	Merthyr Mawr	9. 4. 4
St. Mary Church	13.16. 8	Newcastle Higher	9.11. 7
St. Mary Hill	14. 9. 4	Newcastle Lower	49. 8. 3
Monknash	7. 9. 4	Newton Nottage	37.19. 6
Penlline	32. 7. 0	Pyle	34. 3. 9
Ystradowen	11. 5. 2	Tythegstone Higher	19.12. 6
Bettws	27.11. 4	Tythegstone Lower	15.10. 8
St. Brides Minor	15.13.10	Wick	32. 0. 0
	550. 6.11		1210. 3. 3

*N.B. The original spelling has been retained.

Dietary for able-bodied men and women — 9th February 1839

DAYS	BREAKFAST		DINNER						SUPPER			
	Bread	Gruel	Meat	Pots	Soup	Rice	Bread	Cheese	Bread	Cheese	Soup	Pots
	Oz	Pints	Oz	lbs	Pint	Oz	Oz	Oz	Oz	Oz	Pints	lbs
Sun												
Man	7	1½	3½	1	0	0	0	0	7	0	1½	1
Woman	6	1½	3½	1	0	0	0	0	6	0	1½	1
Mon												
Man	7	1½	0	0	1½	0	7	0	0	1½	0	0
Woman	6	1½	0	0	1½	0	6	0	0	1½	0	0
Tues												
Man	7	1½	0	0	0	1½	0	0	7	2	0	0
Woman	6	1½	0	0	0	1½	0	0	6	2	0	0
Wed												
Man	7	1½	3½	1	0	0	0	0	7	0	1½	1
Woman	6	1½	3½	1	0	0	0	0	6	0	1½	1
Thurs												
Man	7	1½	0	0	1½	0	7	0	0	1½	0	0
Woman	6	1½	0	0	1½	0	6	0	0	1½	0	0
Fri												
Man	7	1½	3½	1	0	0	0	0	7	0	1½	0
Woman	6	1½	3½	1	0	0	0	0	6	0	1½	0
Sat												
Man	7	1½	0	0	1½	0	7	0	0	1½	0	1
Woman	6	1½	0	0	1½	0	6	0	0	1½	0	1

Old people: of sixty years of age and upwards may be allowed 1oz of tea, 7 ozs of sugar, 5ozs of butter in lieu of porridge and cheese for breakfast if deemed expedient to make this change.

Children: under nine years of age to be dieted at discretion.

Sick: to be dieted as indicated by the Medical Officer.

Women with children on the breast: to be allowed the same as the men.

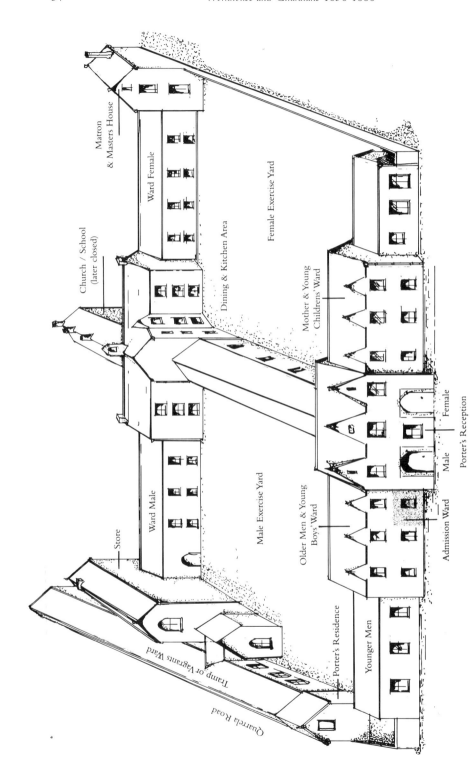

Matron & Masters House

Ward Female

Church / School (later closed)

Dining & Kitchen Area

Female Exercise Yard

Mother & Young Childrens' Ward

Female

Porter's Reception

Male

Store

Ward Male

Male Exercise Yard

Older Men & Young Boys' Ward

Admission Ward

Porter's Residence

Younger Men

Tramp or Vagrants' Ward

Quarrela Road

Schematic architectural plan of the Workhouse in the late 1840s.

Note – the top right-hand section was later demolished and replaced by the Workhouse Infirmary which subsequently became wards for the elderly.

Chapter 4

The Guardians (1839-1844)

Fraud by Overseer, Changes in Composition of Board, Temporary Appropriation of part of the Workhouse by the Glamorgan Constabulary, Departure of Bicheno (the Chairman).

At the Election of '39 two members were returned for Coity Lower, Cowbridge and Llantwit Major, with one each from the remaining parishes. Mr Bicheno was again elected Chairman and William Truman, Vice-Chairman.

The salary of the Medical Officer of Cowbridge was reduced by £10 and added to that of the Medical Officer of Bridgend because he attended to the Workhouse inmates in addition to his district work. A watchful eye was kept on the three Medical Officers, the three Relieving Officers and the Overseers of the parishes, and from time to time they were asked searching questions. Meetings were chaired by David Lewis(one) and William Truman (two) and the remainder by Bicheno.

Overseers of the Poor were not paid in early times, and because of this and the fact that the task was onerous, suitable people could not always be found. Coercion had to be resorted to and there were parishes where such posts remained vacant. Sometimes the Overseer was illiterate or dishonest and funds had been known to disappear. But in the period we are discussing Assistant Overseers were paid about £11 a year and most of them were highly responsible. The work was increasing rapidly in some parishes with the result that additional Overseers had to be appointed. Before doing so permission had to be obtained from the Commissioners. In May '39 they sanctioned the appointment of Evan Williams, Tŷ-dan-y-coed, Penlline, as Assistant Overseer for that parish at an annual salary of £6: 'For collecting rates and keeping accounts and fulfilling all lawful directions of the Board of Guardians.'

Collecting money from parishioners was not always an easy task. There was great difficulty in Coity Lower at one stage. It was overcome when the Board allowed David Jenkins to be their Collector and Vestry Clerk, provided he continued to perform satisfactorily his duties of Relieving Officer and Registrar of Births, Marriages and Deaths. He was to receive threepence in the pound from the money collected.

In October '39 the Guardians announced that they were going to enquire into a case of fraud and if guilty the parties concerned would be proceeded against. It appears that William Lewis, one of the Overseers of Llangeinor, was being accused by the Auditor of having altered receipts. The High Constable of the Hundred of Ogmore concurred. Apparently he had altered the sum due for the County rate from £5.7.3 to £5.17.3, and that to the Treasurer of the Union from £18.17.6 to £18.19.6 - and had then altered them back to the original figures.

The Board did not consider this to have been a heinous crime and thought that a reprimand was all that was necessary. The Auditor had corrected the anomalies by deducting 12/6 from the account of the Overseer and was complimented by the Board for his vigilance.

There they thought the matter rested.

The following week, however, Richard Franklen, John Nicholl MP and the Reverend Robert Knight produced a signed statement protesting against the way William Lewis had been treated, because:-

1) 'Having denied altering the receipts despite the report of the Auditor, Chief Constable and Vestry Clerk the Guardians were not justified in reprimanding him - thereby assuming guilt.'
2) 'A reprimand was a totally inadequate punishment for the offence so assumed to have been proved, and which possibly in law amounted to forgery and embezzlement. Inadequate punishment instead of deterring would encourage. Such offences were difficult to detect, but not it is feared of rare occurrence.'
3) 'The decision was entirely at variance with, and departed from the course pledged by the Board on the twelfth of October'.
4) 'Lastly - that such a decision exposes the Board to the suspicion (however unfounded) that it acted from motives of personal consideration for the individual, rather than for the principle.'

The tone and content suggest that it was John Nicholl, a lawyer, who had written it. The Board merely noted the protest and moved to the next item on the agenda, which was a request from the Overseer of Newton Nottage for permission to apply to the Magistrates for a warrant to apprehend Thomas Hardee for ignoring a Filiation Order.

The relationship with other Unions was not always harmonious. In June '39 the Board received an application from friends of a parishioner of Cowbridge, an indoor patient at the Cardiff Royal Infirmary, for an allowance 'in order for her to be able to wash herself and to have tea and sugar.' A letter was immediately sent to the House Surgeon to find our whether the 'rules of the Establishment require patients to supply themselves with these necessities.' His reply the following week was: 'The patient will be discharged next Tuesday.' The Board asked the Relieving Officer to call and assess her home circumstances.

Bills had to be paid and they seemed never ending. The main staff was paid quarterly and the tradesmen weekly. The printers, John Bird of Cowbridge, received around £8 every five or six months, and the Editors of the Cambrian and Merthyr Guardian about £5 each when their newspapers contained advertisements for posts or tenders. Lawyers were expensive: Messrs Jones,

The Bridgend Workhouse, c. 1848.

Bateman and Bennet, solicitors for Sir Digby and Colonel Mackworth, charged £21.4.4 for conveyance of the land, and William Lewis, the solicitor in Bridgend, £4.19.7 for the part he had played. Ten guineas was the fee for the loan from the Royal Exchange Assurance Company.

There was nothing unusual in the Election returns of 1840 and Bicheno and William Truman remained Chairman and Vice-Chairman. Morgan P. Smith and William Major were now taking a more prominent part in the affairs of the Board. They, the Reverend Robert Knight and William Truman chaired a meeting each, while Bicheno chaired the remainder. His enthusiasm was undiminished.

In March 1841 Mr. Betherton, of the Wyndham Arms Inn was elected for Bridgend, Mr. James Reynolds, a tailor, for Cowbridge (as before) and Nathaniel Thomas, a painter and decorator, for Ewenny. The composition of the Board was beginning to change. There were fifty-five farmers. David Howell was returned for Pyle instead of Bicheno, but, as an interested Magistrate, he remained a member of the Board and was re-elected its Chairman, the Vice-Chairman being William Major. The Gents were: William Jarrat (Lletai, Pencoed), David Thomas (Pwll-y-Wrach, Colwinston) James Evan Hughes (Newcastle House, Bridgend) William Howells (Laleston), William Wood, (Ash Hall, Ystradowen), the Reverend Thomas Edmondes (Llanbleddian), Evan Wilkins (Llantwit Major) and Richard Price (Great Hampton, Llantwit Major).

In July the Guardians were asked by the County to release a part of the

Workhouse for use as a Station House. Some supported the idea but the majority were against it. The following October, Captain Napier, the Chief Constable of the County, applied to the Board for rooms to be set aside in the Workhouse 'for the temporary accommodation, in lodging and victualling, of the new Constabulary Force about to be assembled in the town of Bridgend, for the purpose of being clothed and drilled preparatory to their being sent to their respective stations'. The request was acceded to. The right wing of the Workhouse was: "Appropriated for a period not exceeding three weeks commencing on the twenty first, with the use of a sufficient number of bedspreads and bedding and such clothing as may now be in store with such coal as may be required. Captain Napier agrees to reimburse for such accommodation at the rate of 1/6 per week for each man, and will leave clothing and bedding with the Master in a good and clean state." It was agreed that the Master be allowed to contract on his own account for the 'messing' and that 'he be allowed to use the House's cooking apparatus and coal for that purpose'.

Early in November they received a letter from Edwin Chadwick, Assistant Poor Law Commissioner, Somerset House, enquiring why the Guardians had allowed a part of the Workhouse to be used by the police. The Clerk explained that: "The men were congregated from different parts of the kingdom and sworn in on the 23rd October last. Their board and lodging in one building under the watchful eye of their superior officers would preserve discipline far better than if they had to find their own lodgings in the town. The Workhouse at the time contained only two paupers, so there was no probability that the arrangements would make the House less effectual. The Board thought it their duty to promote public service if it could be done without injury to their own department".

Captain Napier applied for two extensions because of 'non-arrival of clothing'. The first was for a week and the second for five days. It is not clear how many Constables were accommodated but it was probably thirty as that was the recorded strength of the Force two months later – the authorized full strength being thirty-four. Superintendents supervised the men and reported to the Chief Constable every twenty-four hours. They were woken at 7 am. and the lights were extinguished at 10 pm. Breakfast was at 8 am, dinner at 1 pm, and supper at 7 pm.

In December, the Reverend Robert Knight requested that the women's day room and the one adjoining be released for 'the temporary accommodation of the Magistrates of Newcastle and Ogmore for the transaction of public business.' It was allowed. One can only hazard a guess how long this arrangement lasted, but it could not have been for more than a month or two, because in March the Master was criticized for being too lenient with the inmates. There were about forty-five of them by then.

At the Election of '42 Dr. Abraham Verity (Senior) was returned for Bridgend and Morgan P. Smith (Gent), New house, re-elected for Llangynwyd. He was another of the interesting persons on the Board. He was born in Cardiff in 1779, the son of Thomas Smith, a Surgeon and Catherine Price, a relative of the famous Dr. Richard Price of Llangeinor. At the age of 14 years he inherited an estate which contained land in the parishes of Cefn Cribbwr and Tythegston. He was listed as a Surgeon in the Medical Directory of 1845, being a member of the Royal College of Surgeons. In the Census of 1851 he was entered as a Fellow of the College but this was not correct. His wife was Mary Bennet of Laleston, who was related to John Wick Bennet - a Guardian and a well known member of the Gentry. Their predecessor, Thomas Bennet, had been a Surgeon. There were no children of the marriage and he died in 1854 - the same year as his alleged adversary, the Reverend Robert Knight.

The General Purposes Sub-committee, which had also been the Building Sub-committee, was replaced with the Finance Sub-committee and the Visiting and Clothing Sub-committee. Members of the former committee were: the Reverend Robert Knight, Richard Llewelyn, Richard Price, Watkin Bevan and Dr. Abraham Verity; while the latter consisted of the Reverend H.L.Blosse and Dr. Abraham Verity. The Reverend Henry Lynch Blosse, of Newcastle Church, had recently attended Board meetings. He soon became a prominent member and took a leading role in the development of the Psychiatric Services in Bridgend. He was an Archdeacon of the diocese of Llandaff by then.

J. E. Bicheno remained the Chairman and he attended regularly until September when he left for Van Diemen's Land to be its Colonial Secretary. Before leaving he chaired a committee that assessed the rateable value of properties within the County and probably the Reverend Robert Knight assisted him with Newton Nottage, Tythegston and Pyle. He died in Hobart in 1851. A seaside resort was named after him and the two thousand and five hundred books he bequeathed to the colony became the basis of the first Tasmanian Public Library, sited in his old house. His work as a Magistrate was referred to in the Cambrian: "Lord James Stuart expressed the indebtedness of the Magistrates to their friend, Mr Bicheno. Sir John Morris, Bart, seconded." The last meeting he chaired was on the third of the month, various people chaired afterwards including David Thomas, Richard Franklen and the Reverend Robert Knight.

The Election results of 1843 showed that the composition of the Board was becoming progressively wider based. It now contained a contractor, a tailor, an innkeeper (Mr Betherton of the Wyndham Arms), an agent, a surgeon (Dr. Verity), an iron master (William Malins of Dan-y-graig House, Newton), a new Cleric (Reverend Charles R. Knight of Nolton, Chapel of Ease), and fifty-five farmers with several Gents and Esquires. David Thomas was elected Chairman.

It was realized that the Visiting Sub-committee was more important than had been previously visualized because it was essential to oversee what was taking place in the Workhouse and so they decided that the Finance Committee could take over the task while still fulfilling its previous role. The members chosen to serve on it were: the Reverend Robert Knight, the Reverend Blosse, William Malins, Richard Llewelyn, James Reynolds and Watkin Bevan. William Malins left the neighbourhood soon afterwards and was replaced by the Reverend John Harding of Coity Lower.

In 1844 David Thomas, Pwll-y-Wrach House, Colwinston, was elected

Chairman and Richard Price, Llanmaes, Vice-Chairman. Robert Charles Nicholl Carne (the Mayor of Cowbridge in 1851) became a member and was soon active in the affairs of the Board. They toyed with the idea of forming a new North Eastern district around Llanharan, but did not pursue it to fruition.

Resignations were frequent among the staff and they continued over the years. Payments from the parishes, which had been tardy at first, were now being received punctually. The Workhouse was running smoothly despite difficulties with porterage and the education of its pauper children.

Lord Adare came for the first time in July and attended irregularly during the succeeding years. This was the year the Guardians sent their first petition to Parliament. They were against adoption of the Parochial Settlement Bill by which it was intended to substitute Union boundaries for parish limits in the 'settlement of paupers.' (It is considered in Chapter 17).

Chapter 5

The Guardians (1845-1854)

Cholera, Resignation of Treasurer, Census Returns, Committee for the Removal of Nuisances, Disagreement with the Directors of local Bank, Chaplaincy.

At the Election of '45 the Reverend Arthur Deere became a new member. David Thomas (Pwll-y-Wrach House) remained Chairman and Richard Price (Frampton House, Llantwit Major), Vice-Chairman. The new Finance and Visiting committee consisted of: the Reverend Robert Knight, James Reynolds, John Garsed, William Thomas, Watkin Bevan and Rees Powell. Robert Knight, James Reynolds and Watkin Bevan gave continuity.

The Election of '46 was almost a replica of the previous year, with a few new members, such as: William Yorath (Waterton Court for Coychurch), Charles Bowring (Llynfi Iron works), the Reverend Richard Pendril Llewelyn (for Llangynwydd Middle), the Reverend John Powell (for Llanharry), the Reverend Thomas Hughes Jones (for Cwmdu), William Thomas (a Miller of Haw Mill for St. Hilary), and Thomas Lewis (Innkeeper for Cowbridge). Most of those elected were farmers, but there were eight listed as Esquires, Gents or Clerics. Two were freeholders. The Chairman and Vice-Chairman were David Thomas and Richard Price, as before.

Morgan P. Smith, at sixty-six years of age, still participated actively in the affairs of the Board. In May he proposed that a gratuity of £20 be paid to the Reverend Samuel Jones for voluntarily ministering to the inmates of the Workhouse over the previous two years. Thomas Williams seconded it. After a somewhat brief discussion the motion was 'negatived', but the Clerk was asked to ascertain what the practice was in other Union Workhouses within Glamorgan and adjacent Counties.

The Poor Law Commissioners were replaced by the Poor Law Board in 1847 and the same close contact was maintained. The removal of 'Nuisances' following the Health Act of 1848 led to an avalanche of correspondence, mainly with the General Health Board but often with the Poor Law Board. Problems relating to the education of the pauper children who were inmates were numerous and the resulting correspondence with the Education Authority was protracted.

During the year the Reverend Robert Knight became dissatisfied with Dr. Price Jacob, the Medical Officer for Bridgend, and eventually accused him of neglecting his duties. This was the beginning of a saga that had an unfortunate ending. It is considered further in Chapter 11.

There is no information regarding what happened in 1847 and 1848 but in 1849 David Thomas was still Chairman, though the Vice-Chairman had changed. It was now Leyson Morgan, Gent of Tremains, Coity Lower. The Reverend John Griffiths of Llangan had joined Thomas Edmondes and Pendril Llewelyn as elected Cleric members of the Board. Isaac Mathews (Glazier) represented Newcastle Higher, Charles Hampton (Manager of Iron Works) represented Cwmdu, Richard Griffiths (Gardener) represented Llanbleddian, and the remaining forty-five were farmers – inclusive of Watkin Bevan for Newton Nottage.

The Visiting and Finance Committee consisted of: John Garsed, Charles Hampton, Reverend John Griffiths, Richard Jenkins, Gronow John, Thomas Williams, Daniel Llewelyn, Rees Powell, James Reynolds and Watkin Bevan. The last two were becoming permanent members of the committee!

The Reverend John Harding and the Reverend Charles R. Knight were taking a leading part in most of the discussions. David Thomas, the Chairman resigned in August for personal reasons. He was thanked profusely and Leyson Morgan took over with Nicholl Carne as Vice-Chairman.

This was a worrying year for the Guardians because of the Cholera epidemic in Maesteg, Bridgend and neighbouring hamlets; and the fact that incomes in general had diminished relative to the cost of living,with the result that parishes were finding it difficult to pay their contributions. The Tithe Commutation Act of 1836 (followed by the Tithe maps of 1847) was diminishing the amount of money that was freely available in the agricultural community because by the terms of that Act the tithes had to be paid in money rather than in produce. Besides, the price of corn was not controlled after the Corn Law was repealed in 1846. There was no means of predicting how long the difficulty would last and so the Guardians decided that corrective action should be taken. The easiest way of doing so was to reduce outlay (Chapter 14).

The Treasurer, Mr. William Llewelyn, who had been appointed in 1836, resigned, and was replaced by Thomas George Smith – also an agent of the National Provincial Bank of Bridgend.

There had been no irregularity in the voting so far, but in the following year – 1850 – the Election in Llangeinor had to be repeated. The hundred voting papers that were necessary cost 7/6.

Religious services to inmates received attention and the Reverend John Harding was asked: 'to procure a dozen Bibles and a dozen Prayer books from the depot of the Christian Knowledge Society, Bridgend'. Vaccinations were paid for, 'lunatic paupers' were sent to the Asylum in Briton Ferry, and visiting paupers 'removed' to their last place of 'legal settlement.'

A letter was received from John Nicholl MP in February 1851. He was in Rome at the time. It stated that he was uncertain when he would be returning as the illness in his family was continuing. He therefore thought it best to resign as Chairman. He thanked them sincerely and wished them well. The Guardians reciprocated and hoped that his domestic difficulties would soon pass.

Leyson Morgan (Gent, Tremains) replaced him as Chairman at the Election the following year and William Llewelyn (Esquire, Court Colman) became Vice-Chairman. There were twelve Gents or Clerics and most of the remainder were farmers. Watkin Bevan was still the member for Newton Nottage. William Davies (Mineral agent) represented Maesteg, Morgan Howell (Glazier), Newcastle Lower, and Richard Griffiths (Gardener), Llanbleddian.

An ad hoc Sub-committee was convened in January to consider the 'provision of the Act regarding better management of the highways in South Wales.' The County Roads Board had intimated their intention of fixing one large district under the management of a local board, called the Highway Board. The Guardians were to consider what salary should be paid to its Chief Surveyor. They decided that £100 would be an appropriate sum.

The Visiting Committee of the Workhouse paid close attention to its sanitation, heating, 'smokiness', organization, ventilation, general appearance, upkeep and, to a certain extent, its comfort and practicality.

The number of inmates can be ascertained from the occasional comment made by the Guardians and from an analysis of the Census returns. There were only two in the House when the right wing was appropriated for five weeks by the Glamorganshire Police at its inception in October and November 1841, but there were none the previous June when the Census was taken. The two that were mentioned, Mary Thomas, aged 13 years, and Jennet M. Griffiths, aged 46 years, were registered as servants – and the latter certainly was. The two witnesses were William Edmondes, the Superintendent Registrar for Bridgend and David Woodwall Davies, the Relieving Officer and Registrar for Bridgend.

Quarella Farm nearby was occupied by John John (45 years), his wife, son, daughter and two carpenters; while in Wild Mill farm – beyond the far side of the House – there lived William Morgan (40 years), Mary Morgan (70 years), Richard (30 years), John (25 years) Ann (15 years) and John John, a labourer, aged 40 years. That was the total number of residents in the vicinity at the time, and shows that the Workhouse was almost an isolated building in a field. In July '45 there were forty-seven inmates, seventeen of whom were children (Chapter 13).

When the Census was taken in 1851 William Davies enumerated, Thomas Arnott – the Registrar – checked the population of Coity and William Edmondes signed. The number of paupers in the House was 77, but as the Master, Matron and Assistant Matron were included the total was returned as being 80. The number of children of 13 years and under was 36, eight were below a year old, five between one and two, six between two and five years, and seventeen of school age. Fourteen were over 60 years of age, with 9 over seventy. The ages of the remainder were: 13 – 19 years, 4; 20 – 39 years, 16; 40 – 59 years, 7. Twelve of the children had been born in the Workhouse. There were 15 single females between the ages of 16 and 40 years; and of the total population of the Workhouse over the age of two years, 21 were male and 28 female. The oldest inmate was a man of 82 years who had been a seaman. One woman, aged 36 years, was of unsound mind. Twenty of the adults had been born outside the Union area – 17 in Wales and 3 in England. The previous occupation of the inmates varied greatly. Most had been house servants (20 in all) or farm labourers

(6), but other occupations were also represented. Three of the inmates had been farmers, two dressmakers, one a collier, two seamen, one a blacksmith, one a malster and one a cooper.

The Workhouse was less isolated than it had been ten years previously. There were now three families in Quarella Road:- a cattle dealer with his wife and daughter; a husband and wife aged 86 years and 75 years from Ireland who were Chelsea Pensioners; and a stonemason with his widowed mother. Four families were living in Tram Road; a cattle dealer and farmer with his wife, daughter and grandchild; a superintendent of the Inland Revenue, born in Scotland, with his wife, two sons and servant; a bailiff of the County Court, born in Bristol, with his wife, son and servant; and also another officer of the Inland Revenue from Ireland, who was living with his wife, two daughters and servant.

Membership of the Guardians in '52 included David James (Dyer) for Bettws, Thomas Lewis (Innkeeper) for Cowbridge, and George Hamilton Verity (Solicitor) for St. Bride's Major. There were six Clerics – the only new one being the Reverend William Somerset for St. Athan. There were three Gents. David Thomas, who had previously resigned from the chair, still represented Colwinston. Leyson Morgan remained Chairman and William Llewelyn, Vice-Chairman.

The Finance and Visiting Committee consisted of: the Reverend John Griffiths, Reverend Thomas Edmondes, Morgan P. Smith, John Garsed, David Thomas, Gronow John, Watkin Bevan, William Major and William Smith.

Land and property liable for taxation were revalued from time to time. The Guardians decided it was the turn of Llanharry. Messrs Jones and George undertook the task for £48.15.0. Revaluation was necessary in order to adjust the distribution of the Poor Rate that was being paid by the Parish and to ascertain its amount relative to the changing population.

Four local committees were established under the authority of the Nuisances Removal and Diseases Prevention Act of 1848, to supervise the efforts of Mr Richard Sadler, Police Superintendent Bridgend, to remove 'Nuisances' and to improve the sanitation of all the parishes and hamlets within the Union – apart from Bridgend, which had been granted its own Local Board. The only parish to object was Cowbridge on the grounds that it was a Borough with its own health responsibilities. Weekly reports were received from Mr Sadler and in many instances the Board had to take legal measures. The removal of 'Nuisances' was such a major undertaking that it is discussed separately in Chapter 15.

Early in '53, Llansannor was revalued by Messrs Evan Jones and William George. They charged £20.7.6 though a map of the area was already available.

The Election results in March that year were much as before and there was no significant change in the composition of the Finance and Visiting Committee.

Difficulties arose between the Board and the National Provincial Bank, which was responsible for their financial affairs. Thomas George Smith, the Treasurer of the Bank, and their own Treasurer, wrote to say that the Bank declined to give security unless a fixed remuneration was paid. They offered £5 per annum. The following week (23 April '53) they received a letter from him stating that the Bank 'will relieve itself of their duty to the Board at the first opportunity.' The letter was referred to the Finance and Visiting Committee. On the 7th of May the Clerk informed the Board that he had offered a sum of £20 to the Bank for their trouble and that he had sent notice of this offer, with the agent's letter, to the Directors in London. They had replied: "We object to an agent of ours acting in an official capacity for the Board, but banking transactions can continue. The Treasurer should be someone unconnected with the Bank." The Board then suggested that £30 a year be paid – and thought that if the Bank accepted they would write to the Poor Law Board informing them that a new Treasurer was not necessary.

Mr Smith accepted the money on behalf of the Bank and added that if they paid the appropriate sum for the preceding five months the Bank would waive the £7 or £8 they had been charging for overdraft. The terms were considered reasonable. The Poor Law Board indicated that £10 a year would be an appropriate fee for a Treasurer – implying that one was necessary. His 'place of business could be within the Workhouse'.

The Guardians then threatened to withdraw their account from the Bank: "Because the Poor Law Board wishes us to appoint a Treasurer at terms we will not accept." Nevertheless, they advertised the post and when there was no applicant, asked for further advice. They then authorized the Clerk to call at the Bank, collect their money, close the account and take over the duties himself.

The following month the Board heard that Henry John Randall was prepared to be Treasurer. There was no difficulty about this and he was soon appointed. The salary was £10 p.a., but the penal sum that had to be guaranteed was £1500. John Randall (Agent to the Dunraven estate) and Egbert Moxham (Architect in Neath) were accepted as guarantors.

At the Election of '54 there were more changes in the composition of the Board. Hesekiah David, Innkeeper at the Ship and Castle, Porthcawl, replaced Watkin Bevan as representative for Newton Nottage, and Evan Morgan, Tydraw, Cornelly, was chosen by the parishioners of Pyle. The most surprising development, however, was the election of John Jones, an Unitarian Minister, for Coity Lower. The Cowbridge district returned two grocers, a draper, a wine merchant, a saddler, a solicitor (Charles Thomas Rhys) and the ever present Reverend Thomas Edmondes. He was Rector of Cowbridge and Llanbleddian. The family had been influential in the Borough for many years and he himself wielded great power within the County. He was born in 1806 and died in 1892. His wife was the sister of the Principal of Jesus College, Oxford and a son became the Archdeacon of Llandaff. His eldest son, Charles, at one time a curate in Bridgend, became the Principal of Saint David's College, Lampeter.

William Llewelyn (Court Colman), who was High Sheriff of the County, and Richard Jones (Park Farm) – a new member – were elected for Newcastle Higher. Cwmdu was represented by the Reverend Pendril Llewelyn and Charles Hampton (Llynfi Lodge) – a works manager. George Hamilton Verity (Sarn Fawr) – a solicitor – was re-elected for St. Bride's Major. Leyson Morgan (Tremains, Coity Lower) remained Chairman and William Llewelyn (Court Colman), Vice-Chairman.

One of the first items they discussed was the payment of a Chaplain for the Workhouse. The Reverend John Griffiths proposed and William Llewelyn, the Vice-Chairman, seconded, that a paid Chaplain be appointed, but the motion was rejected. The Reverend John Jones and William Powell did not think 'it was expedient to do so.' The payment of a gratuity of £10 a year to the Reverend Christopher Edwards for 'rendering religious services and instruction to inmates' was then considered, but the overall view was 'that a gratuity was not justified because the service was entirely voluntary.'

The Poor Law Inspector attended an inquiry into the delivery and collection of the voting papers at the Election of Guardians four months previously in Coity Higher. It was decided that a new Election was necessary.

The removal of 'Nuisances' was continuing and various publications for their guidance were received from the General Board of Health. Cholera returned to Bridgend in November, but it was not as severe as in '49 and was soon controlled (Chapter 11).

Mr. Randall, the Treasurer, resigned in December and claimed interest of £14.11.6 on 'the difference between the weekly sum he had been allowed and the £500 agreed by the Board to leave with him as a standing balance'. The Poor Law Board allowed payment of £7 'as compensation for the deficiency of the funds in his hands'.

In March 1855 Mr. Morgan Phillips, a Malster of Bridgend, was appointed Treasurer with a security bond of £2000 guaranteed by his brother William Phillips a farmer in Wick, and Thomas Loughor – a farmer in Wenvoe. The brother withdrew his guarantee in March 1858 and his mother and two cousins – Evan John and William Smith of Boverton – were accepted instead.

Morgan Phillips continued to work as a publican. In 1859, Robert Leyshon, the then Relieving Officer for Bridgend, complained about sarcastic comments made by Phillips in front of customers relating to the supply of money for the out-door relief of paupers. The Guardians told Mr. Phillips in no uncertain manner that such behaviour was unacceptable.

Chapter 6

The Guardians (1855-1861)

Suicide of the Clerk, Petition to Parliament about County Taxation, Appreciation of Bishops of Llandaff and St.David's, Census Returns 1861.

A new Cleric, the Reverend John Price (Marlas) was returned for Kenfig at the Election of 1855, but otherwise the Board's membership was much as before. John Jones, the Unitarian Minister, was re-elected and Leyson Morgan remained Chairman.

By then the Clerk, Mr. William Edmondes, was the backbone of the Board, but, on 14th April of that year the sad news was received that he had died suddenly that morning. It was announced by the Chairman, Leyson Morgan, immediately after he had presented the list of Guardians returned at the Election.

Thomas Stockwood agreed to help and John Stockwood, Edmondes' partner in Cowbridge, indicated that he was prepared to attend temporarily to the duties involved provided a replacement was found as soon as possible. An advertisement to that effect was placed in the Cambrian newspaper, the Merthyr Guardian and the Swansea Herald. But before any applications were received three local persons indicated their interest in the post. One was Samuel Cox, proprietor of the Bridgend Gas Works, and the other two were also solicitors – George Hamilton Verity of St. Bride's Minor, and Charles Thomas Rhys of Cowbridge. They interviewed the three and decided to appoint Samuel Cox. He was son-in-law to Dr. Verity (Senior) and was well known in Bridgend.

The cause of Edmondes' sudden death had been kept a secret, but by the middle of May it was generally known that 'he had died by his own hand'. Furthermore, on the nineteenth of that month the Guardians were told that Mr. Leach, the proprietor of the Lunatic Asylum in Briton Ferry, had not received the money that was due to him for the care and treatment of the Union's 'lunatic paupers' over the previous six months, although the Chairman had signed the necessary cheques. Moreover, none of the accounts had been attended to over that period, and there were many other discrepancies.

The Poor Law Board advised them to 'get a competent person to study the late Clerk's books and to update the accounts'. William Llewelyn, a wine merchant, was approached but he wanted £50 for checking the books from September 1853 onwards, as was apparently necessary. The Board considered such a fee excessive and instead accepted John Stockwood's suggestion that he would help Samuel Cox, the new Clerk, to do so.

Photograph of the empty Bridgend Workhouse in 1985 showing that it had been enlarged over the years and the old buildings on the right replaced by wards.

Five hundred pounds had been deposited by Edmondes as security. It was with the Poor Law Board, but, though a considerable sum in those days it was not enough to cover the deficiency. Consequently, the late Clerk's executors were informed that there would be a claim against his estate and that it might be considerable. A sad epitaph to a useful life.

Unfortunately little is recorded about 1856 and the Election of 1857, but it is clear that J.C. Nicholl became Chairman and William Major Vice-Chairman. At the Board's meeting on the 23rd of May the following were present: Dr. Leahy, Reverend T. M. Davies, Reverend Samuel Jones, William Llewelyn Esq, J. D. Jones, Thomas Powell, William Williams, Thomas Preece, Robert Leyshon, Gronow John, William Powell and William Llewelyn. A few of these were new members. Dr. Leahy had been Medical Officer for the Workhouse and the Bridgend District (Chapter 11).

At the meeting it was decided to send a petition to Parliament complaining about the amount of money the County was claiming in taxation, and also their method of levying it. The Guardians were 'praying for the separation of the financial from the judical duties of the County Justices; and the setting up of Financial Boards on which ratepayers would be fairly represented.' The idea had originated at a meeting of the Corn Exchange in Bedford two weeks previously. The County rate for Glamorgan had hitherto been fixed by the Magistrates at the Quarter Sessions and collected by Mr E.P. Richards, who was the County

Treasurer, and a solicitor in Cardiff. He was also the main official of the Bute Estate.

By July the petition was ready and C.R.M. Talbot was asked to present it. The gist of it was: 'The County Justices (in whom the power to levy and expand is vested) are not responsible to the ratepayers. The power of taxation without representation is at variance with the principles of a free Constitution. The method of collection is highly objectionable as the County Rates are merged in the Poor Rates and are concealed.'

The Reverend W. H. Downes, Chairman of the Vestry at Llansannor, informed them that Mathew Lewis, the Parish Overseer of the Poor, had died and that therefore an election was necessary to appoint a successor. The Clerk wrote to the Poor Law Board requesting their authorization to do so. It was obviously granted.

They sold St Athan Poorhouse (Parish Workhouse) and with the proceeds bought 3% consols with the Bank of England. (For follow up see Chapter 9).

The monthly statements of the Assistant Overseers of St Bride's Major and of Sarn were studied and seemed to be satisfactory (as were those of Coity and of Pyle two months later). This close supervision of the accounts of the parishes was a recent innovation. Returns from the parishes of Laleston and Llanharan soon followed.

Circulars were received from Dr. Hall and Dr. Michael asking them to support their applications for the post of Surgeon to Swansea Infirmary. Evidently, the Guardians' influence extended beyond the Union's boundaries! (Dr. Michael became the first Medical Officer of Health for Swansea).

The General Board of Health enquired about sanitation in Cwmdu and Mr Ranger, Superintending Inspector, was asked to investigate it.

In April '58 John Cole Nicholl was re-elected Chairman and William Major, Vice-Chairman. The Visiting and Finance Committee was larger than usual and consisted of: Leyson Morgan Esq, Reverend Samuel Jones, Reverend R. Pendril Llewelyn, Gronow John, John Thomas (Cowbridge), William Llewelyn, Robert Leyshon, James Clark, Dr. Leahy, James Brogden, John Garsed, Thomas Preece, Rees Powell, J.D. Jones and William Williams with the Chairman and Vice-Chairman as ex-officio members.

The balance in the Bank was £951.5.11¼,d in the Union's favour. At long last their financial affairs were satisfactory. They had been less so in earlier years.

A new valuation was carried out of Newcastle Lower, and Penlline was valued soon afterwards. Each parish had its turn.

Mr C.R.M. Talbot, M.P. reported that their petition to Parliament had been successful. It had been agreed that the County and Police Rates should be distinguished from the Poor Rate.

The new Clerk, Samuel Cox, soon proved himself indispensable. He was well connected with experience in the handling of financial affairs. He had successfully adjusted the finances of the Gas Works when they had become precarious in 1831. He was familiar with the stresses of business, but he soon found that work with the Board entailed more effort than he had expected relative to the remuneration that he was receiving. He consequently applied for an increase of salary, pointing out that the amount had been £80 since 1836 when the Union's population was around 18,000 and the outlay £5,000 a year. The population had now reached 30,000 and the annual expenditure £13,000, so that the volume of work was greater, and was continuing to increase.

He listed what he had to attend to: Vaccination returns, County and Police Rates for fifty-two parishes, Lunacy Acts (with heavy penalties for neglect), copying and forwarding the reports of Medical Officers, auditing every six months, making out the annual Poor Rate, corresponding with the Overseers and secretaries of the Poor Law Board, and with Members of Parliament. He was also involved in interpreting the law – much as a solicitor would.

He stressed that he had straightened out entangled accounts when he came, that there had been several changes of Mastership and that some had been inefficiently held. He claimed that his salary was only half what was paid in many places – and a third what was paid in some. At the next meeting on the 26th June 1858, it was agreed that his basic salary should be increased to a hundred pounds. A proposal that it should be a hundred and ten pounds was defeated.

The post included the role of Superintendent Registrar with payment for extra duties for which a special office in the town was rented at £5 a year.

At the Election of '59 sixty-one Guardians were returned, most of whom had served the previous year. There were six Clerics: Samuel Jones (Flemingston), R. P. Llewelyn (Llangynwyd), J. B. Price (Marlas, Kenfig), Samuel Evans (Llangan), Morgan Davies (Llanilid) and Morgan Morgan (Llanmihangel) with one Unitarian Minister – John E. Jones; thirty farmers, a freeholder, a clothier, a wine merchant, an auctioneer, a draper, a merchant, a solicitor (Charles Thomas Rhys of Cowbridge), iron master (James Brogden of Tondu), a printer and stationer, a doctor (Dr. Leahy), a metal breaker and a surveyor. The Board's composition had changed greatly since about 1840. The previous year's Chairman and Vice-Chairman were re-elected.

The first notable action that the Board took was to request their Clerk to write a 'letter of appreciation to the Right Reverend Lord Bishop of Llandaff and Right Reverend Lord Bishop of St. David's for refusing to appoint and to licence non-Welsh speaking Chaplains to jails in their diocese.' They added: "We hope the Bishops will continue to support such a righteous cause." It was a matter of great concern to them that in the past Chaplains 'who were ignorant of the Welsh language' had been appointed to County jails. The Guardians of the Merthyr Tydfil Union had the same sentiments.

Furthermore, these Guardians objected to the way County finance was being administered and a petition to this effect was dispatched to Parliament, a copy of which was sent to the Clerk of the Bridgend-Cowbridge Union. He in turn wrote a supporting petition on behalf of the Board and submitted it to C.R.M. Talbot for presentation to the House.

Another item that worried the Union's Guardians was the 'irremovable poor.' They questioned the accuracy of the list that they had in their possession and so they formed an ad hoc committee to study it. This consisted of: John Garsed, John Thomas (Cowbridge), John Lewis, John Rees, William Williams, Reverend

T. B. Davies, Robert Leyshon, Gronow John, Rees Powell and William Llewelyn. The group that they were particularly interested in was the one charged to the 'common fund' and not to the parishes.

Details of the 1860 Election were announced on April 14th. A total of sixty-three members represented fifty-two parishes. Cwmdu and Llanbleddian had three representatives each, while Cowbridge, St Bride's Major, Llantwit Major, Llysworney, Coity Lower, Laleston and Llanmaes had two, and the remainder, one. The member for Newton Nottage was Watkin Elias. The Clerics were five in number: Pendril Llewelyn for Cwmdu, Samuel Jones for Flemingston, E. Powell Nicholl for Llandough juxta Cowbridge, Morgan Davies for Llanharan and Morgan Morgan for Llanmihangel. There were forty-four farmers, including one who was a gardener and another who was a publican. There were four Gents, an innkeeper, an auctioneer, a maltster, a builder, a miller, a courier, a merchant, an engineer and a surveyor.

The Visiting and Finance Committee consisted of: the Reverend H.L. Blosse, Reverend Pendril Llewelyn, Reverend E.P. Nicholl, Reverend Samuel Jones, James Brogden, John Garsed, William Williams, Thomas Preece, William Powell, John Lewis, James Clark, J.D. Jones, Robert Leyshon, Gronow John, John Thomas and David Jenkins.

In May they discussed the need to 'secure the road to the Workhouse in the event of the Bridgend Railway being closed,' but as the Llynfi Valley Railway Company had not yet taken possession of it, they decided that 'it was premature to negotiate.'

The garden yielded potatoes worth £8.4.3¾ d and well justified its up-keep because plant seeds and the work involved only cost £2.16.9d. There were four funerals that month costing a total of £5.8.0d. These data illustrate the meticulous care that was being taken of the accounts.

In early 1861 the Poor Law Board asked Thilman Thomas, a newly appointed Assistant Overseer for St Athan, to resign because he had not given the required security to the Guardians. On the other hand, James Reynolds of Cowbridge, Assistant Overseer for the parish of Llanbleddian, at a salary of £18 a year, was acceptable because Thomas Nicholas (Timber Merchant in Cowbridge) and Thomas Reynolds (Ironmonger in Caerphilly) had agreed to be sureties for him 'with a bond of £200.' It is clear that the finances of the parishes and also their Officers were being constantly checked. The Board's control of such affairs was firm and decisions made, irreversible.

The usual annual General Election of Guardians 'conforming with the order of the Poor Law Board' was held in March and the Clerk was paid £15 for organizing it. There were a few changes. The Clerics now consisted of: Walter Evans (Marlas, Kenfig), Edward Powell Nicholl (Llandough), Rees Pritchard (Garth Hall for Llandyfodwg), Thomas M. Davies (Llanilid Rectory for Llanharan), Lewis Thomas (Cross House for St Hilary), R. Pendril Llewelyn (Llangynwyd Vicarage for Cwmdu) and Samuel Jones (Llandough Cottage for Flemingston); The Gents were: Charles Drummond (Laleston), William Griffiths (Llanharry), John Garsed (Llantwit Major) and Richard Franklen

(Clemenston). The last on the list had been a prominent member of the Board since its inception. He was born in 1801 and died in 1882. His father was Thomas Franklen and his mother was Anne – the daughter of Richard Crawshay (the Iron King of Cyfarthfa). He was thus a cousin of Sir Benjamin Hall III (of 'Big Ben' fame) who was President of the Board of Health in 1854 and later the Minister of Works. Franklen was High Sheriff of Glamorgan in 1846. He married the fifth daughter of Thomas Mansel Talbot of Margam thereby becoming the brother-in-Law of C.R.M. Talbot and of John Nicholl. Forty-two farmers were elected with an auctioneer, a draper, a malster, a contractor, two millers, and an iron master (James Brogden), a courier and a surveyor.

The Census returns of April 1861, witnessed and checked by Isaiah Lewis, Richard Leyshon and Samuel Cox, showed that the total number of inmates had not changed. It was now 78 (compared with 77 in '51), and consisted of 36 males and 42 females. Closer inspection, however, pin-pointed differences that were in keeping with the improvement in transport since the main railway had come to Bridgend in 1851, and with the longer existence of the Workhouse itself. Thirteen of the inmates had been born outside Wales – seven in Ireland – compared with three in 1851 (2 in Bristol) and none in Ireland. Of the seven born in Ireland 5 were adults and two children. They were aged 9 years and 7 years and were probably brothers, but their parents were not inmates. The number born in Wales, was almost equal – 17 in '51 compared with 20 in '61, but when those born outside Wales are included there were 20 in '51 (2 being children) and 33 in '61, of whom 12 were children. Analysis of the children also showed differences although their total number was similar. The disturbing fact was that more of those born in the Workhouse had not left. In '51 there were two between 2 years and 5 years but no one older, whereas in '61 there were 5 over 2 years and 3 over 5 years – one being 8 years of age and 2 were twelve years old. Twelve babies were entered as having been born in the Bridgend Workhouse in '51 and 10 in '61, but an additional 3 had been born in the Cardiff Workhouse. Five of the older children had a brother or a sister in the House, but it was difficult to decide whether their parents were there as well because the same surname was frequently repeated. It is unfortunate that all the children were grouped together separate from the adults. There were 14 over 60 years of age in '51 as against 10 in '61, but they were older. One, a male hawker born in Llanelly, was 91 years of age and there were others aged 83 years, 84 years and 86 years. The occupation that was entered varied, but, as in '51, general labouring (8) and serving in a house (13) were the most common. Three had been masons, one a blacksmith, one a carpenter, one a collier and one a sieve maker. One female was the wife of a seaman, another the wife of a moulder and one lady, aged 86 years, born in Llandaff, was the widow of a landed proprietor. There were two hawkers, one already mentioned was from Llanelly, and the other, a widow of 42 years, had been born in Middlesex. There was only one dressmaker. It was surprising to find that one pauper, a married man of 59 years of age, had been a Police Superintendent in Ireland. One single female of 27 years was an 'idiot' from Bridgend.

The Master, James Wells, a widower aged 39 years had been born in Surrey; the Matron, a widow 45 years old had been born in Oxfordshire, and Mrs Jane Warnum the Schoolmistress, aged 31 years, was born in Middlesex.

Evidently the Workhouse, which in 1841 had been occupied by mainly local people had by 1861 become more cosmopolitan.

The sum of money requested from the many parishes varied with their population. In June it was £201 from Coity Lower, £198 from Cwmdu, £110 from Llantwit Major, but only £4 pounds from Flemingston. The total rate paid to Mr E.P. Richards was £1067.11.11, and £124.10.0 was obtained from the Paymaster General towards the salaries of Medical Officers and Schoolmistress.

In October they decided to reconsider Porterage for the House as there had been no official Porter since 1845 (Chapter 13). Evan Jones and later Evan Lloyd had acted in that capacity, but they were both inmates and the employment of such persons in an official capacity was prohibited. However, after a brief discussion they decided to leave the matter in abeyance.

Memorabilia of Old Workhouse. Photograph of Plaque taken 1985.

Probably the original Workhouse Clock – still in the possession of the Hospital. Clockmaker: Samuel Marks of Cowbridge (1835-44).

Chapter 7

The Guardians (1862 – 1871)

Formation of Assessment and Visiting Committees, Resident and Non-resident Poor, Burials, Calls, Drainage and improvements to Workhouse, Union Boundary Changes, Resignation of Treasurer, Future of Bridgend Tramway.

It was believed by the Board in May 1862 that the Overseer of Nash had misappropriated funds and so Robert Charles Nicholl Carne was requested to "institute proceedings to have the money recovered". They claimed that parish money "had not been handed over". This was denied by the Overseer and he left soon afterwards. The Magistrates in Cowbridge refused to issue a warrant or levy the amount, and the Poor Law Board was not contacted, so there must have been confusion about the affair.

The "Calls" in October showed that the sum requested from Cwmdu had increased to £331 – while Flemingston remained at £4.

In May '63 they received a circular from the P.L.B. drawing attention to the Herbert Bill by which the Irish Poor Law Authorities had been given the same power regarding destitute Irish born in Great Britain and resident in Ireland, as British authorities had on destitute Irish born in Ireland and resident here. The same applied to Scotland. In both countries there would now be the categories of resident and non-resident poor.

The money paid by Unions for their non-resident poor was considerable. In June the Bridgend-Cowbridge Union received £11.10.2d from Pontypridd for the previous quarter, £15.1.6d from Merthyr, £1.12.6d from Newton Abbot, £28.3.2d from Neath, £5.5.6d from Swansea, £2.7.11d from Bristol and £1.19.0d from Newport. The district rate for the Workhouse at 1/0d in the £1 was £6.11.3d and this sum was paid to James Brooke, Clerk to the Bridgend Local Board of Health.

A David Howell of Newcastle Higher, discharged from the Briton Ferry Asylum in June at the request of the Visitors, was proceeded against a month later for neglecting to maintain his wife and two children aged 5 years and 2 years. This illustrates the speed, and perhaps the lack of consideration, with which they sometimes acted. At the same time a nearby mother and her child were 'removed' to Ireland (Chapter 17).

A suggestion that Board meetings should be held fortnightly instead of weekly was debated in August. Many supported the idea, but when it came to the vote there were 14 against and 10 for so the meetings continued to be held weekly. This enabled the agenda to be more manageable than would have been the case had the meetings been held fortnightly.

The front of the Workhouse in 1985 showing the male entrance on the left and the female on the right. The plaque that has 'Bridgend and Cowbridge Union' written on it is visible in the centre.

Consideration was given to the collecting of money from the inhabitants of Maesteg and it was proposed by Gronow John that William Powell, the Assistant Overseer, be appointed Collector of the Board at an annual salary of £75 paid quarterly. This was accepted, with David Phillips and Illtyd Morgan being insurers for £500.

The Treasurer, Morgan Phillips, appointed in 1855, resigned in October 1863 and the Guardians requested that all the accounts be handed over forthwith to their Clerk. William Llewellyn, Manager of the Bank of Wales, Bridgend wrote to them saying that his bank would honour cheques until the new appointment was made. He added that Thomas George Smith, Manager of the National Provincial Bank, might apply.

Among the 47 Guardians present at the meeting on 17th October were the Rev. Lynch Blosse, Rev. C. R. Knight, E. P. Nicholl, Richard Franklen, J. R. Homfray, William Llewelyn, James Brogden, Major Traherne, Dr. Leahy, W. B. Popkin, John Garsed, Gronow John, Watkin Bevan and William Yorath. They appointed William Llewelyn, as Treasurer, with a security of £2,500 guaranteed by J. N. Daniel (Chairman of the Alliance Bank London and Liverpool) and J. W. Johns (Director of the Oswestry Newtown Mid-Wales Railway). He indicated that the Dean of St David's and the Rector of Coychurch were prepared to be sureties if they preferred local personnel. They did not think that this was necessary. William Smith of Boverton, being a surety for the Treasurer, paid £800 on his behalf "to balance the books".

At the same meeting, Richard Franklen, who had always been an active member, announced his retirement. This was regretfully accepted and it was decided that Theodore Mansel Talbot be approached to take his place.

In April '64 the Clerk of the Pontypridd Union wrote to them enclosing a copy of a petition they had sent to Parliament praying for "alteration in the law which exempted certain mines from liability to Poor Law assessment". It was supported. The Board of Guardians frequently dealt with such matters of County or of National importance, but mundane problems had also to be attended to, such as the issuing of proceedings against a son in Coity Higher for "neglecting to support his father since January", and requesting the Neath Union to give 3/6d weekly (on account) to a pauper from Cowbridge who was residing in Llangynwyd Higher.

At the annual Election W. B. Popkin (Chemist, Fairfield House) and George Taylor (Clerk, Glan Llynfi) were chosen for Cwmdu; Thomas Powell (Farmer, Tongwyn) and Benjamin Price (Farmer, West House) for Newcastle Higher; William Davies (Grocer) for Newcastle Lower; Watkin Bevan (Farmer) for Newton Nottage; John Griffiths (Bear Inn) and John Lewis (Heronstone) for Coity Lower; and Dr Leahy (Newcastle) for Ynysawdre. William Davies and Leyshon Morgan (Tremains) refused to serve. Of the 66 elected 45 were farmers. There was no nomination for Llandyfodwg, Nash, St Andrew's Minor, Sker or Tythegston Lower. J. C. Nicholl was re-elected Chairman with John Garsed as Vice-Chairman, the previous holder, William Major being thanked.

The Visiting and Finance Committee consisted of the Chairman, Vice-Chairman and 19 others among whom were the Rev. Lynch Blosse and C. Lloyd Llewelyn, W. B. Popkin, Benjamin Price and Gronow John.

An Assessment Committee (for the rates) was also formed as delineated in the Assessment Act 1862. Members of it were the Chairman and 11 Guardians, inclusive of the Rev. C. R. Knight, Robert Leyshon and William Major. The Parish Overseers were to submit fresh yearly valuations, and Tithe Assessment was to be included. Railways and Ironworks were to be assessed but Collieries and Electric Telegraph had not yet been finalized. They requested sanction from the P.L.B. to pay its Clerk £45 a year with £5 out-of-pocket expenses. This committee became an important separate entity and it was evident from its inception that the duties would be onerous. William Llewelyn, Court Colman, recognized this and wished to resign: "Because I cannot find the time to attend". The Rev. Thomas Stacey replaced him. Its annual reports were presented to the Board.

The behaviour of the Workhouse inmates was sometimes troublesome and in June '64 seventeen were referred to the Magistrates "each for destroying his clothes". Mr Stockwood, the Magistrates' Clerk, received £3.16.6d for presenting them at the Petty Session.

George Fletcher was paid 10/6d for sweeping the chimneys of the Workhouse. It was also entered in the accounts that potatoes valued at £11.10.4½d had been grown in the garden and that the total County rate was £2882.4.1¼d.

In February '65 the P.L.B. sent them a copy of an "anonymous letter" they had received in which it was claimed that management of the Workhouse was "deficient". The Guardians considered such "anonymous" communication unworthy of notice and in reply enclosed the inspector's last comments – which had been favourable.

New boilers and cooking apparatus were obtained for £20 in March and the chimneys had to be re-swept after only six months.

The P.L.B. suggested that a professional Valuer might be appointed to assess the railways and works, but the Guardians decided that they preferred their own Assessment Committee to do it "to the best of their ability". The Rev. Stacey resigned from it and Henry John Randall filled the vacancy. John Lewis also found the membership too difficult and he was replaced by William Davies.

The money paid for the non-resident poor in August was £14.12.0d to Merthyr, £1.19.0d to Newport, £1.12.6d to Newton Abbot, £1.12.6d to Swansea, £3.5.0d to Bristol, £3.5.0d to Greenwich, £4.2.4d to West London, £4.17.6d to Crickhowell, £8.15.6d to Cardiff, £39.6.0d to Pontypridd and £21.9.0d to Neath. By definition these paupers were "settled" within the Bridgend - Cowbridge Union and it is surprising that they were so widely scattered.

The High Sheriff acknowledged correspondence from them regarding Cattle Pestilence (September 16) and agreed to write to the Lord Lieutenant and County members requesting a County meeting to discuss the problem.

Income Tax on the Workhouse in '66 was £2.10.0d, the Fire Insurance £3.17.0d and the cost of the previous Christmas dinner to the inmates £7.6.8d.

The Directors of the Llynfi Valley Railway Company informed them in March that they "wished to retain the site of the old Bridgend Tramway in case it might become expedient to build a locomotive line over it. It could not therefore be released for a Public Road" – as had been requested by the Guardians –"but would not object to allow its use as a road, to be kept in repair by them, for £5 per annum subject to 6 months notice to quit on either side". In other words the Board could utilize the road under the terms of a tenancy. The charge was later reduced to 1/0d a year.

The curate of Coity, Rev. D. Roberts, was paid £1.6.8d for the burial of 4 paupers. This was the first time such payment was made (24 March).

"Calls" to the parishes at 6 monthly intervals continued to be requested in four instalments, the dates of receipt being specified. Those of the March "Call" were April 14th, May 26th, July 7th and August 15th. The total for Cwmdu was £600, Coity Lower £406, Newcastle Higher £256, Llanbleddian £234, Llantwit Major £366, Pencoed £114, St Bride's Major £214, Cowbridge £140, Nash £16, St Andrew's Minor £18, Merthyr Mawr £60, Newcastle Lower £108, Newton Nottage £188, Pyle £154, Sker £6, Tythegston Higher £164, Tythegston Lower £36 and Llangan £58. They numbered fifty-six in all.

The valuation lists as compiled by the Overseers were received, but supplementary lists had to be drawn up in sixteen parishes inclusive of Cwmdu and Newton Nottage, and a totally new one for Newcastle Higher. The Assessment Committee was then re-elected. On it were the Chairman, the Rev.

C. R. Knight, J. Samuel Gibbon, H. J. Randall, Robert Leyshon, William Williams, D. H. Davies, David Rees, John Howell, William Davies, Watkin Bevan and John Lewis.

In July Mr. Graves expressed doubts about "the quality of the drainage of the Workhouse" and suggested that "a competent person be called to study it". William Williams was asked to give his opinion. He thought that new pipes and chutes would be necessary and that the cost of the whole undertaking would be about £205.

The Rev. David Roberts received £5.6.0d for burying seven paupers. Payment of 6/8d for each burial became the accepted practice though a sum of up to £2 was sometimes allowed.

At this time the P.L.B. were being inundated with complaints from Workhouse inmates throughout the Country and they wondered whether perhaps some of them were being hidden by the staff. To counteract this possibility they sent a circular to each Union suggesting that a notice be placed "in each room of the Workhouse" indicating that all complaints should be "sent by letter to the Clerk or verbally to the Guardians" and that a "record of them should be kept" and "information supplied on how they were dealt with". The Bridgend – Cowbridge Board received it on September 29th.

The money for the October "Calls" was due on 20th October, 24th November, 5th January and 16th February, that for St Athan being £114, Cowbridge £140, Llanbleddian £202, Llantwit Major £354, Penlline £116, Cwmdu £712, Llanharan £136, Llangynwyd Lower £82, Llangynwyd Middle £74, Coity Higher £132, Coity Lower £380, Merthyr Mawr £54, Newton Nottage £188, Sker £6, Tythegston Higher £64 and Tythegston Lower £38.

This was the year the fourth epidemic of Cholera occurred (Chapter 12) and a committee was formed to note its progress. On it were:- the Chairman, Vice-Chairman, the Venerable Archdeacon Blosse, Robert Leyshon, William Williams, Morgan Williams, John Lewis, W. B. Popkin, John Thomas and the Rev. C. R. Knight.

A new cemetery for Coity was ready in December (1866) and the Vestry of St Bride's Major thought that the cost of pauper burials had to be discussed: "because the ancient custom for payment is not proven".

Glanrhyd Mental Hospital, then known as the County Lunatic Asylum (Chapter 16), had already been built and the Guardians formed a committee to visit the hospital in order to ascertain how the Union's "lunatics" were progressing. Robert Leyshon, William Williams and James Clark agreed to be members of it (February 1867). Its composition was changed annually.

The Assessment Committee (and the Board) thought that Mines, Wood and Plantations should not be exempt from parochial taxation and so a memorial to this effect was given to C.R.M. Talbot, M.P. for presentation to the House of Commons.

By now it had been decided that the drainage and water supply of the Workhouse were both defective, and how they could be improved was deliberated. The first serious suggestion was that they should acquire a stone tank lined with cement and holding 10,000 gallons of water for flushing purposes, but this was later modified because Mr Williams, their adviser, thought that a well 24 feet in depth and new chutes were also necessary. Finally, it was decided that the tank should be of cast iron, holding 5,000 gallons and that it should be placed near the well. Mr Williams then withdrew his services and Mr Collier was asked to continue. He bought a "lifting force pump with a crank" for the well, costing £9.15.0d. The tank was supplied by Charles Shepherd for £30, and William Roberts charged £4.17.5d for the carpentry. The pump was repaired six months later and new taps supplied at a cost of £6.10.0d.

The Land Tax for six months on the Workhouse premises was 12/3d and the County, Police and Cattle Plague rates £709.17.8d. Expenses incurred in pursuance of the Nuisances Removal and Prevention Act was £50.5.4d (Chapter 15).

Mr John T. Graves, the Poor Law Inspector, commented in December: "The Workhouse is unsatisfactory in structure, and despite the efforts of the Board of Guardians to improve it, is not a pleasing place to visit. The ward for "itch" patients at the top of the Workhouse is dirty and there is lack of cupboards in several of the Day rooms. There is not enough difference in wards between the actually sick and the infirm who are bedridden. Men are in bed in many scattered dormitories, and there are more bedrooms as day rooms than is usual". The P.L.B. commented on this report and pointed out that there was: "No paid Nurse to attend the sick". They indicated that the Guardians should consider remedying this deficiency after obtaining the opinion of Dr Verity, the Medical Officer in charge. He reported that the nursing was satisfactory as it was (Chapter 12).

A new floor was put in the children's rooms in February '68 by William Roberts, the carpenter, for £12.9.3d and other essential carpentry was also carried out by him at a total cost of £72.11.9d.

The burial of pauper inmates had been a sensitive subject from the time the Workhouse was established and the Rev. Stacey now added fuel to the controversy by stating that he would not allow all the burials to be in the new Coity cemetery. The Clerk requested the opinion of the P.L.B. and their reply was: "He is fully empowered to do so. Why bury non-parishioners there?".

At the Election in March, 66 were nominated but 3 refused to serve. 49 were farmers, 4 were Clerics, and among the remainder were an innkeeper, a draper, a builder, a grocer, a miller and a surveyor. The new Assessment Committee consisted of the Chairman, with the Rev. C. R. Knight, H. J. Randall, Robert Leyshon, David Jenkins, William Williams, David Rees, John Howell and Watkin Bevan.

The doctors submitted a report on the condition of the Workhouse in August (Chapter 12). What worried them most were the lack of cleanliness, the poor ventilation and the dirty state of the privies, particularly those in the Itch Garret, the Fever Hospital and the old lying-in ward.

Money from the Paymaster General towards the salary of the Schoolmistress and the Medical Officers was £124.10.0d. The money was received annually and increased in later years.

The October "Calls" sent on the 3rd of the month demanded payment by October 10, November 21, January 2 and February 13. The sum for Cwmdu had increased to £828, Newton Nottage to £264 and that for Tythegston Higher to £222.

Mr. Graves indicated in March that the "woodwork needed re-painting, that coconut fibre should be placed between the beds in the sick wards, more chamber pots placed in the adult wards, a few armchairs procured for the sick and more tables for the old male and female wards". He also commented that the bells they had were unnecessary and that their cooking apparatus was "useless". Although the general tone of the report was critical the Guardians did not demur and took steps to plan a new laundry and to add to the kitchen for which Mr Hurley's tender of £156.11.0d was accepted. The cost of the new "cooking apparatus" was £200. Other suggestions made by Mr Graves were that gas should be used instead of oil and that the "Dead house" should be moved to the outside of the Workhouse. The only disagreement the Guardians voiced was: "Pails are more useful than chamber pots"!

Out-door relief for the Union's paupers was considerable and in April the following resolution was passed: "No out-door relief is to be paid to the wives of persons emigrating to the colonies, or elsewhere for longer than four weeks after 22nd May and only in selected cases before then". Deserted wives were thereby given an additional burden and perhaps they thought that this would encourage the bread-winner to stay at home or take his wife and family with him if he left. The problem of desertion was ever present. In the same month as this resolution was passed three children had to be taken into the Workhouse because both parents had left home without them, and a man in Yorkshire died leaving a widow with six children who moved to Wenvoe. The Cardiff Union granted them 8/0d a week, but as the husband had been a parishioner of Flemingston the sum was covered by the Bridgend – Cowbridge Union.

An imbalance had developed between the population of the four districts which complicated the Union's administration, and so in September the Board decided to alter their boundaries: Llanharan was transferred from the Eastern to the Bridgend district in exchange for Marcross, Monknash, St Mary Hill and Llangan; Llangeinor and Llandyfodwg were added to Bridgend from the Northern as was St Bride's Minor from the Western; while Ewenny, St Bride's Major, St Andrew's Minor and Wick were transferred to the Western from the Bridgend district. These moves approximated their population - that of the Eastern becoming 6,508, the Northern 5,531, Bridgend 5,716 and Western 8,732 - the final population of Newton Nottage being 1,082, Cowbridge 1,094 and Cwmdu 4,154.

In January 1870 the Visiting Committee of the Workhouse recommended that a Cook be appointed who could also be a Nurse and Assistant Matron (Chapter 10). The Board sent a memorial to the House of Commons regarding "the unequal distribution of burdens caused by the Poor Rates". This kind of inequality troubled them greatly.

Thomas Phillips, the undertaker was liable "to a duty of 2 guineas in respect of his hearse" and the Guardians agreed to pay it for him. They must have felt rather generous at that meeting because they also considered the feasibility of having visiting hours for the Workhouse inmates. There had not been any so far. It was decided that Tuesdays and Thursdays would be suitable, between 10.00 a.m. and 4.00 p.m., provided the inmate was not "sick".

Newton Nottage was offered £15 for the "purchase of their "ruinous Poorhouses" in April and they were allowed to proceed with the transaction. (The money was used in 1872 – Chapter 8).

At the yearly Election two were nominated who were not qualified because of non-residency and two, the Rev. Edward Evans and John Garsed (Moorlands), refused to serve. Among the members were the Rev. Charles LL. Llewelyn (Coychurch), Gronow John (Norton Hall), Titus Lewis (Commercial traveller - St Quentin's Cottage) and Daniel Owen (Ash Hall, Llanbleddian). The Chairman and Vice-Chairman were as before with Robert Leyshon as 2nd Vice-Chairman.

The Visiting Committee consisted of the Chairman, Vice-Chairman and 21 others inclusive of Dr Leahy, the Rev. Blosse, the Rev. C. R. Knight and Gronow John. As its size made it unmanageable they passed a resolution: "That any member of the Board of Guardians can visit the Workhouse at any time". This was an important development which confirms the view that they desired to make life in the Workhouse as humane as conditions would allow.

Elected to the Assessment Committee were the Chairman, Vice-Chairman and 8 others among whom were the Rev. C.R. Knight, H.T. Randall, Robert Leyshon and Watkin Bevan. The new Visitors for the Union's "lunatics" in the asylum were Watkin Bevan, Thomas Thomas (Maesteg) and David Llewelyn.

A portion of the boys' Schoolroom was partitioned off to give the new Schoolmistress, Miss Ridewood, a bedroom (Chapter 13) and the old washroom and laundry were converted into two wards by John Morgan for £27.

Monthly statements were received from the Assistant Overseers and a new Assistant Overseer was appointed for Coity Higher with two acceptable sureties. Burial of in-door paupers in the Coity Cemetery was no longer automatic, as shown by the fact that Thomas Thomas was buried in June in his home parish church at St Mary Hill for £1.3.10d, although William Blake and Thomas Evans were both buried in Coity for £1.0.6d each and a child, John Trihan, for 9/3d.

The "Calls" in October were generally higher than those issued at the same time the previous year – that of Cwmdu was £790; Newton Nottage £300; Laleston £232; Newcastle Higher £354; Pyle £204; Llangeinor £314; Llantwit Major £424; and Coity Lower £504 - but it is difficult to be certain how much of this increase was due to the boundary changes.

The Assessment of mines was causing difficulty and the P.L.B. suggested in August that a Valuer be appointed. The suggestion this time was accepted by the Board and William Adams was appointed to the post. There was agreement with the Pontypridd Union that the collieries in Neath were rated too low as this had resulted in the Assessment Committee receiving 110 appeals during the year. A combined meeting of the Assessment Committees of Merthyr Tydfil, Pontypridd, Bridgend, Neath and Swansea was held at which it was decided to

A close-up view of the Quadrangle and part of the male section of the Workhouse. The overgrown area was the Male excercise yard.

ask R.O. Jones, the Chairman of the Quarter Sessions, to adjourn the appeals and to nominate a local Valuer for each colliery.

Mr Longe, the new Poor Law Inspector, visited the Workhouse in November after which the roof and windows were repaired for £5.12.7d.

A strange episode occurred a fortnight later. The Assistant Overseer of Pencoed, Thomas Griffiths, claimed that £40 had been paid by him on behalf of the parish of which there was no record and the P.L.B. wished to know why he was not being prosecuted. The reply was that he had not been properly appointed and was not therefore recognized by the Board – and so: "It is not expedient for the Guardians to prosecute him". The £40 was later disallowed and the "Treasurer debited for the six months".

The chutes of the House received further attention in January 1871 for £3.12.0d, and bedsteads were repaired for £1.0.0d, the fire insurance came to £7.12.0d, and rates to £6.11.3d, Mr Wrigley was paid £9.0.0d for shaving and cutting the hair of inmates, and Knight and Co. (Stationers London) received £7.16.6d while the local stationers, John Hemming and Wesley Williams, were paid £3.1.7d and £1.10.4d respectively.

The Merthyr Union sent a petition to the House of Commons in February in which they opined that representatives of ratepayers should have a say in assessing county finance. A copy of it was sent to the Clerk of the Bridgend-Cowbridge Union and, at the request of the Guardians, he wrote a supportive memorial.

The Colliery Valuer's report was now available and showed that he agreed fairly closely with what the Assessment Committee had considered reasonable. This was very satisfactory and he was paid £30.

The Census showed that there were 104 inmates in the Workhouse, 39 of whom were aged 14 years or younger compared with 36 in 1851 and 40 in 1861. Six were under a year old.

At the Election the Rev. R.P. Llewelyn refused to participate leaving Thomas Thomas (Merchant, Commercial Street), David Phillips (Postmaster), and Illtyd Morgan (Innkeeper, Commercial Street) to represent Cwmdu. Watkin Bevan was re-elected for Newton Nottage and the Rev. John Evans for Pyle.

The importance of sureties or guarantors was well illustrated in July when one of the Treasurer's sureties died and the other ceased to be a Director. He was asked to name possible replacements so that a new bond could be formalized.

The possibility of paying superannuation was introduced by the P.L.B. in August. The Guardians were asked to give their opinion on the payment of such an allowance to Officers "when they retired or gave up work because of illness". They supported the idea but felt that "public bodies should have discretionary power" either to grant or to withhold it "so that there would be no abuse". They added: "To pay superannuation to those who have worked in different Unions successively would make smaller Unions stepping stones to larger Unions, and besides pensioning those only partially employed would make compulsion far too wide". Therefore the principle was accepted by them, but, as will be seen, in later years its application was far from universal (Chapter 12).

The September "Calls" requested £870 from Cwmdu, £296 from Newton Nottage, £308 from Llangeinor, £130 from Llangynwyd Lower, £116 from Llangynwyd Middle, £166 from Pencoed, £584 from Coity Lower, £444 from Llantwit Major, £70 from Merthyr Mawr and £110 from Wick.

There was a circular letter from the P.L.B. in October enclosing a copy of the Vaccination Act of 1871 by which they were directed to appoint and pay one or more lay Vaccination Officers. The Board decided that the Registrars of Births, Marriages and Deaths could undertake the additional duties (Chapter 14).

56

Balance Sheet for the Half-Year ending Michaelmas, 1870.

	£	s.	d.
Langeinor	1	1	3¼
Pencoed	5	8	0¼
Langonoyd Higher	13	8	1
Nonsettled Poor	44	7	0
Provisions	14	11	2
Necessaries	14	9	7
Clothing	143	5	6¾
Wine	11	12	3¼
Cod Liver Oil	2	11	2
David Lloyd	74	9	0½
Richard Leyshon	55	11	4
Treasurer	1313	16	11
	£1694	11	5¾

	£	s.	d.
Saint Athan	31	17	3¾
Colwinstone	24	16	10½
Cowbridge	40	0	2¼
Saint Donatts	15	5	3¼
Eglwysbrewis	6	3	6¼
Flemingstone	11	6	11
Gileston	8	5	9¼
Saint Hilary	18	14	6¾
Lanblethian	63	6	8
Landough	10	7	7¼
Landow	17	1	1¼
Langan	17	9	5¾
Lanharry	18	14	7¾
Lanmaes	22	12	2¼
Lanmihangel	9	3	11¼
Lansannor	17	2	0¾
Lantwit Major	99	10	8
Lisworney	16	9	8¼
Marcross	12	1	11
Saint Mary Church	4	10	11½
Saint Mary Hill	16	17	6¾
Monknash	21	15	10¾
Nash	2	4	8
Penlline	34	5	11½
Stembridge	0	13	11
Ystradowen	16	14	3¼
Bettws	25	3	8½
Saint Brides Minor	18	17	2
Coychurch Higher	15	19	10
Coychurch Lower	25	14	10
Cwmdu	215	3	0½
Landyfodwg	43	6	4¼
Langonoyd Lower	28	16	6¼
Langonoyd Middle	24	17	3¼
Lanharran	39	0	10¾
Lanilid	11	0	0¼
Peterstone	16	4	11
Ynisawdre	1	17	0¼
Saint Andrews Minor	3	17	3
Saint Brides Major	62	10	11¾
Coity Higher	38	1	8¾
Coity Lower	140	10	10½
Ewenny	31	5	0
Kenfig	18	4	9¼
Laleston	39	15	10½
Merthyrmawr	14	19	5¼
Newcastle Higher	81	5	0¾
Newcastle Lower	34	11	6
Newton Nottage	53	4	4½
Pyle	52	19	2¼
Sker	0	3	11
Tythegston Higher	48	4	3¾
Tythegston Lower	12	1	10
Wick	21	16	5½
Invoice Account	13	15	11
William John	3	7	9
	£1694	11	5¾

4

Elected Guardians.—Continued.

PARISHES.	ELECTED MEMBERS.	OVERSEERS.
Langan	Thomas John	John Jenkins
"		Rees Jenkins
Langeinor	Richard Thomas	David Thomas
"		Gwilym Traherne
Langynwyd Lower	Michael Leahy	Jenkin Rees
"		John Maddock
Langynwyd Middle	Rees Thomas	Jenkin David
"		Richard Daniel
Lanharran	Thomas Richards	Thomas Davies
"		Gwilym David
Lanharry	Evan Lewis	Evan Howell
"		Thomas Jenkins
Lanilid	John Lewis	Miles Watkin
"		Thomas Thomas
Lanmaes	John Rees	Thomas Jenkins
"		Thomas Williams
Lanmihangel	David Evans	David Evans
"		William Jenkins
Lansannor	John Lewis	John Lewis
"		David Reynolds
Lantwit Major	William Smith	John Harris...
	Thomas Evans	Phillip Harry
Lisworney	Jenkin Thomas	David John
"		Thomas Arnott
Marcross	John Jenkins	John Jenkins
"		Thomas Thomas
Merthyrmawr	William Powell	Thomas Jones
"		William Morgan
Monknash	Thomas Alexander	Daniel Thomas
"		William Lougher
Nash	Hopkin Hopkin	Hopkin Hopkin
Newcastle Higher	Thomas Powell	Daniel Jones
"		Rees Thomas
Newcastle Lower	Alfred B. Price	George James
"		David Brown
Newton Nottage	Watkin Bevan	Robert Floyd
"		William Hopkin
Pencoed	John Howell	John Griffith
"		William Howell
Peniline	John Williams	Noah Rees ..
"		Evan Jones...
Peterstone-super- montem }	Edward Gronow	Edward Gronow
		William Lewis
Pyle	Rev. John Evans	Rees Jenkins
"		Rees Powell
St. Athan	Rev. Hanmer Morgan	Rees Thomas
"		William Donne
Saint Brides Major	Gronow John	Edward Hopkin
"	Leyshon John	Jenkin Rees
		Cadogan Thomas
St. Brides Minor	William Williams	William Williams
"		Morgan Edward
Saint Donats	Edward Wilde	John John ...
"		Edward Wilde
Saint Hilary	Thomas Thomas	John Jones
"		Henry Maddick
Saint Mary Church	Robert Howe	Evan Evans
"		William Gwyn
Saint Mary Hill	Morgan Williams	Richard Howells
"		Thomas John

5

Elected Guardians.—Continued.

PARISHES.	ELECTED GUARDIANS.	OVERSEERS.
Sker	Thomas Morgan	John David
Stembridge	John David	John Edmund
Tythegston Higher ...	Hopkin Williams...	Thomas Smith
,, ...	... ...	Edward Howells
Tythegston Lower ...	Morgan Jones	William Thomas
,, ...	... ...	Thomas Preece, jun.
Wick	Thomas Preece	Thomas Cooke, jun.
,, ...	... ...	Thomas Williams
Ynisawdre	Rev. George Phillips	Watkin Henry
,, ...	... ...	Jenkin Donne
Ystradowen	Howell Harris	William Matthews
,, ...	... ...	

Chairman :
JOHN COLE NICHOLL, ESQ.

Vice-Chairmen :
THE REV. CHARLES LLOYD LEWELLIN.
MR. ROBERT LEYSHON.

Visiting and Finance Committee :

The Chairman
The Vice-Chairmen
The Ven. Archdeacon Blosse
The Rev. C. R. Knight
Mr. Gronow John
Rev. John Evans
Mr. Lewis Jenkins
,, Thomas Powell

Mr. Watkin Bevan
,, David Rees
,, John Howell
,, Morgan Williams
,, T. Thomas (Cwmdu)
,, John Lewis (Lansannor)
,, William Williams
,, David Lewellin

Mr. William Powell
Dr. Leahy
Mr. Evan Lewis
,, Thomas Preece
,, John Jenkins
, Edward Wilde
,, David Jenkins
,, Dd. Evan (Coity Lower)

Assessment Committee :

The Chairman
Henry J. Randall, Esq.
Rev. C. R. Knight

Mr. Robert Leyshon
,, William Williams
,, David Rees

Mr. David Jenkins
,, John Howell
,, Watkin Bevan

Relieving Officers' Districts :

1st. *The Eastern or Cowbridge District.*—Parishes : St. Athan, Colwinstone, Cowbridge, St. Donats, Eglwysbrewis, Flemingstone, Gileston, St. Hilary, Llanblethian, Landongh, Landow, Langan, Lanharry, Lanmaes, Lanmihangel, Lansannor, Lantwit Major, Lisworney, Marcross, St. Mary Church, St. Mary Hill, Monknash, Nash, Penlline, Stembridge, and Ystradowen.

Mr. *DAVID LLOYD, Relieving Officer, Cowbridge.*

2nd. *The Northern or Maesteg District.*—Parishes : Bettws, St. Brides Minor, Coychurch Higher, Coychurch Lower, Cwmdu, Landyfodwg, Langeinor, Langynwyd Lower, Langynwyd Middle, Lanharran, Lanilid, Pencoed, Peterstone, and Ynisawdre.

Mr. *WILLIAM JOHN, Relieving Officer, Aberkenfig, Bridgend.*

3rd. *The Central or Bridgend District.*—Parishes : St. Andrews Minor, Saint Brides Major, Coity Higher, Coity Lower, Ewenny, Kenfig, Laleston, Merthyrmawr, Newcastle Higher, Newcastle Lower, Newton Nottage, Pyle, Sker, Tythegston Higher, Tythegston Lower, and Wick.

Mr. *RICHARD LEYSHON, Relieving Officer, Bridgend.*

3

EX-OFFICIO GUARDIANS,

Blosse, The Venerable Archdeacon, Newcastle, Bridgend.

Carne, John Whitlock Nicholl, Esq., St. Donats, Castle.

Dunraven, The Earl of, Dunraven Castle. Bridgend.

Edwardes, the Rev. Frederic Francis, Gileston Manor, Cowbridge.

Edmondes, Rev. Thomas, Cowbridge.

Franklen, Richard, Esq., Clemenstone, Bridgend.

Gibbon, John Samuel, Esq., Newton House, Cowbridge.

Homfray, John, Esq., Penlline Castle, Cowbridge.

Homfray, John Richards, Esq., Pwll-y-wrach, Cowbridge.

Jenkins, John Blandy, Esq., Llanharran House, Cowbridge.

Knight, The Rev. Charles Rumsey, Tythegston Court, Bridgend.

Lewellyn, William, Esq., Cwrt Colman.

Morse, Thomas Robert, Esq., Glanogwr, Bridgend.

Nicholl, George, Whitlock, Esq., Ham, Llantwit Major.

Nicholl, John C. Esq., Merthyrmawr, Bridgend.

Randall, Henry John, Esq., Bridgend.

Salmon, William, Esq., Penlline Court, Cowbridge.

Stacey, The Rev. Thomas, Bridgend.

Thomas, Hubert de Burgh, Esq., Llanblethian.

Traherne, George Montgomery, Esq., St. Hilary, Cowbridge.

ELECTED GUARDIANS.

PARISHES.	ELECTED GUARDIANS.	OVERSEERS.
Bettws	Oliver Heywood Jones ...	John David
„ ...	... ...	Oliver Heywood Jones
Coity Higher ...	David Lewellin ...	John Thomas
„ ...	... ...	David Jenkins, jun.
Coity Lower ...	Robert Leyshon ...	Thomas Treharn Thomas
„ ...	David Evan ..	William Williams
Colwinstone ...	Thomas Thomas ...	Daniel Thomas
„ ...	... ...	Thomas Thomas
Cowbridge ...	David Rees ...	John George
„	Lewis Jenkins ...	Thomas John
Coychurch Higher ...	Jenkin Thomas ...	John Rees
„ ...	... ...	David Griffiths
Coychurch Lower ...	Rev. Charles Lloyd Lewellin	William Thomas
„ ...	... ...	John Thomas
Cwmdu ...	Thomas Thomas ...	Thomas Thomas
„	Rev. R. P. Llewelyn ...	Robert William Tolfree
„ ...	David Phillips ..	....
Eglwysbrewis	Daniel Holford Davies ...	Daniel Holford Davies
Ewenny ...	Anthony Lewis ...	Jenkin Lloyd
„ ...	... ...	David Phillips
Flemingstone ...	David Jenkins ..	David Jenkins
„ ...	... ...	William Williams
Gileston ...	Christopher Spencer	Christopher Spencer
Kenfig Borough	Thomas Loveluck ...	Thomas Loveluck
„ ...	... ...	Rees Thomas
Laleston ...	John David ...	John Rees
„ ...	... ...	John David
Lanblethian ...	Ebenezer Davies ...	John Butler
„ ...	... ...	William Jones
Landough ...	David Thomas ...	David Thomas
„ ...	... ...	Thomas Morris
Landow ...	Robert Thomas ...	William Thomas
„ ...	... ...	Hopkin Hopkin
Landyfodwg ...	Jenkin Williams ...	Edward Williams
.. ...	... ...	John Evans

Chapter 8

The Guardians (1872 - 1878)

Becoming Rural Sanitary Authority, Further Improvements to Workhouse, Death of District Auditor, Chaplaincy, Outlay of Union over 6 months, Settlement of Paupers, More Boundary Changes.

The contents of the Regulation Act of 1871 were considered in January 1872. As a first requisite "notice to quit" was given to all the inmates of the Workhouse retaining those who wished to remain - "for a specific period". This period could of course be extended if need be, but the procedure did introduce a time factor into their stay.

The Local Government Board, which had replaced the Poor Law Board the previous year, informed them that their Officers could be paid monthly and not quarterly if the Board desired. This apparent easing of conditions stimulated them to request an attendance allowance of 2/6d for each Guardian and 3d mile travelling allowance, but there is no record regarding its acceptance or refusal although permission was granted for the undertaker to receive 8d a mile: "from the Workhouse to the place of burial provided it is not in the churchyard of Coity".

At the Election the Rev. R.P. Llewelyn agreed to represent Llangynwyd Middle; the Rev. H. Morgan, St Athan; the Rev. John Evans, Pyle; and the Rev. Charles C. Williams (Nash Manor), Llysworney. There were 58 others. Twenty-two of them were asked to serve on the Finance and Visiting Committee of the Workhouse, eight on the Assessment Committee and twelve on the Asylum Visitors' Committee. Samuel Cox, the Clerk was paid the usual £15 for arranging it.

Information was received that the Swansea Union was paying 2/6d weekly to a Nurse for attending to aged and bed-ridden non-resident paupers. This was merely noted in passing, but it must have had some effect on their attitude to the medical care of ill people although no paid nurse was employed in the Workhouse until August '83 (Chapter 10).

In March the L.G.B. wished to know how the £15 obtained from the "sale of the site and ruins" of the Newton Nottage Poorhouses was going to be used. The Rev. Robert Knight's suggestion that the parish well could be repaired and a new pump placed in it was approved. It was "arched over" in October and a pump erected. The total cost was £24.8.0d for which the £15 was accepted as part payment.

By the Public Health Act of 1872 the Board became the sole Rural Sanitary Authority. This important development is discussed later (Chapter 15).

Samuel Cox applied for an increase of salary in September on the following grounds: "Apart from attending the Board's meetings on Saturdays I am employed daily in the Board room (except Sundays) and often at home till a late hour. My son acts as assistant in the routine work several days a week. I have had to discontinue almost entirely my private work as solicitor because it is too important to delegate to a clerk. The Union's expense in 1858 was about £13,000 - now it was £20,000, but the proportional work is much more because of legislative demands and orders of P.L.B. especially since 1865 when all paupers became chargeable to the common fund of the Union (led to enquiring about settlements of paupers, obtaining and appealing against orders of removal previously transacted by solicitors of parish, often at great cost). My salary has been unchanged since 1858 although the P.L.B. has directed B or G to adjust remuneration because of additional trouble imposed on Officers. Being a solicitor I am obliged by regulations of the P.L.B. to transact legal business of the Union (with few exceptions) without charge which should entitle me to a higher salary than a non-professional Clerk. I should have applied sooner". The application was successful and his salary was increased from £110 to £150 per annum.

Renewed interest was being taken in the Workhouse building and the L.G.B. thought that the improvements envisaged by the Guardians were inadequate. They were advised to consult an architect "who knows about Workhouse buildings if possible". A comment that: "The wooden building you have for Cholera should be superseded by a permanent building" was added.

The report of the Assessment Committee was now available: they had re-valued the rates of the collieries within the Union at £21,000.

The "Calls" in October had not materially changed though that for Newcastle Higher was £380. The County, Police and Cattle Plague rates paid to Mr Luard, the new County Treasurer, amounted to £1,356.4.10d.

Early in '73 a circular was received from the L.G.B. stating that if the Workhouse could not cope "owing to vast increase in unemployment" a task of work e.g. breaking stones or oakum picking, should be given to those who could not be admitted, in exchange for out-door relief. A place of work should be provided for the task and each case referred to them for approval. Fortunately, this did not apply to the Bridgend- Cowbridge Union.

A petition from the Ulverstone Union to the House of Commons that: "All real property now exempt and all personal property be made liable to poor and other rates" was supported and a memorial given to Mr Vivian M.P. for presentation.

Sixty-two Guardians were elected in March but seven refused to serve, inclusive of three from Cwmdu - David Grey (Rockhouse, Manager of the Tin Works), David Thomas (Farmer) and William Rees (Grocer) - leaving Illtyd Morgan (Innkeeper) and Thomas Thomas (Proprietor of the Tin Works) as representatives. Dr Leahy was elected for Llangynwyd Lower and Thomas Major (Gadlys) with Rees Thomas (Bryn-y-Fro) for Llangynwyd Middle.

Mr Courtney Doyle, the L.G.B. inspector, visited the Workhouse in July and enumerated his instructions:-

1) "The Deadhouse to be disused and another made from the sickhouse (presumably this was the wooden structure they had built for patients with Cholera).
2) Get a bath of tin on wheels so as to be movable.
3) Stop piling ashes in the girls' yard".

What the reaction was to these demands can only be surmised but a committee was formed to investigate "the lighting and water supply" and on it were Mr. Nicholl (the Chairman), Mr. Collier, Mr. Rees, Dr. Leahy, Mr. Morley and Mr. Illtyd Morgan.

In March '74 Mr. J. Hemming of the Newspaper Company was paid £15.10.0d to supply 250 copies of half-yearly abstracts and a list of paupers. This appears to be the first time that such a list became generally available although it was supplied regularly thereafter.

At the Election David Grey again refused to serve as did Thomas Thomas (Gent, Llwydarth Villa) the previous member, leaving Illtyd Morgan and two new members – James Barrow (Mineral agent) and Morgan Jones (Land agent, Tymaen) to do so. Newcastle Higher elected Robert William Llewelyn (Gent, Court Colman), and Llanbleddian, Dr. John Watkin Phillips – as a new member. Forty-three were farmers.

Examples of the "Calls" were: Cwmdu £860, Newton Nottage £196, Tythegston Higher £208, Llantwit Major £286, Coity Lower £384, Merthyr Mawr £46 and Newcastle Higher £432.

The Rev. C. R. Knight objected to secret voting in the meetings. He obviously felt that a show of hands was fairer because it pinpointed the views of prominent members.

There had to be two sureties for every Assistant Overseer and if one of them died a replacement, suitable to the Board, had to be promptly found. This happened in August to William Lewis, Assistant Overseer of Cowbridge, when Mr Jones, the District Auditor, died. He had been appointed in 1853. Thomas John (Malster, Aberthin) agreed to fill the vacancy and a new bond was drawn up. At the same time the Assistant Overseer of Penlline, Ebenezer Davies, had "neglected" to name anyone and he was therefore asked to do so "at once". He later became Overseer of Cowbridge (Chapter 9).

The establishment of the Cottage Homes and Industrial School came to the fore in January '75 (Chapter 13). The Paymaster General granted £293.16.0d towards the salaries of the Medical Officers and the Schoolmistress.

In March they considered the contents of a letter from the Clerk of the Peace which indicated that at the Quarter Sessions the Magistrates had decided to apply to Parliament for an amendment of the Turnpike Road and Highways Act in so far as South Wales was concerned. The Guardians were asked to comment. They thought that there was: "No point focusing on South Wales with special legislation because the whole country will soon be considered".

A disturbing letter was received about the same time. It was from the Rev. F. W. Edmondes, the new Rector of Coity, and in it he strongly expressed the view that a Chaplain should be appointed for the Workhouse. This had been discussed in 1854 and considered to be unnecessary (Chapter 5). The same verdict was again reached, but the Rector was loathe to accept it and wrote to the L.G.B. for advice. Their reply was: "There are too few inmates for the appointment of a Chaplain. Analysis of the Creed Register shows that frequent religious services are held in the House of Nonconformist Ministers and that on Sundays the inmates go to church or chapel - only two are not fit to do so and they are Anglican".

Sixty-eight Guardians were elected in March but 6 refused to serve, including William Rees (Farmer, Garnllwyd) for Cwmdu. Its representation was as before. William Hopkin was elected for Newton Nottage, Thomas Rees (Hall) for Pyle, Dr. Leahy (Newcastle) for Llangynwyd Lower and Thomas Major (Gadlys) for Llangynwyd Middle.

The report of the Assessment Committee showed that they had held meetings in several parts of the County regarding the revision of the County Rate. In general they considered the rates to be too low, as did the Assistant Overseers – although their co-operation had been poor.

In May the Board focused on the placement of Llangynwyd Higher. In their opinion it should be part of the Bridgend-Cowbridge Union. A letter to this effect was sent to the Clerk of the Neath Union which up until then had contained the sub-district, but a month later it was clear that Neath would not agree to the transfer.

The total of the June "Calls" amounted to £6,298.1.11d of which Bettws was to pay £203, Llangeinor £418, Coity Lower £377.13.9d, Newcastle Higher £401, Newton Nottage £193.2.8d, Cowbridge £114.6.6d and Cwmdu £845.12.0d.

Mr Bircham, Assistant Local Government Inspector, gave full support to the building of a separate establishment on the Cottage System (Chapter 9): "As otherwise additional accommodation will have to be found for the children within the Workhouse".

At the Election, Dr. John Watkin Phillips agreed to represent Nash, and George Morley (Manager Llynfi Iron Works) Ynysawdre. The Clerics were: Frederick William Edmondes (Llwyn On) for Coity Lower, Charles Lloyd Llewelyn for Coychurch Lower, H.T. Nicholl for Llandough and John Jones for Marcross. Thomas Major (Gadlys) continued to represent Llangynwyd Middle, Thomas Morgan, Sker and Thomas Rees (Hall), Pyle.

Any member could visit the Workhouse at any time. Twelve were asked to serve on the Assessment Committee and they were the Chairman, Major Turberville, John Blandy Jenkins, G.M. Traherne, R.W. Llewelyn, John Spencer, James Barrow, Evan Bevan, Lewis Jenkins, John Lewis, William Thomas and Thomas Rees. The knowledge and expertise of the members had to be wide because the rateable value of all property and industry within the Union's area was being assessed. Its influence is illustrated by the support given to a memorial from the Merthyr Union: "That all landlords be compelled to pay a fair share towards the local rates".

The outlay of the Union over the previous six months was tabulated thus:- for inmate maintenance £687.2.10d, out–door relief for resident paupers £3,755.7.5d and for the non-resident £199.15.11d, Vaccinations £150.16.6d, Registration £61.17.0d, "Lunatics" in Asylum £882.19.7d and funerals of the in-paupers £9.18.0d To this should be added the salaries of the staff. The "Calls" to the parishes were for £5,834.0.6d.

The salary of the Assistant Overseer of St Bride's Major was increased to £26 and that of the Assistant Overseer of Pencoed to £20. The surveyor of Bridgend was informed that the Board was willing for its resident casuals "to break stones at a shilling a yard", if he arranged: "To bring the stones and to take them away".

In January 1877 the Board received from the L.G.B. the provisions laid down by the Elementary Education Act of 1876. These increased their responsibility and considerably widened their influence (Chapter 13).

H.J. Randall, previously their Treasurer and now the Clerk of the Bridgend Board of Health, wrote to them in March stating that the L.G.B. wished to know what steps were being taken to improve the town's sanitation as laid down in the Rivers Pollution Act, and it was therefore necessary to assess the Workhouse's "disposal". He suggested that an outlet other than the present "Lord Dunraven's Culvert" should be used. They replied: "We cannot consider the problem in isolation – it is necessary to know the plans for the town before doing so".

The "settlement" of paupers was still one of the most worrying items they had to deal with. A poor Law Amendment Act had been passed in 1876 creating "settlement by residence" and they now sent a memorial to the L.G.B. supporting the one sent by the Bristol Union requesting clarification of certain points so that the envisaged improvements could be applied.

It was not unusual for a committee member to resign in mid–term for personal reasons and when it occurred they always requested another Guardian to take his place so that the original number would be maintained. This happened in May. Lewis Jenkins resigned from the Rural Sanitary Committee and was replaced by John Thomas of Cowbridge. Similarly, G.M. Traherne replaced H de Burgh Thomas on the Cottage School Attendance Committee (Chapter 13).

The small committee set up in 1873 to study the lighting and water supply of the Workhouse decided that the "water supply" needed considerable improvement and so they formed another ad hoc committee to indicate what should be done. The temporary Chairman, Rev. F. W. Edmondes; the Vice-Chairman, Morgan Williams; and James Barrow agreed to give their considered opinion.

The L.G.B. Inspector, Mr Bircham, visited again in August and suggested that a Porter and a paid Nurse be appointed. He also commented that: "Discipline within the Workhouse is poor" and that: "Another committee should be formed to suggest wider improvements than just the water supply". The Board did so and the Rev. F.W. Edmondes, Mr. Ferrier, Mr. Watt and A.B. Price became members of it. Their report in September listed these requirements:- repairs to windows, bath, doors, privies; supply of water to the girls' yard with a force pump and a boarded floor in their dayroom; repairs to the pavement yard and more bedding and furniture.

The Guardians returned to the question of religious worship in November. Despite, or perhaps because of, the absence of an appointed Chaplain they were most anxious that it should not be neglected and that each inmate should have denominational choice. Consequently, they passed the following resolution: "Any inmate can attend Newcastle Church or Nolton Church or Chapel on Sundays, Good Friday and Christmas Day provided it is under the control and inspection of the Master or Matron".

The Board was asked by the Swansea Union in March 1878 to indicate what they thought should be included in the County Administration Bill. They did so a month later in a memorial for presentation by Mr Talbot to the House of Commons. It contained these views: "That the limits of every Union and every Sanitary District should be within the boundary of the County, and the Union area be the basis of County administration; that members of County Boards should be elected for 3 years and thereafter a third to retire each year; that the number elected by the Board should be greater than the number nominated by Justices; that the County Boards, not Quarter Sessions, should be Courts of appeal on assessments, and that full publicity be given to their activities with publishing of accounts in local newspapers".

It is not surprising that they referred to appeals against the decisions of the Assessment Committee because they were numerous and probably subject to local prejudice. It was certainly appropriate because in April the Assessment Committee reported that the re-valuation of railways, collieries and iron works as suggested by Mr. Hedley, the Valuer, had been accepted. That of the Llynfi railway had been reduced by £1,000, but the others, such as the Cowbridge railway, had been increased from a nominal sum to £265 and the G.W.R., within the Union area, by 45 per cent.

At the Election Dr William Hopkin Thomas (Bron-y-garn House) became a member for Cwmdu, as did John Evans. John Howell, George Ferrier, Dr Leahy and Dr Watkin Phillips were among the others re-elected by their parish. William Hopkin (Tŷ Talbot) represented Newton Nottage.

Indicative of the general level of the "Calls", to be paid in four instalments as before, were: Cwmdu £776, Llanbleddian £216, Llantwit Major £354, Llangeinor £348, Coity Lower £620, Laleston £158, Newcastle Higher £360, Newton Nottage £254 and Pyle £164. The monthly statements of the Assistant Overseers of the various parishes were checked as usual. William John, the Relieving Officer for Cowbridge, who was also their Collector (Chapter 14), had his payment fixed at 6 per cent of the money he received, and William Powell, the Collector for Cwmdu, a salary increase of £20 - from £75 to £95 per annum.

More changes were made to the boundaries of the districts in August: Pencoed, which had been part of the Maesteg District, was transferred to that of Cowbridge - as was Wick from Bridgend; while Coychurch Lower was added to Bridgend from Maesteg. The L.G.B. wondered whether the Cowbridge district would then be too big, but the Board thought otherwise pointing out that without the change Maesteg was too extensive. The changes were then confirmed, but the L.G.B. explained that the salary of the Relieving Officers would have to be modified accordingly though that of the Medical Officers could remain unchanged as their district would be as before. The Registrar General announced that he was not disposed to alter the boundaries of the Registrar districts. This of course would greatly complicate the envisaged plan and could well make it unworkable. But, after further correspondence he relented, and the boundary changes were allowed to proceed.

Photograph taken from the Men's excercise yard showing store-rooms with Tramp Ward left

Chapter 9

The Guardians (1879 -1886)

Attempt by Cowbridge to Form Separate Union, Further Alterations to Workhouse, Treasurer, Census, Leave of Absence to Mr. J. C. Nicholl (Chairman), Burials, Tramroad, Request of Pencoed Vestry, New Clerk (R. Harmar Cox), Apprenticing, Sunday Closing, Ogmore and Garw, Investments.

In February 1879 the Rev. Lynch Blosse, the Dean of Llandaff, died and the Chairman expressed condolence to the family adding that he had been a most valuable member of the Board for many years.

The following month Mr. Bircham, the Inspector, stressed that further modifications to the Workhouse were necessary for which he would advise if need be. The Assessment Committee reported that there was: "Depreciation of housing property and stagnation in industrial concerns, especially of Iron Works and Tin Works, and that there had been many objections to their valuations because of it": The report was signed by T. Picton Turberville, its Chairman.

At the Election Mr Nicholl remained the Board's Chairman and Mr Blandy Jenkins the Vice-Chairman with James Barrow as his deputy or 2nd Vice-Chairman. The Rev. Henry Lewis represented St Bride's Major and Charles Lloyd Llewelyn, Coychurch Lower. The four established committees were formed, namely, the Finance and Visiting Committee, Assessment Committee, Visiting Committee of the Asylum, and the School Attendance Committee. To these was now added The Management Committee of the Homes. (These last two committees are referred to in Chapter 13).

The relationship between Bridgend and Cowbridge had not always been harmonious as exemplified by the latter's objection to the clearing of Nuisances in the borough by the Union's Inspector of Nuisances in 1853. That had been settled when the Commissioners stated that he had a right to do so (Chapter 15). Nevertheless, the members for Cowbridge district had participated fully in the affairs of the Union and it was with surprise that the Board learnt that a memorial had been sent to the L.G.B. expressing the view that the district should become a separate Union in conjunction with adjacent parts of the Cardiff Union. The L.G.B. enclosed a copy of the memorial and suggested that its contents required urgent consideration by a full committee. This was held on June 14th. Sixty attended under the Chairmanship of Mr Nicholl. Six of them were Esquires - G.M. Traherne, Blandy Jenkins, William Llewelyn, B.A. Jenner, H.J. Randall and R.T. Bassett; six were Clerics - F.W. Edmondes, H. Nicholl, Samuel Jones, Henry Lewis, C.R. Knight and Thomas Edmondes; three were

Modern photograph of the Workhouse and Bridgend General Hospital in relation to the Railway, Quarella Road and Ogmore river.

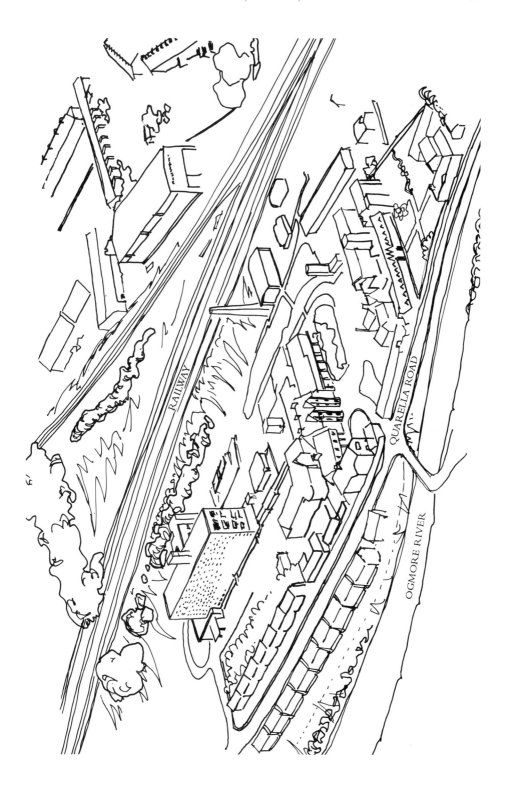

doctors – Carne, Phillips and Leahy and among the other influential persons present were Colonel Morse, Colonel Turberville, John Garsed and Gronow John. The memorial had been signed by "Ex-Guardians, Ex-officio Guardians and some Active Guardians". One of the leading Ex-Guardians was the Rev. Thomas Edmondes and it would be interesting to know what discussions he had with his son, the Rev. F. W. Edmondes who was very active in the Union as constituted. It had been rumoured for about ten years that Thomas Edmondes was promoting the formation of a new Union, but the main advocates for it at the meeting were G. M. Traherne and Dr Carne. It soon became evident that there were strong reasons for maintaining the status quo, such as: "that the Union paupers had been reduced by a third since 1869 despite the increase in population; that the poor were having no difficulties that would be removed by formation of the new Union, but the restricted area would be injurious to their interest and liberty; that division would impose additional burden on ratepayers without sufficient promise of ultimate benefit". Thirty-one voted in favour of remaining as they were and 28 against, so, despite the closeness of the vote the change was considered to be "inexpedient" and the L.G.B. accepted that view.

Mr. Bircham's suggestions regarding the provisional alterations to the Workhouse were discussed in July. They were: "Widen the boardroom, receiving wards and bathroom; remove the partition in the lying-in ward, and join room 3 and 22 to make a dayroom for one class of male inmates".

Examples of the October "Calls" were: Bettws £156, Penlline £110, Ewenny £92, Kenfig £74, Merthyr Mawr £58, Newton Nottage £246, Cwmdu £790, Coity Lower £592 and Llangeinor £360.

Mr Randall inquired in March 1880 whether the alterations to the Workhouse meant that the sanitation would be affected, but he was assured that this was not so because the changes did not involve drainage or an increase in inmates.

The following month the Board received a letter from the Vestry Clerk of Pencoed stating that their "ratepayers desired to sell cottages and premises of the parish and use the money for sanitation and a burial ground". This request led to a prolonged correspondence with the L.G.B.

The April "Calls" were slightly higher than in the previous October – for Cwmdu it was £804 and for Newton Nottage £256.

At the Election, Thomas John Edwards (Gent, Court House) became the member for Pencoed and James Barrow (Fairfield House) was re-elected for Coychurch Lower. The Assessment Committee reported that there had been 15 supplementary and one new valuation during the year. Out-door relief over the previous six months amounted to £4,448.15.8d for resident paupers and £131.8.0d for the non-resident.

The Medical Officers had been asked to give their opinions on conditions in the Workhouse and their report was now ready (May 1880). They considered the water to be of such poor quality that arrangements had to be made to get a supply from the new Water Company, and in order to expedite matters they had enlisted the aid of Mr Dyer, its secretary. He had said that the company was prepared to lay a pipe to the back of the Workhouse at a rental of £7 per annum, supply a meter at a charge of 1/6d per 1,000 gallons, and fix pipes and taps within the House for £5. A sub-committee composed of the Vice-Chairman, A.B. Price, William Jenkins, Thomas Morgan and Hugh Bevan supported the plan.

Structural changes to the Workhouse were also necessary - for which G.F. Lambert was appointed Clerk of Works at a salary of 2½% of the contract. A separate sub-committee was formed to superintend the alterations and the Chairman, Vice-Chairman, Colonel Turberville, Blandy Jenkins, Rev. F. W. Edmondes, A.B. Price, Hugh Bevan, Thomas Morgan and William Jenkins were elected members of it. Nine tenders were received ranging from £400 to £624 and that of £418 from Robert Jones was accepted. Mr Lambert commented: "The whole of the west side needs demolishing".

While all this was taking place the routine work of the Board was not neglected as shown by the dismissal of John Williams, the Assistant Overseer of Pyle, for inefficiency. Richard Davies replaced him with sureties from Rees Thomas and Joseph Joseph. Evan Matthews, the Assistant Overseer of Coychurch Lower was also asked to resign because he was: "Not a fit person to hold office".

Mr J.C. Nicholl, the Board's Chairman for many years, informed them that he wished to relinquish the office because he was going away for six to eight months, but it was prevailed on him to continue and take "leave of absence" instead. Others would chair in the meantime. (His second son, Lewis, at Clifton College, was going on a long sea voyage, because of illness, and he intended accompanying him).

The October "Calls" were generally lower than those of April, that of Cwmdu being £544, Llangeinor £416, Newcastle Higher £324, Newton Nottage £238, Llantwit Major £306 and Coity Lower £548.

Mr Lambert was paid £23 for altering the stairs, £18 for modifying the drainage, £3.7.6 for inserting plate glass in the windows instead of "leadlights" and £30 for raising the ceiling of the kitchen. Robert Jones had already received £78.8.0 as part of the contract and he was paid a further £80 in January 1881 when the new rooms were inspected for furnishing.

These new rooms were:- "The Committee Room, the Clerk's office, the men's receiving ward, the women's receiving ward, the Matron's room, the women's front dormitory, and the old men's new bedroom". It was agreed that an "earth closet" had to be provided in the lobby, ventilation "on top of the new staircase" and fireplaces (with a stone curb) in the "women's front dormitory, new old men's dayroom, men's receiving ward and new old men's bedroom". A note was left to the architect that the "urinals were inefficient" and that the "chimney piece in the old women's new room had to be of stone or slate - not wood" Laying hot water for the bath cost £3.15.0d. The balance of £39.9.1d was paid to Robert Jones on March 19th and £19.0.9d to Mr Lambert. The cost of the fireplaces was £36.19.0d and that of the laundry £26.18.0d.

Administrative problems were never far away and a troublesome one surfaced in February. Several Guardians wished to dismiss Mr Llewelyn, their Treasurer, but the L.G.B. maintained that, as his appointment had been permanent: "He can hold office till he dies, resigns, is removed by the Board or becomes insane". The causes of the dilemma were his desire to move the Union's account from the London and Provincial Bank to the National Bank of Wales, and his wish for a new bond of £3,000 to be drawn up, with Francis R. Crawshay, Forest House, Pontypridd (Chairman of the Bank) and F. R. Howell, Oaklands, Aberdare (its Vice-Chairman) as sureties. The Guardians' first reaction was to refuse to accept them though Mr Bircham, the Inspector, who was present at the meeting reminded them that "he could deposit the money wherever he liked". Mr Moon (Manager of the National Bank of Wales, Bridgend) and Mr Payne (Manager of the National Provincial Bank, Cowbridge) were both prepared to assist. But Board members were still dissatisfied and so they formed an ad hoc committee to study the implications of the change. The Vice-Chairman with J.B. Jenkins, Rev. F. Nicholl, Rev. F. W. Edmondes, Henry Lewis, William Howell, Hugh Bevan, Phillip John, Thomas Morgan and William Thomas were members of it. Their view was that the L.G.B. should be requested to investigate the "significance of the change of banks". This was done with the result that the storm in the proverbial teacup had settled within a month and the new bond signed.

Meanwhile other matters had to be attended to. A memorial was received from the Salford Union regarding the abolition of the office of Overseer of the Poor, but before discussing it the Guardians wished to know what the combined salary of the Union's Officers was. When they discovered that it was only £719.10.0d they decided to leave the memorial "on the table".

At the March Election thirteen refused to serve on the Board inclusive of the Rev. Spencer (Flemingston), Rev. Robert Thomas (Llandough juxtra Cowbridge), John Garsed and A.B. Price – though the latter was still on the Management Committee of the Cottage Homes. Mr. Nicholl was re-elected Chairman, James Barrow first Vice-Chairman, and William Jenkins – a farmer of Llanmihangel Place – the second Vice-Chairman.

The attention of the L.G.B. returned to the Workhouse and they requested the Guardians to fix its ward accommodation by "size and number". There was no immediate hurry but it had to be done carefully.

The cost of out-door relief over 6 months was £3,926.10.9 ½ d for the resident poor and £169.1.1d for the non- resident; £127.2.11d for vaccinations; £55.8.0d for registration; £947.11.5d for the Asylum "lunatics"; £12.10.0d for extra medical treatments and £532.10.7d for the Cottage Homes.

According to the Census the total number of inmates was 75 but most of the children were in the Homes (Chapter 13) though there were still 14 in the Workhouse – 3 of whom would soon be transferred there as they were 5 years of age or over. It had been arranged that a child going to the Homes would spend the first week in the Workhouse in order for a medical examination to be carried out and clothes supplied. The number of adults was slightly less than in the previous Census returns – 61 as against 65. There were 2 babies present, 4 a year old, 3 two years of age and 2 aged 3 years. Six males and 2 females were 80 years or over – the oldest being a male widower of 87 years from St Bride's. Thirteen were from Ireland, 4 from England and 1 from Scotland. Two females were recorded as being "imbeciles". One of the inmates, born in Carmarthen, had been a local Baptist Minister, Evan Howells – who was at Ruhamah Chapel in 1851.

Burials received attention and it was decided that elm coffins with four handles would be used at a cost of 16/0d each, and that 5/0d would be paid for digging the grave and taking charge. The payment for a similar coffin for a child under 16 years of age would be 6/0d.

A subscription of 2 gns a year each was paid to the funds of Swansea Hospital, Cardiff Infirmary, Bristol General Hospital and the Royal Hospital of Bath. This replaced the previous method of paying a fee direct to the Hospital authorities.

The "tram road" to the Workhouse had recently been bought by the Earl of Dunraven from the Llynfi Valley Railway Company and he agreed to honour the previous arrangement whereby it was to be handed over to the Board of Guardians for a peppercorn rent of 1/0d a year. The L.G.B. wondered what the implication of this was if an accident occurred on it. (The road became the responsibility of the Local Authority in August 1883).

Early in January 1882 the L.G.B. enquired about the envisaged occupancy of the wards. Mr Barrow, the Vice-Chairman, was asked to comment. He thought that further minor changes were necessary: "The present female sick ward should become the store room and vice versa, the lying-in ward should be the convalescent ward and the small one next to it for lying-in, and the two rooms by the washhouse should be bedrooms for children". The alterations were approved.

The L.G.B. returned to the request of the Pencoed Vestry regarding sanitation and a burial ground. They wished to know whether the burial ground was to be purchased or enclosed and what was meant by: "The burial ground is granted by the Court Leet of the Manor of Coity Walia? and "What is meant by the special sanitary rate"? The queries were referred to the Overseer of the parish. (The Court Leet was an ancient court that operated until about 1885. It was held twice a year and one of its functions was to settle boundary disputes. About 24 people attended and the expenses were met by the Lord of the Manor).

In March the Clerk, Mr Samuel Cox, requested that his son be appointed Assistant Clerk. He wrote: "I've needed clerical help for ten years or so. There are frequently two meetings at the same time on Saturdays and on these occasions my son has attended one of them. I think that this should be recognized". The appointment was duly made and confirmed by the L.G.B.

Seventy-two Guardians were elected, 55 of whom were farmers and 3 Clerics – S.H.F. Nicholl, F. W. Edmondes, and Henry James Humphrey (Llangan) who was new. J. C. Nicholl was re-elected to the Chair, an office he had held for twenty-five years, and Gronow John thanked him on behalf of the members. Samuel Cox was paid £36 for being Clerk to the School Attendance Committee.

Examples of the six monthly "Calls" were: Cowbridge £130, Llantwit Major £318, Cwmdu £662, Llandyfodwg £486, Llangeinor £570, Pencoed £162, St Bride's Major £182, St Bride's Minor £112, Coity Lower £560, Coity Higher £130, Newcastle Higher £356, Newcastle Lower £76 and Llangynwyd Middle £86.

The Workhouse needed further modification because the L.G.B. desired them to find accommodation within it for "contagious diseases" that would be separate from the wards for "infectious fevers – Smallpox and Cholera".

An important letter arrived in July from The National Providence League requesting support for the Government's Annuities and Insurance Bill in which universal insurance against destitution in sickness, infirmity or old age was being promoted. A petition to this effect was sent them for presentation to Parliament.

In March 1883 the L.G.B. wrote to say that the request of the Pencoed Vestry was "dragging on" and that it was time "a decision was reached". In the same month their long-serving Clerk, Samuel Cox, resigned owing to illhealth and great regret was expressed by all.

The following month there were two significant occurrences, one was the receipt of a memorandum from Mr Randall supporting the Ogmore Dock and Railway Bill, and the other the resignation of the Assistant Clerk, R. Harmar Cox.

At the Election, Thomas Thomas (Innkeeper, Bear Inn) and John Thomas (Chemist) were returned for Cowbridge, Thomas Lewis Roberts (Schoolmaster) and James Barrow for Cwmdu – though the latter also represented Ynysawdre; Rev. Henry James Humphreys for Llangan and George Birbeck (Mining Engineer) for Newcastle Higher.

The Assessment Committee reported that there had been fifty-three objections during the year – mainly from farmers.

The Pencoed affair came to the fore again in April and the Guardians, acting on a suggestion made by the Rev. F. W. Edmondes, asked the Overseer to hold a full Vestry meeting to reconsider the request they had made three years previously.

The Rev. F. W. Edmondes was elected Chairman and James Barrow and William Jenkins, Vice-Chairmen as before. It was announced that A.B. Price (West House, Bridgend) had died and that therefore it was necessary for William Thomas, the Assistant Overseer of Newcastle Lower, to find a new surety. David Rees (Park Farm) stepped into the breach.

The post of Clerk was advertised in the Bridgend Chronicle and Central Glamorgan Gazette (24th March 1883) at a reduced salary of £130 with £20 for arranging the Election of Guardians, also to be Clerk to the Rural Sanitary Authority at £50 p.a., and Clerk to the Assessment Committee and School Attendance Committee at a salary determined by the Guardians and approved by the L.G.B.. Mr. R. Harmar Cox, the previous Assistant Clerk, was appointed on 5th May.

Information was received from the Pencoed Vestry that they were "not now desirous of selling". Perhaps the Rev. Edmondes had had prior knowledge of the change of mind!

A letter arrived from the Northampton Union explaining that they were "endeavouring to change the method of electing Guardians" and its contents were debated at some length. Finally they agreed by a narrow majority (9:7) that the voting should be by ballot. Soon afterwards the Swansea Union sent them a copy of a memorial they had sent to Parliament regarding, not only the Election of Guardians, but also that of Town Councillors and members of School Boards. They were told by the Clerk that: "In the Election of Guardians the number of voting papers supplied to a ratepayer is proportional to his assessment and he puts his initials opposite the candidate of his choice; that in the election of Town Councillors each ratepayer has one vote and puts a cross opposite his chosen candidate; and that with School Boards the voter has as many votes as members with the right of putting all of them for one person. They preferred a cross to be put opposite the candidate in the election of Guardians. They also thought a triennial election was more appropriate then the present annual one, and that the payment of "Calls" should be in two instalments rather than four – but this latter suggestion was later rescinded. They favoured the triennial election so strongly that they informed the L.G.B. of their wish, but it was not supported by them at the time. On the other hand, the payment of "Calls" by two instalments was approved – despite the final negative vote of the Guardians.

The County rate at a farthing in the £1 was £227.11.11d, the Police rate at a halfpenny in the £1, £455.3.10d and the County Roads rate at an eighth of a penny in the £1, £113.15.11d.

Several paupers were being apprenticed with payment of £5 at the beginning and £5 the following year if progress was satisfactory. Two suits of clothes were also supplied. Occasionally the apprenticing was more enlightened than one would have expected, as when a blind boy, Joseph Davies, sent to the Blind Home, Swansea, showed considerable talent as a piano player and was given appropriate lessons paid for out of the Union's funds. When, a few years later, someone suggested that he might be able to earn a living as a basket-maker the answer was: "No, but he could as a piano-player or an organist". Unfortunately it is not known what the outcome was.

The Rev. R.P. Llewelyn, Llangynwyd sent them the following letter in November: "The old churchyard is full, also the northern portion of the new one, and only six grave places are left in the southern. **All the spaces must be kept for parishioners.** The new cemetery is ready in Maesteg – portion set apart for use of Church of England, consecrated 19th inst for Nonconformists and Roman Catholics. During my incumbency 4,628 have been buried in two small churchyards.

I'm compelled to **refuse** further bodies from the Workhouse. Inform the Director of Burials and ask him to consult the Clerk of the Burial Board re. regulations and fees for the cemetery".

The running costs for the previous six months were noted in December:- maintenance of inmates not charged to the parishes, £385.4.7½d, out-door relief £3,146.14.1d, non-settled poor £131.0.0d, vaccinations £370.10.0d, Registration £81.6.6d, lunatics in Asylum £535.9.6d., pauper school fees

£57.11.3d, Cottage Homes £535.9.6d and the School Attendance Committee £125.13.3d.

Mr Bircham commented on the Workhouse: "The wards are clean and in good order". He had reservations though about the record-keeping in that the Medical Officer's book was not properly filled and the comments of the Visiting Committee too sparse. He suggested that when they inspected the Workhouse they should do so in the company of the Medical Officer.

The earlier request that Cowbridge should become a separate Union must have had some effect on their attitude despite its refusal because in March 1884 it was decided that the Union: "Be divided into two for purposes of relief", and thereafter Cowbridge was dealt with as a separate entity. Another innovation introduced at the same time was the allowing of Dissenting Ministers to visit the Workhouse during the week – provided permission was granted by the Master.

The amount of money received from the Paymaster General the previous year was £230.4.11d with £762.12.0d for the pauper 'lunatics' (Chapter 16).

Mr Llewelyn, the Treasurer, left in July and Mr Moon, Manager of the National Bank of Wales, Bridgend, replaced him. Thomas Payne (Manager of the National Provincial Bank, Cowbridge), John William Pritchard (Manager of the London and Provincial Bank, Bridgend) and Thomas George Smith (Manager of the National Provincial Bank, Bridgend) were also candidates.

A new district, by the name of Ogmore and Garw, was formed in November. It consisted of Llandyfodwg, part of Llangeinor and part of Coychurch Higher – with a population of 4,931. The salary of its Medical Officer was to be £15 (Chapter 12).

The sad news was received in December that their Ex-Clerk, Samuel Cox, had died and sincere sympathy was extended to the family. His demise precipitated an unexpected problem in that it left the post of Superintendent Registrar vacant and apparently if it was not filled within 14 days "the post would lapse to the Registrar General". A hurried advertisement was put in the press and the new Clerk, R.H. Cox, appointed.

In February 1885 Mr Cox became Clerk to the Eastern Districts Roads Board – a post previously held by his father – which meant that he would be sometimes absent from meetings of the Board of Guardians.

A rather amusing directive came from the L.G.B. around the same time which was worded in a very positive manner: "Drop the word Cwmdu and call the area Maesteg – Maesteg Higher, Maesteg Middle and Maesteg Lower – because that is the term used by the local people". As if the local people did not know!

A petition regarding the Sunday closing of Public Houses arrived in March and they replied that they had already discussed the subject and were supporting it.

There was a rare occurrence in April. Ebenezer Davies, the Assistant Overseer of Cowbridge, 'absconded' without warning though he had given notice to the Provident Clerks' Guarantee Society regarding his £200 security. A David Evans replaced him. It later transpired that the Overseer had owed £220.16.9d and the balance was duly received but not before a threat to summon him had been made.

The Assessment Committee reported that the rateable value of houses in Bettws, Llangeinor, Llandyfodwg, Newcastle Higher and Ynysawdre had to be raised. Colonel Franklen was now its Chairman.

The L.G.B. requested changes in representation to the Board of Guardians in April. Sker, Sternbridge and Nash were to cease to be represented; Llandyfodwg was to have 3, Llangeinor 3, Bettws 2 and Newcastle Higher 2. New sureties were necessary for John Deere, Assistant Overseer of Llantwit Major and John Deere, White Hart and Alban Watts, Brewer, were accepted.

The Rev. F.W. Edmondes was re-elected Chairman with William Jenkins and William Howell (Pencoed) Vice-Chairmen.

The Board's opinion on the distribution of Polling districts was requested in June and minor changes were suggested by them, such as: "One of the polling stations should be at Tynewydd instead of Nantymoel" but, on the whole, they were satisfied with the arrangements as they were.

Attention was again focused on the Workhouse because it had become necessary for the Medical Officers and the Guardians to decide on the "number of inmates per ward according to a scale issued by the L.G.B.". It was agreed that the sick men's ward could accommodate 7, the infirm ward 2, the married couples ward 2, and the lying-in ward 2. The projected maximum total of inmates was fixed at 126 excluding Vagrants (Chapter 17).

The October 'Call' of £4,689 was to be received in two instalments, that for Llangeinor being £480, Pencoed £96, Coity Lower £320, Newton Nottage £100, Pyle £124, Llanbleddian £116, Llantwit Major £196, Bettws £164 and Cwmdu £468.

Out-door relief over six months amounted to £553.12.0d for Cowbridge, £1,067.16.4d for Maesteg and £1,045.12.5d for Bridgend. The total for the non-resident poor was £81.3.0d.

Further changes in boundaries were made in November such as the joining of Llanmihangel to Llanmaes and Eglwys Brewis to Flemingston, but they were of minor significance and were not commented on by the L.G.B.

Several Vaccination Centres had to be paid for. The one for Pontycymmer was in the long room of the Temperance Hotel for which Evan Thomas, the proprietor, received £3 a year; that for Porthcawl in the home of a Mr. W.E. Davies for £4, and in Llantwit Major a Mr. Dark was paid £2. There were also others in suitable locations. Printed notices in both English and Welsh were placed on the walls of these stations pointing out the duties of parents under the Vaccinations Acts and the penalties for ignoring them.

A somewhat strange demand came from the L.G.B. in November. They wanted to know forthwith what the Board's investments were, and this was followed three months later by another epistle containing the information that £128.4.7d of their money invested in Consols with the Bank of England was going to be transferred to the Commissioners "for reduction of the National Debt as dividends had been unclaimed for over ten years". The problem was immediately referred to the Finance and Visiting Committee with the object of getting "the stock to the Board's Bank and the dividends to the Guardians". This was money·

invested by the Board from the sale of Poorhouses and parish properties, as exemplified by the sale of St Athan's Poorhouse in 1857 – Chapter 6.

The L.G.B. instructed them to increase the representation of St Bride's Major, Llangeinor, Bettws and Newcastle Higher and authorized them to summon Coychurch Lower for "non-payment of the Call". There were several parishes "in arrears" and they were all warned that they could be summoned, but in no instance did this become necessary.

The employment of a short-hand typist by the Assessment Committee "to take evidence in Colliery appeals" was approved, and the Guardians were told that William Evans of Glyn-neath, who had been appointed the previous year at a salary of £30 per annum, was a great help in valuing collieries and in coping with disputes.

At the Election the Rev. F.W. Edmondes remained Chairman, Thomas Rees became the first Vice-Chairman and William Howell the second as before. Mr. Tucker, their funeral director informed them that he was going: "To use a dark wagonette in future for the conveyance of coffins instead of the dog-cart as at present".

In August they decided to obtain a "bedstead with sides" for a man with epilepsy. At long last the sick wards were beginning to look like those of a hospital.

Chapter 10

Masters and Matrons

Husband and Wife Partnerships (6), Other Masters (5),
Other Matrons (6), Combined Cook and Assistant Matron (4),
Combined Nurse and Assistant Matron (4), Complaints, Enquiries,
Misbehaviour, Oakum Picking, Birching.

The Workhouse could not be administered statisfactorily without an efficient Master and Matron. Success or otherwise depended on their ability to co-operate with the Guardians, the Relieving Officers and the Medical Officer in charge. Order had to be maintained without excessive zeal or unfairness that would cause disharmony. The sexes had to be kept apart, even when married, as conjugal life was not allowed. Drunkenness had to be avoided. Work had to be found for the inmates, and Vagrants had to do their quota in order to pay for their keep. The activites of children had to be organised and arrangements made for illness to be treated. Food had to be ordered, meals cooked and served, clothing attended to, and the building maintained in a reasonable state of repair.

The first Master and Matron were Mr John Tussell, aged 32 years, and his wife, Mary, from Carmarthen. They were bilingual and were appointed in August 1838 when the Workhouse was nearing completion. His salary was £40 a year, and hers £25 – 'exclusive of board and lodging.' It was Mr Tusssell who bought clothes for the incoming paupers, as well as other necessary items such as soap and candles. He always asked the Guardians for permission before buying, and it was usually granted, the cost being met the following week. In May 1839 he was allowed to employ a woman servant in the Workhouse, and a month later the Board agreed that he could have someone to dig and hoe the garden.

Their salary was reconsidered in April 1840 and it was decided to pay them £52 with an additional £52 for food. The garden was for their own use. If they did not accept the terms they could leave in three months' time. This autocratic attitude of the Guardians was not unusual. A committee of five prominent members of the Board visited the Workhouse every week to make sure that all was well.

There was a strange development in October 1841. Captain Napier, the Chief Constable of the County, was permitted to use the right wing of the establishment 'for the housing and victualling of the new Constabulary about to be assembled in Bridgend.' They were there for 5 weeks while waiting for their uniforms. The Master was allowed to contract 'on his own account for the messing and to use the cooking apparatus and the coal of the Workhouse for that purpose' (Chapter 4).

There were only two paupers in the House at the time, but the number must have increased rapidly, because in March 1842 Mr Tussell was criticized for his treatment of the able-bodied men: "He is much too lenient, and this is subversive of the intention of the Poor Law Act and the necessary and wholesome discipline that was intended". He was warned that he would be dismissed 'unless a much more strict and rigorous supervision was forthwith adopted'.

A special meeting of the Guardians was convened in April 1844 to "further discuss the medical cover and possible increase of salary to the Master and Matron with discontinuation of the ration money allowance". It was agreed that £65 be paid provided the garden was relinquished.

Numerous tasks had to be supervised, such as sweeping the chimneys, opening and checking the drains, cleaning the cesspools, washing the privies, pitching the yard, moving the smoky stove from the kitchen 'in a workmanlike manner', leading the base of the chimney in the boys' bedroom, attending to the clocks, repairing the locks and many others, not forgetting the keeping of accurate and legible accounts.

Everything was going reasonably well until the following month. A tragedy then occurred. A young woman was admitted in the evening with convulsions, which continued all night. Dr Pritchard, the House Medical Officer, was not contacted until 8 o'clock the following morning. He could not come at the time and Dr Abraham Verity came instead. He prescribed medicine. Dr Pritchard arrived two days later and bled her 'because it was necessary'.

The Commissioners were informed. They took the view that the Master was guilty of neglect for 'admitting a pauper direct to the House without first placing her in the receiving ward (as per regulation) and sending for the doctor'. He had also been neglectful in not sending for the doctor until the following morning when she had been 'fitting' all night. It was also his duty to contact another doctor when he found that Dr Pritchard was not available. They instructed the Guardians to admonish him, and to tell him that should that type of neglect recur he would probably be dismissed. They accepted his word that the receiving ward was being used for something else and wanted to know why that was so. No explanation was forthcoming. The Master took umbrage at the severity of the reprimand and promptly resigned giving a month's notice. Mr. Thomas Williams, one of his guarantors wrote to the Board withdrawing his name, but the Clerk replied that although Mr. Tussell was leaving, liability remained for a further month during which time the books would be checked.

An advertisement for his replacement was placed in the Cambrian, the Cardiff Advertiser, the Great Western Advertiser and the Naval and Military Gazette. Both Master and Matron had to be bilingual and have a 'knowledge of accounts'.

Mr. Thomas Phillips, a coal merchant of Llandaff, and his wife Catherine, were appointed in September 1844. The 'penal sum' was £100. Two hundred pounds was suggested but 'negatived'. The salary was £65 per annum and it was made clear to them that the post was full time.

The garden was the responsibility of the Guardians because it was no longer used by the Master. He was asked to obtain half a sack of 'early farmers' potatoes, two sacks of the 'white Lancashire' variety, two sacks of the 'late red' as well as four ounces of leek seeds. A gardener was later employed. Twenty loads of manure were received and three hundred-weight of early potatoes planted.

In March 1849 the Master was paid £1.9.0 to take the wife and family of William Powell, "now in Cardiff jail for absconding from the Workhouse with the Union clothes on his person, to Cardiff to be delivered to the said William Powell on his discharge from jail".

The Visiting Committee noticed that several infants had a skin eruption and the Master was asked to obtain the opinion of the Medical Officers (Chapter 11).

His accounts were carefully studied in an effort to reduce the high cost of maintenance. It transpired that the principal cause was 'the arbitrary charging of a penny per day for the clothing without reference to the actual cost'. The charge had been made to 'liquidate the balance loss when a halfpenny a day was charged'. There was no explanation why this administrative exercise was justified and no mention made of who had authorised it. At one stage he employed a woman with a 'base-born' child to assist in the booking for the House and was told to discontinue doing so immediately, as 'women with base-born children should be kept strictly in the ward'.

In June 1849 he asked permission to keep his father-in-law in the House as a member of the family', he, the Master, 'providing food, clothing, bedding and other necessities at his own expense'. The father-in-law was 75 years of age and 'nearly helpless'.

The Guardians were doubtful about their power to comply, but promised to explain matters to the Poor Law Board and to request their guidance. Permission was refused and the Master was told 'to send his father-in-law from the Workhouse and never to admit him again'. (The Poor Law Board did not appear to be more considerate than the Commissioners had been!)

The following December, the Visiting Committee reported adversely on the state of the 'Vagrant Wards'.

Mr. and Mrs. Phillips decided they had lost the Board's confidence and resigned. A reference was refused. Mrs. Howells, their servant, also left (Chapter 17).

Mr. and Mrs. Jenkins were then appointed from among many applicants. They were aged 57 years and 61 years respectively. The husband was to receive £35 and the wife £17 'with rations'. The £65 previously paid had been reduced to £52 although there were 'fifty paupers on average in the House'. Mr. David Jenkins was one of the Relieving Officers and so had to relinquish that post as well as his Registrarship of Births, Marriages and Deaths. The Matron's new assistant, previously called a servant, was Miss Elizabeth Deere, aged 16 years, and she received £4 a year.

In July the Master visited the Monmouth jail in order to discuss 'oakum picking' with Mr. Bennett, its Governor. He explained that 'old rope was cut into lengths of 6 inches to 8 inches, separated into single cords, and then beaten with a mallet similar to that used by plumbers. If the quality of the rope was good the quantity required to be picked by each individual should be 7½ pounds.

Anything less would not be penal'. The Board decided to adopt the 'oakum picking' as the task work of all able-bodied paupers within the House.

Soon afterwards the Visiting Committee of the Workhouse reported that some of the 'floors there were stained' and that 'some of the able-bodied women with bastard children were not clean in their persons'. It was also pointed out that the 'irremediables needed special attention' and that 'paupers relieved out of the House should from time to time be admitted'.

Two years later, on the 28th of April 1851, Mr. Jenkins died suddenly. He had been born in Henley-on-Thames and his wife in Llantwit Major. The vacant 'husband and wife post' was advertised in the Cambrian, the Merthyr Guardian and the Bristol Mercury. Fluency in both English and Welsh was essential and the Master had to know book-keeping. Testimonials had to be supplied. The appointments committee consisted of the Reverend John Griffiths, the Reverend Thomas Edmondes, John Garsed, Morgan P. Smith, Rees Powell, Watkin Bevan and Daniel Llewelyn. In May they appointed Mr. and Mrs. Silvanus Dalton.

In October the Visiting Committee suggested that 'from 20 to 30 tons of stones and half a ton of junk be obtained for the purpose of employing able-bodied paupers, should any such apply for relief, and that the Chairman of the Board be requested to apply to the agent of the Earl of Dunraven for permission to deposit the stones on a waste piece of land pointed out by him'.

Soon afterwards the Master was asked to take proceedings against 'a late female inmate for running away with articles of clothing'. She was later found guilty by Bridgend Magistrates and sentenced to six weeks hard labour at the House of Correction, Swansea.

By now pigs were being reared at the Workhouse and in January 1852 the Master sold three of them at 7/0 score pounds. Their combined weights came to 35 score 11 pounds, for which he received £12.8.9d. He paid 4 pence for weighing them and 5/0 for a horse and cart to convey them to the purchaser in Maesteg.

Three months later the Matron complained to the Master, her husband, that she was unhappy about the conduct of two inmates - a man and a woman. They 'countercharged' by claiming that she had been seen drunk in the town. A Sub-committee of William Llewelyn (Vice-Chairman), Reverend John Harding, Reverend John Griffiths, J. N. Nicholl Carne, Watkin Bevan, Rees Powell and Robert Leyshon was formed to investigate the charge. The Poor Law Board agreed that a searching inquiry was necessary. This was carried out and it soon became evident that the circumstances were not straightforward.

It appeared that the Matron had 'passed out' on the road in Bridgend. Captain C.F. Napier, the Chief Constable, had seen her fall and, though suspicious, he did not think she was drunk. Bearing this in mind the Poor Law Board acquitted her of the charge but added that the Guardians should 'tell her to be careful'. The Master had evidently shown his annoyance in no uncertain manner because he later apologised to the Guardians for doing so.

The inmates had to be fed according to the rules, new clothes had to be bought for them every six months or so, good behaviour and sobriety had to be ensured, allotted tasks had to be performed and their health had to be supervised. It was the Master who informed the doctor when they were ill, and it was he who ensured that the treatment prescribed was carried out correctly. By and large the Medical Officer and he were on good terms, but difficulties sometimes arose. This was so in September, 1852, when an infant pauper died under 'suspicious circumstances'. The Master thought there had been 'foul play'. Dr. Verity, the Medical Officer in charge, disagreed. In his opinion the diarrhoea that the baby had had for three weeks was due to a cold, dysentery had then developed and it was this that had killed him. Another infant had also died from what the Master called 'lack of attention'. The doctor had to be called many times before he came. Apparently he was out and came as soon as he could. The baby was dying. He told the Master: "Give him a little wine, but it's hopeless". The Guardians considered all the evidence and decided that no blame was attached to Dr. Verity.

In the same month the Reverend William Sorness 'preferred a charge' of drunkenness against Mrs. Dalton and requested that Dr. Verity and Police Superintendent Sadler be called as witnesses. They said that she had been too drunk to attend to her duties when they saw her.

Three weeks later the Board received a letter from her stating: "Through ill health and continued pains in my limbs I cannot fulfil the arduous duties of the Establishment. I beg leave therefore to decline the situation as Matron here. For all past favours I am grateful and with much respect to the Board". She was allowed to go in a fortnight.

The Clerk of the Guardians, Mr. William Edmondes, then wrote to the central authority requesting permission to continue the employment of Mr. Dalton. John Graves, the Poor Law Inspector of the district, drew attention to article 189 of the Consolidation Order of the Commissioners dated 24th July 1847: 'If Master and Matron be husband and wife and one leaves for some reason, the other or survivor in the case of death, must leave at the end of the current quarter'.

This was contrary to the Guardians' wishes, and so for the time being they decided to cope by appointing an Acting Matron - at £17 per annum. Mrs. Mary Maliphant from Swansea accepted the challenge and they were so impressed with her that in December they made her Matron. They also re-appointed Mr. Dalton as the new Master, despite the contents of the Consolidation Order of 1847. This shows that they had the courage and the authority to act independently when they were convinced that what they were doing was in the best interest of the Establishment.

The Workhouse continued to function as before as evidenced by the fact that two pigs were sold for £3.8.0 and four piglets bought at 10/0 each.

Its smooth running was interrupted sometimes by troublesome events. A large number of people confined in a limited space could not always be expected to follow the rules and they did not do so in September 1854. At the inevitable inquiry that followed the Master said: "David Bryant, an inmate, bought 7/6 worth of rum in Bridgend and brought it back. He often goes to the town for messages and medicine and he always tells me. I lock the outer door after him and open it on his return. On that day I had been to Pyle to a raffle for a pony belonging to a poor woman, the wife of an Exciseman. I returned at eight in the evening and all the inmates had gone to bed. I have a key of my own for the House. I have often been as late as nine-thirty in Bridgend, but never as late as ten. I always attend the paupers at meal times and cut up the provisions myself. I am never the worse for liquor. When I came back that night Mrs. Maliphant was by the door. It seems a visitor had given an inmate some money. It seems Bryant had had 7/6 worth of rum at Phillips' Spirit Shop. The front door is always locked at night. Two women inmates had come with me".

David Davies, alias Bryant, continued with; "Some of the women got drunk. Someone had sent me to town. I fetched six noggins of rum for one of the women, paying three shillings for it. I had been given the money. I was asked again but didn't go though I would get sixpence for my trouble. Ann Davies was the culprit. That time it was one of the painters who went. I share a bedroom with Charles Thomas who is sick, and I attend on him. When Ann Davies spoke to me I was wheeling rubbage out to the river and the door was open for me to go in and out to do so. I was not aware that I was liable to punishment for carrying spirits into the House. I have been an inmate for two to three years and thought that spirit was for a sick person".

Dr. Leahy was asked for his opinion and he said: "Dr. Verity has recently had a severe accident. I attend the Workhouse at all hours - sometimes as late as eleven or twelve because of confinements. I've never seen the Master drunk or confused".

Mrs. Maliphant's version was as follows: "I only leave the Workhouse on business. That evening the women were unruly and I sent them into the yard and locked the door. Then I was told there was spirits in the dining room. I asked how it got there and Ann Davies said: "No business of yours". I found the bottle and took it away. It was an empty quart bottle. Ann Davies followed me and she was very abusive, she swore and threatened to knock me down. I go to bed at nine. The women were all in bed when Mr. Dalton returned about eight. I have never had cause to suspect that spirits has come into the House. Mr. Dalton left at one. I have seen him sometimes worse for drink - not often: a sober man. He is often out when I go to bed - especially lately. Men and women can't go into each other's rooms as the doors are always locked. Neither could the man who brought the spirits go into the female house. Ann Davies was admitted on 5th August last. She was given Union clothes, but she wouldn't wear them, saying: 'I'm here for a short time only - about one or two weeks'. She kept her own clothes. It was not my duty to search her".

Mr. Thomas Arnott, the Relieving Officer, spoke next: "I gave the order to admit Ann Davies. She had been turned out by her husband, and her mother and father refused to have her. So I took her myself to the Workhouse. There was no written order. She was destitute and had not eaten for three days when I saw her. The husband said that he would reimburse the expense. I informed the Overseer of the circumstances but I did not bring it before the Board though I did mention it to the Chairman".

The whole account as quoted was submitted to the Poor Law Board, and the Guardians expressed the view 'that they did not want extreme punishment on the Officers or the inmates'.

However, Thomas Arnott resigned and the Guardians decided to investigate his books. There was a suspicion that they had been 'falsified' (Chapter 14). The eagerly awaited verdict of the Poor Law Board came at the end of October. In their opinion 'the whole episode had shown considerable mismanagement, neglect of duty and ignorance on the part of the Relieving Officer, the Master and the Matron. There had been no written order for the admission of Ann Davies and the Guardians did not have the details. The Master frequently absented himself and kept late hours. His behaviour exceeded the bounds of temperance. There were no entries about the time he entered or left the Workhouse. Regarding the Matron – she had not searched Ann Davies as required, and had not clothed her in Workhouse dress. She did not know when Bryant had returned. All three should be reprimanded'.

The evidence shows the kind of life the Master, Matron and inmates led in the Workhouse. Although there were many regulations their application was not as strict as one might have supposed. In no way was the Bridgend Union Workhouse a jail or a Bastille. It is surprising that rum was thought to be such an evil drink when large quantities of porter, wine and, sometimes, gin were being officially ordered. The quantity of porter in the early years averaged 30 – 40 pints (at $2\frac{1}{2}$d a pint) every week, the wine about 20 pints (at 2/0 a pint) and, on the twenty-eighth of January, 1854, they ordered 5 pints of gin (at 1/9 a pint). Of course the drinking water was of dubious quality despite the water pump that they had, and this may have been the explanation.

On 20th March 1855 Mrs. Maliphant died after a short illness. Her services had been greatly appreciated because the following entry was made : 'The Board deeply laments the death of the Matron who for two and a half years has fulfilled her duties to the perfect satisfaction of the Guardians'. In the advertisement that followed it was mentioned that they were looking for a person who was a good housekeeper, could cut clothes for the women and who would attend the sick. Knowledge of Welsh was indispensable.

Ann Richards of Swansea was appointed at a salary of £20 a year with 'board and lodging'. She resigned in 1857 and Mrs. Margaret Williams became Matron. The post was keenly contested. Mrs. Ann Gair of Bridgend was favoured by the appointments committee but when it came to a general vote she received 10 votes and Mrs. Williams 12. Thomas Lewis of Bridgend promised a surety of fifty pounds.

In the meantime Mr. Dalton resigned and became Master of Cardigan Workhouse (He left that post in 1865 because of illness and died soon after). He was replaced by a Mr. Shaw. His was an unfortunate appointment because 'he did not give proper attention to the books'. According to the Guardians there was 'no intention to defraud'.

In July Mr Shaw took unauthorised leave to attend to business in Merthyr Tydfil and the Guardians suspended him without pay. The following month he promised to get the books up to date if he were allowed to work in the boardroom from ten to four each day. He thought that he could complete the task in a fortnight. Permission was granted. However, he had been too optimistic because, according to the Auditor there was still a deficit of £6.2.0 ¾,d. Mr. Shaw ascribed this to clothes that he had given the Relieving Officers as out-door relief to children - but, apparently, none had been requested. Despite the Guardians' intention to stop his salary when he was suspended the Poor Law Board insisted that he be paid until he left office. During his absence the Matron took over.

A special meeting was held in July, soon after Mr. Shaw's suspension, to discuss whether the Master's salary should be increased. It was decided that henceforth he would receive fifty pounds per annum. They also concluded that it would be wise to advertise more widely for a Master than they had done hitherto. Consequently, two advertisements were placed in the Times, the Hereford Times, Bristol Mercury, Naval and Military Gazette and the usual Merthyr Guardian and the Cambrian.

Mr. James Wells, aged 36 years from Surrey, and Mr. Edwin Wilson were shortlisted. Mr. Wells was appointed, and £3.10.0 travelling expenses given to Mr. Wilson. Henry Jenning and James Wells, both of Farnham, Surrey, were his sureties, and the names of two solicitors in Farnham were given 'as proof of their respectability'. They assured the Board that the two persons concerned were highly responsible.

The Matron was directed in September 'to punish the inmate, Ann Sullivan, by placing her on a disorderly diet for 48 hours for having left her sleeping room to enter the sick ward where she was found between 12 and 1 o'clock.' Around this time an inmate, Peter Jones, was sent to court for misbehaving in the House and the Magistrates fined him 5/6. Elizabeth James and Elizabeth Price were fined 11/0 for misconduct. Elizabeth James was fined a further 7/6 for 'a similar offence'.

There was a strange occurrence in January 1858. Apparently many paupers were escaping over the wall of the front yard. It was decided that; 'the best way of preventing it was to raise the wall three feet and to place iron spikes or glass on the top'. This was done.

Two months later the barber, Mr. Wrigley, refused to shave and cut the hair of Vagrants in the Casual Ward. He maintained that it was not included in his contract. They advertised for a replacement, but no-one applied. Mr. Wells, the Master, then submitted a tender and it was accepted. He was to be paid £1.5.0 a quarter.

Mr. Shaw, the previous Master, was still somewhat troublesome. He had been charged for the deficit in his books, but maintained that it had been due to 'cheese losing 45 ½% in the cutting' and the fact that 'lots of potatoes had gone bad'. Mr. Wells showed that only '15% of the cheese need be lost'. Under the circumstances the Guardians concluded that Mr. Shaw had 'no grounds for appeal'.

The Matron received £8 for the period she acted as Master (18th July to 10th October) together with her salary. For reasons unexplained she resigned in June

1858. Three applicants were shortlisted including Mrs Dunn, the Schoolmistress, who was appointed with more votes than the other two combined. Mr. Wells and her got on well together despite the fact that for a few months she also taught the children. The only criticism was that the 'accommodation and the treatment of Vagrants left much to be desired'.

In February 1859 Mr. Morgan Phillips made the surprising accusation that 'pigs in the town were being fattened with food from the Workhouse' and that 'vegetables from there were being taken to the homes of some of the Guardians'. Apparently, an inmate had claimed that three pigs had been fattened, and that John Lloyd, another inmate, had been obliged to 'carry leeks and vegetables daily to the residence of Mr. Gronow John'. When questioned John Lloyd denied everything. What he had told Mr. Jenkins, the inmate who had spread the rumour, was that he had been going out every day to post letters. He had taken half a dozen leeks to Mrs. John on one occasion - at her request - in order to show 'the quality of the leeks that were being grown from seed in the Workhouse garden'. The Reverend C.R. Knight supported by the Reverend S. Jones moved that no complaint was to be made against the Master.

The atmosphere between the Master, Matron and Schoolmistress was becoming more relaxed and it was agreed that they could eat whatever the Master wished. Their diet would be 'at his discretion in accordance with what was being practiced at the Chepstow Union Workhouse'.

The Poor Law Board inquired in March whether an inmate, Harry Rowland, who suffered from 'fits and excitability' was 'ever placed under restraint, and if so, how often? and of what kind?' The reply was that 'he had been placed in a separate room occasionally (twice last year) because of his threatening behaviour and that some inmates kept out of his way'. No 'restraint' had been used.

The Guardians received a serious complaint from the Matron in August: "Mr. Wells treats me with disrespect before inmates and undermines my authority. No-one can work satisfactorily in such circumstances". She resigned the following month although the Guardians tried to convince her that their differences were 'too minor to justify her leaving'.

The vacancy was advertised in the Bristol Mercury, Hereford Times, Cambrian, Merthyr Guardian, Midland Counties Herald, Bridgend Chronicle and Bridgend Times. The successful applicant had to be a good housekeeper, able to make clothes, attend the sick and be free of any 'encumbrance'. The salary was to be £20 per annum. The ability to speak Welsh was not mentioned. There were five applicants - the Matron of the Llanelli Workhouse, the late nurse of Hay Union Hospital, the late schoolmistress of Merthyr Union, Mrs. Gow (Swansea) and Mrs. Roy (Llysworney). Mrs. Emma Mitchell of Llanelli was appointed. She arrived in September 1860 when there was no Schoolmistress and willingly agreed to teach temporarily 'provided she was paid extra for doing so'. The following December, she relinquished her post having been appointed Housekeeper to the Joint Counties' Lunatic Asylum, Abergavenny.

As Christmas was approaching, the Master arranged a festive dinner for the inmates and suggested that the money for it should come 'from the common fund and not from subscriptions as heretofore'. The Guardians agreed. It cost £7.6.8. Twelve applications were received for the Matron's post - two from London, two from Hereford, and one from each of the following, Hungerford, Usk, Dursley, Worcester, Neath, Taibach, Bridgend and Pencoed. Evidently such posts were becoming popular and the wide appeal showed the success of advertising far afield combined with the efficacy of the recently-established railway system. Discontinuing the need for bilingualism must also have been a factor. Three were shortlisted and Mrs. Caroline Powell, aged 44 years, of the House of Correction, Usk was appointed. She had been born in Oxfordshire. Seemingly, the Guardians, and indeed the public, thought the duties of Matron, Schoolteacher and Housekeeper were the same, and it made no difference whether they worked in a Workhouse, an Asylum or a House of Correction. She arrived in February 1861. The Master and Schoolmistress had done the work while the post was vacant and had divided the money between them. The endless stream of resignations continued. Mr. Wells, the Master, resigned in May having been appointed Master to the Workhouse in Southampton. The verdict on him was: that his 'character and conduct had been exemplary'.

In December 1857 the Workhouse had the services of a Cook-a Mary John of Quarella Road. She was paid an annual salary of £12. She resigned in April 1859 and had not been replaced by June 1861.

There were thirty-six applicants for Mr Wells' post consisting of Workhouse masters, schoolmasters, porters, a police superintendent, a sergeant of the Royal Artillery, a relieving officer and a postmaster from Bethnal Green. One of the masters who applied was Silvanus Dalton who had been employed by them five years previously. Henry Mathews who was a porter in the Bath Workhouse was appointed. Five months later he left to become a Relieving Officer in Knighton and was given a glowing reference by the Clerk.

William Jenkins was the next appointee at a salary of £50 per annum 'with rations'. The shaving of indoor paupers and the cutting of hair were continued by him on a contractual basis of £5 per quarter. He was still the barber two years later. Caroline Powell the Matron was paid £20 per year (June 1864).

The following August the Master resigned having been appointed Clerk of the nearby Lunatic Asylum. He had held the Office for nearly three years. Twenty-eight people applied for the vacant post, ten of whom were schoolmasters. Edward Bevan, lately the master of Swansea Workhouse, and William Leyshon of Island Farm, Bridgend were shortlisted and the latter appointed.

In December Mrs Warnum, the Schoolmistress, and Mrs Powell, the Matron, both applied unsuccessfully for the post of Housekeeper to the County Asylum. A year later the Matron had her salary increased to £30 per annum. In response to a request from the P.L.B. for an explanation of this increase the Clerk replied that she was senior to the Schoolmistres (salary £30), worked hard and in the absence of a Nurse had cared for patients with Cholera. This was accepted and approval given.

In April '68 she became ill and Dr. Verity recommended a fortnight's sick leave with a 'change of air'. This was granted but she continued to feel unwell after returning and the following August resigned. Strangely the Master left at about the same time without giving a credible explanation. Perhaps they had some sort of understanding!

Four married couples applied for the post and Mr and Mrs W .T. Bounds were appointed with a surety of £100. Mr Bounds was 41 years of age and his wife aged 38; they were born in St Pancras. Their daughter, aged 8 years, was to be looked after 'out of House'. If one resigned (having given a month's notice) then the other had to leave at the same time.

The P.L.B. requested the Master to keep a Religious Creed Book of all the inmates as requested by the Poor Law Ammendment Act of 1868. A new method of filing was also introduced. Early in '69 the Master was assaulted by a female inmate: she was sentenced to a month's imprisonment in Swansea Jail. In February, when she was released, her children were taken by the Master to meet her.

Neither Mr Bounds nor his wife were at ease in Bridgend, and in September they applied for a similar 'combined' post with the Lambeth Union but they were unsuccessful. January 1870 proved a troublesome month with a number of complaints brought against Mr Bounds. First of all he was accused of confining a pauper of low intellect in the Tramp Ward 'for lying on a bed when she should have been making it', and on another day she was made to 'pick oakum till her fingers bled'. Then there was a girl of eighteen, with a weak arm and leg, who had refused to nurse children when tired, and had been confined to the Tramp Ward. Another inmate was 'dragged by the hair and kicked'. Finally, parents and their children admitted to the 'Vagrant Ward' had been badly treated. The father had been kept there for twelve days without bedding, while his wife and family had been transferred 'to the wooden Fever Ward because of a low fever'. Dr. Verity discharged them on his first visit, but when they came home 'the boy of eleven years was so weak that the Overseer lodged him in his own house'. It seems that he 'had slept on the floor' and had not been given 'a change of clothing'. According to the Guardians: "Most of these accusations are unfounded, and although there might be a figment of truth in some of them they have been highly coloured. Most of them have been made by Gwenllian Hopkins who cannot be questioned because she has left the country". They rebuked the Master for keeping a person in the Tramp Ward for so long and for not giving a change of clothing to the boy. They stressed that all punishments, however mild, had to be entered in the Punishment Book.

The following April, Mrs Mary Jane Cook, aged 29 years, from Cornwall became Cook and Assistant Matron to the Workhouse at a salary of £16 per annum. This eased the pressure on the Matron, but disharmony continued. In October 1870 'an inmate damaged his shirt and used obscene language'. He was referred to the Magistrates' Court and sentenced to ten days in jail. The Guardians considered the sentence 'far too harsh'.

As previously mentioned Mr and Mrs Bounds had a daughter and by the terms of their appointment she was not supposed to live in the Workhouse, but it became clear in February '71 that she was living with her parents and that her friends called from time to time. This was considered to be an alarming lapse and the parents were given four days leave to devise some other means of caring for her. They were unable to find an alternative, and in March applied for a post with the Woolwich Union, but were unsuccessful. The previous arrangements then continued without further censure.

In April '71 the Master brought a complaint against the Cook for causing a disturbance late at night in the Workhouse and for 'refusing to desist when asked'. She was dismissed with a month's notice and was replaced by a Miss Marion John.

In July anonymous complaints were brought against the Master by 'several inmates and a ratepayer', but their nature was not divulged and after an inquiry it was decided that they were unfounded. A year later he formally approached the Guardians for permission to keep his daughter in the Workhouse when she was home from school. It was allowed provided he paid a sum of 7/0 a week for her keep.

There were more complaints against the Master, but again they were deemed to be 'unfounded', although there must have been some niggling doubts because later, in March 1875, the Guardians considered the management of the Workhouse to have much improved.

In July the Cook resigned having been appointed to a similar post in the Cardiff Workhouse. Mrs Mary Thomas was appointed but stayed for only five months. There followed a Miss Ellen Draddy for a trial period of one month.

In the same month the Visiting Committee stated that they had received complaints about 'the beating of children by the Master'. He was censured for 'using undue severity with an illegal instrument and before the proscribed time had elapsed after the offence'. Furthermore he had 'not entered it in the Punishment Book'.

The following October Ellen Draddy, the Assistant Matron and Cook, resigned and Mrs Mary Morgan was appointed.

In July 1877 Mr and Mrs Bounds, the Master and Matron, resigned probably because they could not control the children. The following events may have precipitated their departure: it had been suggested by the Guardians that the Master should lock the doors between the 'boys' and girls' yard' and allow the Schoolmistress to have a key. He was also to ask the inmates to tell him if they had any complaints which were then to be entered in a Book. Four boys had 'absconded over the wall' and when they were caught the Master had confined them in the Tramp Ward but they again 'broke out' and left the premises. Eventually the Guardians decided that birching was neccessary - 'six strokes with a birch rod in the presence of the Master.'

There were thirty-seven applicants for the post and three married couples were shortlisted. Mr and Mrs Messenger from Swansea were appointed. Both were thirty-four years of age: he had been born in Kidderminster and she in Middlesex. Mr Bounds was allowed access between 9am and 5pm to complete his books but was refused a testimonial though a reference would be supplied if requested by an employing Authority.

Mr Wrigley resumed the task of shaving and cutting hair at £5 per quarter; from 1858 the task had been carried out by the Masters.

Mary Edwin became Cook and Assistant Matron to the Workhouse in September '77 at a salary of £18 per annum.

Perhaps the Management became lax again because in January 1878 Mr Messenger, the new Master, was instructed 'not to give beer to the inmates except medicinally'. A fortnight later one of them returned drunk from Chapel and the Master was told to prevent him leaving the Workhouse for a month.

Eighteen seventy-nine was a reasonably tranquil year for them, but in January 1880 the Master was sued by a Mr Tucker for 'non-payment of work alleged to have been done by him'. He was allowed the services of a solicitor and was defended successfully.

In November, an inmate who had helped in the kitchen, was told to stop doing so because of 'bad behaviour', and this added to the daily chores of the Matron. She contiued to cope through 1881, but in February 1882 they both thought that the additional work merited recompence so they applied for an increase in salary indicating that they had been in post for four years and that during that period had supervised the inmates in various activities which had previously been carried out by outsiders, thus saving about £12 a year. They listed these activities which included repairing clothes, knitting stockings, and cutting out clothes (except men's suits) and in their opinion had thereby freed the Workhouse of 'able-bodied' loungers. In Neath the combined salary was £30 pounds per year more than theirs. Suprisingly, despite due consideration, the Guardians decided that an increase was not justified.

In September the Matron went to the Bristol Royal Infirmary to bring back a boy who was for discharge. (Such work was usually done by the Relieving Officer - Chapter 14).

From August 1883 she had the help of a paid Nurse who was also Assistant Matron (further details Chapter 12). She was paid £20 a year compared with the Matron's, £30 and the Master's £50.

In November it was decided that the inmates should have fish for dinner every Wednesday - brought by the supplier of the Neath Workhouse at two and a half pence a pound inclusive of carriage.

There was a complaint against the Master in February 1886. Apparently an inmate had been sent home from the Workhouse with his feet 'unhealed'. The doctor had seen him prior to discharge but this had not been entered in the Master's Record Book. This omission was viewed as a serious offence and he was 'cautioned'.

The new post of Assistant Matron and Nurse was occupied by Ellen Jones from August 25th to November 17th; she then resigned and was replaced by Mrs Elisabeth Bywaters. In October '84 her wage was increased from £20 to £22, funded by a ban on the provision of beer to the inmates. She left in July 1885. There were two applicants for the post. Mrs Mary Rowe, supported by a reference from the Matron of the Cardiff Royal Infirmary, was appointed. After only three months she resigned and there were no applicants for the post on first advertisement. A second advertisement resulted in seven applications. Margaret Lewis from the Asylum in Bridgend and Mrs Woodlocks from Liverpool were shortlisted. The latter failed to turn up at interview because she did not have the money to pay for overnight stay in Bridgend. The Guardians were obviously attracted by her application because they suggested that if successful at interview she could commence work immediately and if unsuccessful stay the night or weekend free in the Workhouse. In response to this offer she came and was appointed on the 16th of January but at the previous salary of £20 per annum.

Chapter 11

Medical Officers (1836-1861)

Dismissals of Dr. Price Jacob and Dr. Pritchard, Government Money,
Fevers and Infection, Dr. James Lewis, Nursing of Inmates,
Cholera, Skin Eruption, Vaccination.

The Poor Law Medical Officers examined paupers at the request of the Relieving Officers or Guardians. They also decided when an ill pauper should be admitted to the Workhouse and whether a Vagrant was fit enough to continue his travels. The Medical Officer of Bridgend attended to the inmates in addition to his district work. Later, they all became Public Vaccinators. They treated patients during the Cholera epidemic and assisted the Board in the application of the Public Health Act of 1848.

Their salary covered the cost of attendance and medicine. At first, surgical treatment and midwifery were also included, but later 'a cost per item service' was introduced. A fee was also received for the examination of 'lunatics'. Details of visits and medicines were kept in a special book which was submitted monthly to the Board with a weekly abstract.

The Medical Officers in 1836 were: John Llewelyn for Cowbridge (Eastern), Robert Brock Thomas for Maesteg (Northern) and Price Jacob for Bridgend (Central). The future pattern was illustrated by a statement on the tenth of November 1838 that the Board was dissatisfied with the Medical Officer of Cowbridge for not revisiting Margaret Radcliffe - a pauper of Llanilid – who had been reported on the thirty-first of October as being unable to work from 'rheumatism and scalded feet'.

In August 1839 the Parish Officers were presented with details of medical care for the previous quarter: Number of cases visited 113, cost of each case including medicine 8/0d, average visits per patient 3, and cost per visit 2/8d.

A letter of complaint about Dr. Price Jacob was sent to the Commissioners in October 1839. It appears that he neglected his duties and in the opinion of the Guardians: "His continuation in the Office would be detrimental to the Union". The Bridgend Relieving Officer was asked to check the doctor's entries of Home Visits and he showed that at least one of them had been false. The Reverend Robert Knight indicated that he was going to 'prefer' a charge of neglect at the next meeting and Price Jacob was asked to attend, but he did not do so 'because the post did not arrive until 4pm that day'. There the matter rested and Price Jacob continued in office. In March there was a serious development. The Clerk reported that an order of bastardy against Price Jacob

103

had been obtained at the Petty Session in Bridgend the previous Saturday, in response to which he was to reimburse Coity Lower of 18/6d in supporting 'the bastard daughter of E.R.(single) and to pay weekly till the child is 7 years (if the child continues to be chargeable to the hamlet)'. Dr Jacob was 44 yrs at the time and the father of five children ranging from 2 to 9 yrs. The Reverend Robert Knight promptly proposed that the doctor be forthwith dismissed. This was seconded by R.T. Turberville. Dr John Williams took over the post temporarily. He lived by Newcastle Church and had recently retired at the age of 64yrs. (His son, Arthur John Williams became M.P. for South Glamorgan). He was the son of Dr. Jenkin Williams (Stormy) and Catherine (sister of William Morgan FRS). Later that month Dr. William Pritchard was appointed.

Re-selection was carried out annually for the first four years and then discontinued. There was doubt about the suitability of Dr. Llewelyn (Cowbridge) in March 1839 and Dr. William Henry Wood was proposed, but when it came to the vote Dr. Llewelyn had overwhelming support and was consequently re-selected.

It soon became evident that the doctors were loth to submit weekly abstracts, but when it was explained to them that their not doing so inconvenienced the Board they co-operated, though Doctors Llewelyn and Brock Thomas sometimes 'forgot'. They were requested several times to 'forward them punctually'.

In January 1841 the three Medical Officers were asked to meet the Board at the Workhouse; "On Wednesday next at noon to consider the instructions by the Poor Law Commissioners respecting vaccination and to present your report in writing". There was to be: "A contract regarding the vaccinating of all persons who shall apply to you in the Union District, at a reasonable time of day at your residence or where contract states, of persons not successfully vaccinated before". Two books were to be kept – one to be handed to the Clerk each week, while the other was being used. If vaccination was successful the name was to be given to a Guardian and a certificate issued by the Relieving Officer. The fee was to be 1/6 per case. A register of Smallpox was also to be kept and handed to the Clerk every quarter. The contract, having been agreed to, was signed and the common seal of the Guardians 'affixed'.

Later that month it was decided that their Report Book should indicate why a pauper had been seen, and where. If the patient had attended the surgery the letter A was to be entered; if visited at home the letter V; when medicine had been given without examination the letter M; and if examination had been carried out and medicine given the letters VM or AM.

Dr. Pritchard was ordered to buy twelve single trusses for the Workhouse in December – though at the time there were only two or three inmates! Four months later there were complaints about his 'abruptness and hastiness of manner in his visits to paupers'. He was told: "Treat them with more respect and kindness".

Nothing untoward happened between then and February, 1844, but on the tenth of that month the Clerk reported: "Indoor paupers are being asked to attend Dr. Pritchard's surgery in Laleston – which is against the spirit of the Poor Law Act and subversive of the rules and regulations of the Workhouse". He added that he had also been told that 'a pauper with a fever in Coity Lower had not been visited by him for over a fortnight'. Dr. Pritchard was asked to 'attend for discussion' and was told that if he did not do so they would write to the Commissioners.

Two further complaints about his conduct were then received. The first concerned a maternity case in Ewenny, where a woman, aged forty-two years, had been in labour for two days. Dr. Pritchard visited her once and did not return. He sent a midwife instead. The baby lived for only about ten minutes. When asked to explain what had happened his answer was: "She was not in labour when I called, so I sent for the midwife and paid her – they couldn't. I also gave them some money and an order for the Relieving Officer". The second complaint was that he had taken two days to visit a lady with fits in the Workhouse after being requested to do so by the Master. His explanation was that he had intended calling sooner but had failed because he had been too busy with patients: "I called when I could" he said.

The Guardians wrote to the Commissioners about him, but before they had a reply a curt note was received from Dr. Pritchard: "I consider myself no longer in your employment". The Commissioners supported the 'neglect charge' and added that it would have been sufficient to dismiss him had he not resigned. Regarding the maternity case they surprisingly instructed the Board to admonish the Relieving Officer 'for not paying sufficient attention to what was happening at the confinement'. Dr. John Williams replaced him temporarily and then Dr. Abraham John Verity was appointed.

In March 1844 the Board discussed in some detail the 'medical relief' given by the Union. There was general dissatisfaction with its administration. There were too many delays in the treatment of sick paupers. They concluded that an additional Medical Officer was necessary and that the best means of justifying it was to re-divide the area in such a way that a new district was formed. The Central District (Bridgend) could remain unchanged as well as the main part of the Eastern (Cowbridge). The Northern (Maesteg) could include Bettws, St. Bride's Major and Minor, Cwmdu, Llandyfodwg, Llangeinor, Llangynwyd Lower and Middle together with Ynysawdre.; and a new North Eastern District formed which would contain Coychurch Higher and Lower, Llanharan, Llanilid, Pencoed, Peterston and Llanharry.

Oddly enough they then supported their suggestion of 1836 that one Medical Officer, free of private commitments, could be made responsible for the whole Union; but the Commissioners again disagreed. They wrote: 'It is quite inadmissible to have only one Medical Officer. It is contrary to the provisions of the Medical Order. Reconsider the subject and continue to appoint a Medical Officer to each district'. The Guardians capitulated and, moreover, the formation of the new North Eastern District was left in abeyance.

Dr. Brock Thomas resigned, but when he realised that the envisaged boundary changes of the Maesteg and Cowbridge districts were not being implemented he changed his mind and agreed to continue.

The Board doubted the legality of Dr. Verity's medical qualification – 'he not being L.S.A.' – and wrote to the College for information. Edmund Burford, secretary of the Royal College of Surgeons, assured the Guardians that he had been a member since the fifteenth of May 1840.

In January 1845, the Medical Officers received for the first time a full list of 'sick and aged paupers' from the Relieving Officers.

From time to time paupers were visited at the request of a member of the Board. Dr. Verity was asked to give an opinion on a Mr. and Mrs. Llewelyn. He concluded that the husband, Isaac, had 'gravel' and his wife, Gwenllian, 'low typhoid fever'. Both were 'helpless'. He visited them twice, and his assistant, Mr. Cory, once. The immediate question from the Board was: 'Is Mr. Cory a duly qualified Medical Practitioner?' The answer was: "Not at present". He begged leave to appoint Dr. Abraham Verity (Senior) as his deputy, and it was granted.

Like the other Medical Officers he was soon to answer further questions. The first was: 'Why have you omitted two names from your medical list to the Board?' His reply was: "Regarding the first, I was not informed of the illness until too late to send in a report; and as for the second, no illness was discovered – no fractured ribs as I had been told". Other questions were to follow and they were not always easy to answer. One day he was asked to meet Dr. Llewelyn to examine a pauper in St. Bride's Major: 'Because a needle has entered his body and is remaining there'. On another occasion he was asked to attend a Board meeting and explain his treatment of a pauper in Newton Nottage who had had an accident. With exemplary candour he admitted that having walked a great deal that day he had drunk two glasses of ale and was not quite as he should have been. Naturally he was reprimanded and cautioned. They also questioned his handling of a patient with gangrene of leg: 'Is amputation necessary on the pauper in Coity Lower? If so would it not be better to admit him to the Workhouse?' He replied: "His system will not allow of amputation. It should have been done five years ago". A letter was sent to him by the Clerk expressing 'surprise at his asking Lord Adare to pay for attendance on a family in St. Bride's Major when he had already entered it in his book as having been done in his official capacity'. There was no answer to this and he was told to be careful.

A characteristic of his treatment of the sick was the frequent recommending of extra nourishment. In December 1845 he indicated that a pauper in Clemenston should be given a 'little wine with plenty of spice in it, and one mutton chop daily'. He was asked to inform the Relieving Officer and the Board what time the extra nourishment was necessary. In reply he pointed out that the request to see the patient had originated from Mrs Franklen of Clemenston and that he had thought it would be supplied by one of her charities. A copy of the letter was sent her.

Soon afterwards he was asked to attend the next Board meeting and explain 'the items he had charged for'. One was of a male pauper of twenty-three years who had fractured his leg. No treatment had been given so it was decided to admit him to Swansea Hospital as an emergency. The Clerk wrote to the

Hospital Secretary asking whether 'last year's subscription will cover the cost because of lack of time'. Fortunately it did.(The new Infirmary opened in 1837 as replacement for the old one built in 1817. Subscription was 10gns. a year).

By November 1848 Dr. James Lewis had replaced Dr. Brock Thomas who had died of Smallpox. The salaries for district work varied a little as shown by payments for the previous quarter:- Dr. John Llewelyn £13.7.0d, Dr. James Lewis £10, Dr. Abraham J. Verity £12.10.0d; and Dr. Thomas Morgan (Western) £10. This last district covered Newton Nottage, Porthcawl, Tythegston, Pyle, Cornelly, Kenfig Hill, and Cefn Cribbwr. It had only recently been formed.

The diagnoses made were often couched in lay terms. The list in January, 1849, consisted of: 'Low fever, fistula in ano, contusion of leg, pain in limbs, fever, cold, chest affection, fever, severe cold, dislocation of knee, abscesses, debility, palpitation of heart, crushed leg, bowel complaint, 'labor', and 'pain in limbs'. The list was similar in February apart from the addition of miscarriage, accident of hand, and weakness. A pauper with 'fever' was prescribed '3 lbs. of meat and ½ pint of brandy' a week. Out-door relief was given to ill able-bodied paupers by the Relieving Officers and the sum varied from 4/0 to 11/0 a week depending on the circumstances. Around this time considerable attention was being given to the kind of food people ate, and the Board received a letter from the Commissioners stressing 'the importance of diet – particularly of inmates and children'. Dr. Verity was asked to comment and while in the House to pass judgement on 'the ventilation of the day rooms and sleeping rooms'.

Dr. Llewelyn had not been questioned for a long time, but he was now asked: "Why have you not seen the pauper you have been asked to, when you have had four requests to do so?" He explained: "From the first I considered her case hopeless; diarrhoea, chronic bronchitis and debility which at her advanced age (77 years) only required a nourishing diet. Although I considered my service useless I told the husband that if it would afford him satisfaction I would be happy to see her again. This he only once expressly wished me to do, but from unforseen causes I deferred my visit to the day following the one I had promised to see her, when I found her dead". The Board did not consider this explanation a good one, and so Reverend Powell was asked to see the husband and explain what had happened. Furthermore, the Clerk wrote to Dr. Llewelyn advising him that 'recurrence of these complaints will result in referral to the Poor Law Board'.

Dr. James Lewis was also not allowed to relax. In May 1849, he omitted 'medicines' from his report and was asked: 'Why?' Moreover, he was told that he should indicate what type of visit he had made.In addition they wanted to know whether: "Dr. Jacob, who has sent a report on a pauper in Bettws, is a qualified Medical Practitioner? Article 3 of the General Medical Order of the Poor Law Commissioners of 12 March 1842". (This Price Jacob was the doctor dismissed by them in 1840).

The eleventh of August 1849 was an important date in the history of Bridgend and the Board because on that day Dr. James Lewis reported that the previous week he had seen 118 patients with 'premonitory' symptoms of

Cholera in Maesteg, of whom 11 had passed into Cholera and proved fatal'. He recommended that: 'Mr. Burget (London) be appointed Assistant Medical Officer at Maesteg for about two months at a salary of £10 per month; that two 'Visitors' be appointed deputy Relieving Officers at 18/0 per week each; that a depot for supplying medicine be fixed in Maesteg, and that he be allowed to employ a competent assistant to dispense medicine there'. [Another depot was set up in Bridgend and William Morgan (shoemaker of Newcastle Lower) became Assistant to Mr. Arnott, the Relieving Officer, at 18/0 per week]. Dr. Thomas Morgan (Western District) reported that there had also been six fatal cases of Cholera in Kenfig Hill the previous week.

By the eighteenth of August twenty-five further cases of Cholera had been seen by the Medical Officers; a pauper in Cwmdu had died of the disease. On the twenty-fourth of August, nineteen were reported, fourteen of whom had died. They were mainly in Cwmdu. By the first of September the additional number was thirty-five with one death; by the eighth it was twenty-seven with nine deaths; and on the fifteenth, seven with two deaths and ten with severe diarrhoea. Nevertheless Dr. Lewis was convinced that the outbreak was diminishing in Maesteg due, in his opinion, to the vigilance of the 'Visitors'. They had saved lives. The 'public health' of the district had improved sufficiently for him to 'discharge' one of the 'Visitors' at the end of the week – the fifteenth September. The dispenser was paid £5.8.0 and Mr. Burget £10. Undoubtedly, the rapid control of the outbreak was due largely to the administrative skill and able direction of Dr. Lewis.

One special item had worried the Guardians during the epidemic and it concerned Dr. Verity. According to the ubiquitous Reverend Robert Knight a child in Wick had been visited once by the doctor and had died two weeks later. An inquest had been held. The Chairman was asked to write to the Coroner for a copy of the proceedings, so that a committee made up of the Chairman, the Vice-Chairman, James Reynolds, Rees Powell and Daniel Llewelyn could study it and pass judgement. Dr. Verity refused to comment when they wrote to him adding that 'he would reply in the public papers to imputations against him by the verdict'. The Clerk then wrote to the Commissioners pointing out that although it concerned a case in private practice (the son of a labourer) the Guardians were worried that it would affect the 'confidence of paupers'. The Commissioners took the view 'that as the poor boy in question was a private patient Dr. Verity was not answerable to the Board for his treatment; nor was the conduct of the practitioner their responsibility'.

Dr. Thomas Morgan was given a gratuity of £10.10.0 for extra service during the Cholera epidemic and everything returned to normal. The close surveillance of the Medical Officers continued.

In February 1850 Dr. Morgan explained satisfactorily the difficulties he had experienced with a pauper despite the fact that the complaint had been made by Mr. Arnott, the Relieving Officer. Dr. Verity was asked two questions: "At whose request and by what authority did you amputate the toes of a patient in Treoes and then enter him as a pauper? and what were your reasons for not attending Jennet Harry, a pauper, after having been asked three times to do so?" Dr. Lewis had to explain why he had charged £3 for unsuccessfully treating a patient with a fracture. He replied: "The fracture was of the neck of the thigh within the capsular ligament. Such fractures never heal and the patient will continue lame for life". Dr. John Llewelyn was paid £3 for treating a fractured leg of a pauper in Eglwys Brewis without being asked any questions, but they followed it with: Why did you not attend a pauper in Llanharan when asked? He explained that though he had failed to call the same time as the Relieving Officer he had called later. She had : 'Indigestion and hypochondriasis' and admission to the House was recommended. Three and a half pounds of meat weekly were ordered by Dr. Verity for a pauper in Pencoed, and he was asked to state when it was to be 'consumed'. Dr. Llewelyn had neglected to supply a pauper with medicine though two requests had been made by the patient – 'why was this?' It transpired that: "The person calling for the medicines would not wait for me to return from my country visits. The following morning my servant delivered the medicine to the pauper's house". This led to the Poor Law Board being asked: "Should the Medical Officers send all medicines to the residence of paupers?" The reply was: 'That is not necessary'. Soon afterwards he charged £5 for amputating the leg of a pauper in St. Athan. The Guardians considered this fee 'exorbitant' and the Clerk wrote to the Board for guidance. They decided that the money should not be given unless 'another doctor had assisted him and been paid by him'. Dr. Llewelyn stated that Dr. Thomas Griffiths had assisted him and had charged £3. Payment of the £5 was then allowed. Dr. Thomas Morgan received £2 for attending 'a complicated labour with retained placenta'. This was acceptable.

The amount of money paid to the doctors for items of service was considerable and it is not surprising that the Union Board was being careful. Their funds came from the hard-pressed parishes and expenses were high. Dr. Verity on the nineteenth of October, for example, received £6.3.0 for vaccinating eighty-two children, 10/0 for delivering an in-door pauper from Llanmaes, £2 for managing a difficult labour in an in-door pauper from Coity Lower, 10/0 for attending a confinement in Coity Lower, 10/0 for another in St. Mary Hill, and £1 for replacing the dislocated shoulder of a pauper in Coity Higher.

There was a vacancy in Swansea Infirmary in November and a pauper from Tythegston with 'scrofula' was admitted to the bed – 'Dr. Thomas Morgan certified, Mr. Arnott accompanied, and the Common Seal of the Union was fixed on the recommendation'.

It was becoming clear that the official Medical Officers could not personally treat every sick pauper, because their number had increased. Industrial development was progressing, with the result that labourers, mainly from West Wales and Ireland, were coming into the area. Wages were low and farm produce relatively expensive. Pauperisation was accelerating, overcrowding was rife in many districts, sanitation was almost non-existent, fevers and diarrhoea were common complaints – and to these must be added the difficulty of transport and the long distances that had to be covered by the doctors. They usually walked, rode a horse, or went by carriage. The obvious answer was for the doctors to appoint deputies who would be acceptable to the Board. Dr. Llewelyn (Cowbridge) nominated Dr. Edward Bates, L.S.A.; Dr. Verity and Dr. Thomas Morgan chose Dr. Leahy between them, and Dr. Lewis recommended Dr. Joseph Briggs, L.S.A.. of Bron-y-Garn, Maesteg. The Board approved.

Around this time the Master and the Visiting Committee of the Workhouse became concerned about children who had 'a persistent cutaneous eruption'. It had been present for six months before Dr. Verity was asked to explain what it was due to. He was not unduly worried and wrote: "Some of the children have a slight eruption, but most of them have recovered. It's a common rash caused by the diet (consisting mainly of oatmeal, salt meat, salt broth, and little vegetables apart from potatoes). Children coming in are often debilitated and this predisposes them. A slight change of diet with some attention from the Matron will clear the three or four remaining cases. It is not dangerous". (14th June 1851). He was unduly optimistic. Six months later the Board requested 'a combined opinion' on the rash. Drs. Leahy, Llewelyn and Verity supplied the following report, signed by the three: "We have examined the children and think they are progressing satisfactorily, but strict cleanliness is necessary and a more generous diet. The disease they have takes a long time for complete eradication. We recommend: Bread and milk, good broths, fresh meat, and half a glass of beer or porter daily". (14th February 1852). This diet regime was adopted.

In December, Dr. Verity was asked 'to supply particulars of each patient seen by him in the Workhouse especially the five with eruption of scalp and the three children kept separate from the others because of cutaneous eruption'. On the twenty-seventh of August 1853, another joint report was supplied by Drs. Michael Leahy, John Llewelyn and Abraham J. Verity: "The four children are progressing satisfactorily. Removal to the country would hasten cure". The Board decided that the best approach was to send one of the children to Swansea Infirmary for treatment, and for the others to be treated in the House by their own doctors.

Dr. James Lewis of Maesteg was also asked to give an opinion, but he refused to attend. In fact he wrote to the Poor Law Board for clarification of his duties: "Was I compelled to attend to patients in the Workhouse at the request of the Guardians without remuneration?" A copy of his letter was returned to the Guardians and the Clerk explained to them what had happened. They replied: "Dr. Lewis is a District Medical Officer, not Medical Officer to the Workhouse. The request is not one he could be made to comply with". The Guardians did not pursue the matter further.

The skin eruption cleared over the ensuing months and did not recur. (It was generally accepted that oatmeal 'heats the blood and occasions cutaneous eruptions').

Dr. Thomas Morgan had resigned in July 1851 from his post in the Western District and Dr. Michael Leahy had replaced him. He nominated Dr. William Pritchard of Laleston as his deputy and he was accepted despite the previous complaints about him.

In November of that year Dr. Verity claimed £3 for amputating the leg of an in-door pauper and an additional £2 for reducing a fracture dislocation in the same patient. The validity of the second charge was questioned and the Poor Law Boards' decision was: 'No. It is not allowed – only one charge in one person at one time can be claimed'.

The first instance of Typhus being specifically diagnosed was in March 1852. There were three or four others in the ensuing three years. Extra nourishment of one pound of beef and three pounds of oatmeal or two pounds of mutton with a pint of beer daily was the usual treatment.

The kind of administrative medical decisions made by the Guardians can be seen from the following entries for May: a pauper with 'diseased bone' was allowed the three pounds of mutton and the daily pint of beer recommended by the doctor, together with out-door relief of 6/10 per week; another with 'inflamed absorbents' was granted the same quantity of mutton and beer, but without the relief; someone with 'scrofulous disease of the shoulder joint' was not admitted to the Workhouse because it could only be cured 'by time and diet'; a request from the House Surgeon of Swansea Infirmary for a pair of shoes and trousers for John Davies – a pauper from the Union – was granted 'out of stock'.

Dr. Verity's reports sometimes caused confusion. In one he wrote: 'A pauper in St. Bride's Major has Syphilis, which will affect him permanently and he, therefore, needs rest for a week or two'. What he meant apparently was that 'rest and quiet for a short while would enable him to continue his work'.

They were not pleased when the House Surgeon of Swansea Hospital discharged a patient of theirs, because 'the Medical Gentlemen considered he had been there long enough. He was better but not cured. Cure was doubtful and depended on time as much as anything'.

In January 1854 Dr. Verity claimed that a girl of eighteen years, living with her parents in Wick, had Gonorrhoea. The mother would not accept it and requested a second opinion. She did not think there was any foundation for such a diagnosis. What her daughter had, in her opinion, was 'debility following Typhus Fever'. Dr. William Pritchard was asked to see her. He failed to find evidence of Gonorrhoea and reported that there had been a 'slight discharge due to debility following Fever, but it had now gone'. Dr. Verity insisted that she had Gonorrhoea when he saw her and that 'she was no virgin'. The Clerk sent a mollifying letter to the parents, but they remained in an angry mood. Eventually he wrote to the Poor Law Board on behalf of the Guardians citing this case, and sixteen others, claiming that Dr. Verity had 'forfeited their confidence'. The Board did not comment.

On the fourth of November 1854 Cholera returned to Bridgend and Dr. William Camps was sent by the General Board of Health, Whitehall, to take charge. He reported that there was Asiatic Cholera in Coity Lower and Newcastle Lower. Dr. James Lewis suggested that in order to prevent it spreading to Maesteg he should be permitted to employ nurses and house-to-house visitors, and given the right to establish depots in Coytrahen and Maesteg (Crown Inn) for the storage of blankets and cotton sheets.

On the eleventh Dr. Camps reported that he was seeing three or four patients a day with diarrhoea. One had died of Cholera – but he also had Typhus; another definitely had the disease, while a third was convalescing from it. A week later Thomas Jones, a gardener at Merthyr Mawr, died of Cholera and was buried on the same day. His home had been poorly ventilated and was without privies but had been kept clean. John Cole Nicholl promised to 'attend to the house'. There were three fatal cases that week, and three others were suffering from it – one had been ill for five or six days, another for seven days, and the third, a girl of fourteen years, was dying. There were two further cases in Bridgend on the ninth of December but they were the last. It did not spread to Maesteg as had been feared by Dr. Lewis. Dr. Camps was paid £44 by means of a special rate levied on the parishioners of Coity Lower and Newcastle Lower.

Vaccination on request had been practiced since 1841, but in February 1854 it became compulsory 'under the provisions of a recent Act'. The district doctors were asked to organise a service and give details to the Board so that the public could be informed. Their agreed programme was as follows:

Dr Llewelyn

Every day	10am	Surgery Cowbridge.
1st Monday of month	11am	Llanharan.
1st Wednesday of month	11am	Llantwit Major.
1st Friday of month	11am	St Mary Church.

Dr A J Verity

Every day	10am	Bridgend Surgery.
1st Monday of month	2pm	Pencoed.
1st Wednesday of month	2pm	Llangan.
1st Thursday of month	2pm	Wick.

Dr James Lewis

Every day	10am	Surgery Maesteg.
1st Monday of Month	11am	Velin Evan Ddu, Llangeinor.
1st Monday of Month	2pm	Bettws.
1st Monday of Month	4pm	Bayden Llangonwyd Lower.

Dr Michael Leahy

Every day	10-4pm	Surgery Bridgend, Aberkenfig.
1st Tuesday of Month	12-2pm	Mynydd Kenfig.
1st Friday of Month	12-2pm	Newton Nottage.

The numbers vaccinated rose rapidly. Dr James Lewis was paid £15.17.0 in August for vaccinating 166 children; Dr Verity vaccinated 51 the same month and Dr. Llewelyn 143. The fee was 1/6 when a short journey was involved, and 2/6 when longer – as from Cowbridge to Llantwit Major.

The doctors were also paid for examining 'lunatic paupers'. A fixed fee of 2/6 for a visit had recently been introduced. They saw around ten a quarter.

In February 1855 Dr Leahy was asked to explain 'why he had entered visits and medicine for a pauper who had recovered', and 'why he had not visited an ill pauper after Dr Pritchard and his deputy had stopped doing so'. The answers he gave were: "I attended the patient Monday and Wednesday last week, and daily this week, she died Sunday. Entries after that date were mistakes". (She had not recovered as the Guardians had presumed). His explanation for the second mishap was stranger still: "Dr Pritchard hadn't told me he was not attending any more. I saw Dr Phillips (assistant to Dr Pritchard) and asked him were further visits necessary. All he told me was that Dr Pritchard had stopped going – I can't remember". Dr Leahy must have thought he had seriously blundered because he resigned on the same day that he sent the letter.

Dr Pritchard undertook his duties temporarily and the post was advertised. There were no applicants. Dr Phillips, the assistant, then took over but the post was re-advertised, not only in the county papers as before, but also in the Lancet and the Midlands Counties Herald of Birmingham. Again there were no applicants. After a fruitless search extending over two months they condescended to ask Dr William Phillips to be their permanent Medical Officer for the Western District. One wonders why they had not done so sooner.

By 1857 an occasional operation was being performed in the Workhouse though there was no indication that a special room had been allocated for the purpose. In May of that year Dr Verity amputated the arm of a male inmate and the Poor Law Board sanctioned the procedure and allowed payment of £2.0.0. The fees charged for special services were as before and were debited to the pauper's settlement parish when it was known. This was so the following July when Dr Verity was paid 10/0 for delivering an inmate from Penlline, 10/0 for delivering another from St Bride's Major, 10/0 each for the same service to inmates from Cwmdu, St Athan, Newton Nottage and Llysworney. In each case the parish paid. When the pauper had not been 'settled' the bill was paid from the 'common fund'.

A large number of vaccinations continued to be carried out as shown by the £10.14.0 paid to Dr Verity in April 1858 for the 102 he had performed the previous month. An active case of Smallpox was diagnosed in Maesteg in October, but the disease did not spread, which, if the diagnosis was correct, shows how effective the vaccination programme was.

The following January another attempt was made to re-organise the medical service. The Reverend C. R. Knight and William Llewelyn of Court Colman commented on the ideas that had been expressed from time to time by their colleagues, and tabulated their views:- "The appointment of two Medical Officers to each parish is impracticable and objectionable as it would give rise to jealousy between them, and collusion against the Relieving Officer."

"The alternative of paying a fixed salary to payment per head was an experiment – tending to multiply cases without giving a better service".

"A permanent contract with the Medical Officers leads to more stability than periodic renewal would."

"We agree there should be better facilities for the poor to obtain medical assistance. Quantities of nourishing diet should be discontinued except in special cases, provided the Medical Officer has the power to order more expensive drugs from a table drawn up and supplied by a Chemist."

Pigs were being reared on the premises as one way 'of consuming refuse', and the doctors were asked in March 1859 to give their views on the sanitary problem that this might be causing. They thought the drainage should be improved and the drain flushed periodically, because, as things were then, 'the practice was injurious to the inmates'.

Dr John Llewelyn of Cowbridge resigned in March 1860. He had been appointed in 1836 and the Guardians sent him 'their official thanks' and added that they 'regretted losing his service'. There were two candidates for the vacated post, Dr Edward Bates, of Cowbridge (who had been his deputy) and Dr Ruscombe Lansdown of Canton, Cardiff. The Clerk wrote to the Poor Law Board enquiring about their medical qualifications and the reply was that Lansdown held the Diploma of the Faculty of Physicians and Surgeons of Glasgow, which allowed him to practice surgery, but not medicine. They added: 'This body cannot grant any legal degree in medicine, so Mr Lansdown is only partially qualified – and Mr Bates is in the same position'. Nevertheless, a loophole was offered in the remarks that followed: 'A diploma or degree is not so absolute a requisite as to prevent Guardians employing such a person when a fully qualified person cannot be obtained'. The excuse was grasped and Edward Bates was appointed at a salary of £52 per annum, with additional payments per item of service. He received £4.12.6d for thirty-nine vaccinations a month later.

Three cases of Typhus were reported in June and one of Asthma, both being unusual entries.

The work in Maesteg had become more onerous owing to a minor population explosion, and Dr James Lewis applied for an increase in salary, which was granted. It was agreed that he be paid £65 per annum. The quarterly payment to doctors in September 1860 was: Edward Bates £13, Abraham J. Verity £12.10.0d, J.W.Phillips £12.10.0d, James Lewis £16.5.0d.

In January 1861 Edward Bates joyfully announced that he had passed the examinations of the Royal College of Surgeons, England, last December and that he now had the necessary diploma.

More medical diseases were being treated than hitherto and the diagnoses were more variable. Twenty-seven were reported in the last week of January 1861 and they included:- Fever, Phthisis, Nephritis, Pericarditis, Pneumonia, Haemoptysis, Dysentery, Partial Paralysis, Gunshot wounds, Loss of sight, Neuralagia and Ulceration of leg. (Strokes, Parkinson's disease, and Heart attacks were not mentioned).

Additional Information

The Commissioners informed the Board in June 1842 that a 'gratuity' of fifty guineas would be paid annually by the government towards the "several accounts" of each Medical Officer (article 10 of the Order of March 12th), and it is recorded that from January 1849 to 1861 the Board received £91 annually from the Paymaster General "as a moiety of the salaries paid to the doctors. (It was increased in later years).

'The Fever' that was being repeatedly diagnosed is difficult to explain. Dr Verity referred to it as "Malaria" in his evidence to the Sanitary Committee of Bridgend (1849), but this is unlikely to have been correct – though it was indigenous in marshy areas until the end of the century. Typhus is a possibility, but the enteric fevers (Typhoid and Paratyphoid) have to be included because when they were clinically distinguished in the eighteen-eighties several small epidemics of Typhoid were recognised, and in some places – such as Pontycymmer -it was endemic. Food poisoning also has to be considered. Scarlatina (or Scarlet Fever) was diagnosed fairly frequently, but it had not yet been separated from Diphtheria (or Croup). Whooping Cough occurred and also Rheumatic Fever and Measles. It is strange that Respiratory Tuberculosis (Consumption:Phthisis) was not reported more often as it was an important cause of death. Joint and Glandular Tuberculosis were known as Scrofula (King's Evil).

ATTACHMENT 1

Medicaments advertised in the Cambrian and Merthyr Guardian. 1835 – 1840.

SCOT'S PILLS: Invented by Dr Anderson, physician to King Charles 1st. – For Bileous, Gouty, and Dropsy Conditions, Headache, Disorder bowel and stomach.

Dr WRIGHT'S PEARL OINTMENT: Patronised by Clergy, Nobility, Gentry, Family Nobility. Cancerous, Indolent Tumours and inveterate Ulcers. Glands, scurvy, evil, ringworm, scald head, chiblains, ulcers legs, sore nipples, weak and diseased eyes.

Dr WRIGHT'S FAMILY CATHARTIC PILLS.

C.S. CHEDDON'S HERBAL TONIC PILLS.

GRAHAM'S: Losenges and earache tincture.

ROWLAND'S MACASSAR OIL: for the hair.

WEIR'S DIGESTION POWDERS.

PRITCHET'S VEGETABLE VERMIFUGE

Dr JOHN ARMSTRONG LIVER PILLS.

MRS JOHNSON'S American soothing syrup for teething.

Dr RADCLIFF's ELIXIR- Purifies blood. Measles. Smallpox, scurvy, worms, (etc).

Dr GREEN'S ANTISCORBIC DROPS – good for every impurity of the blood, weakness, debility (etc).

FRAMTON'S PILL OF HEALTH: Stomach, bowels, depression in females (etc).

PAUL'S EVERYMANS FRIEND: Corns, bunyons.

Dr. PAUL'S FAMILY APERIENT: For clear skin and long life.

POWELL'S COUGH ELECTUARY: Grand restorer of the right tone of the lungs. winter coughs, asthma.(etc).

BLAIR'S GOUT AND PHEUMATIC PILLS.
BARCLAY'S ASTHMATIC CANDY.
SYDENHAM'S ANTIBILEOUS APERIENT.
Dr SIBLEY'S RE–ANIMATING SOLAR TINCTURE: Debility,
consumption, nervous and rheumatic complaints, spasms, indigestion (etc).
ATHERIAL ESSENCE OF GINGER: For cholera (etc) from King William
Street, London Bridge. Bottles 2/6, 4/6, 10/6, each.
ANTICONSUMPTIVE LINIMENT: V.D., also occult losenges.

ATTACHMENT 2

An important inquest was held at the Wyndham Arms Inn at 12 noon on the
9th of March 1839 (Glamorgan Monmouth and Brecon Gazette and Merthyr
Guardian).

A female, aged 23 years, with abdominal pain for 4 mths had died about an
hour after taking medicine supplied by a visiting doctor from Swansea, known as
Baron Spolasco. A verdict of Manslaughter was passed at the inquest but the
Baron was deemed not guilty at the Glamorgan Assizes in Swansea. He was later
fined and imprisoned for issuing false prescriptions, but soon released. Another
Court case was held in July 1840 when a further 25 charges were brought against
him, but somehow he was again found not guilty. He was undoubtedly a quack
with an amazing ability to take advantage of the superstition and ignorance of the
age. There was no further mention of him in the local press after 1845.

PRÉCIS OF POST MORTEM REPORT ON THE ABOVE.

On that day Dr ABRAHAM VERITY, surgeon of Bridgend, in extensive
practice for 30 years.(Not a member of the College of Surgeons or Licentiate of
Hall) produced a Post Mortem report on Susannah Thomas, aged 23yrs, (at
request of the Coroner).

"My son assisted and also nephew. Wall of stomach thickened with patches of
gangrene. Perforation near middle. – peritoneum inflammed. Fluid present, took
fluid from stomach into house. Evaporated it and tasted. Bitter? aloes 10-12g.

Fluid in abdomen strained, decanted, filtrated and evaporated – light brown,
greyish powder.- probably jalap with oat meal. Tasted and gave to dog. Purged.
Quantity 55g (10-12g of jalap)".

JOHN LLEWELYN (Cowbridge): "I attended her for 2 months and then
she went to live in Bridgend. Irritability of stomach from sluggish state of liver and
intestine. Sent medicine to her. Last time I saw her was 6 weeks before death."

WILLIAM HENRY WOOD: (Cowbridge) – MRCS, LRCP

"I attended physician's practice at St George's Hospital London, for 4 years
and was clinical clerk to Dr Hope for 3 years. <u>Post Mortem</u>. Liver and spleen
healthy. Perforation size of 6 pence centre of greater curvature – margins
thickened. Small ulcers near pylorus. Blood extravasated between muscular and
mucous coat simulating gangrene. Medicine was not cause of death."

Verdict : Manslaughter.

 Post Script: Dr John Llewelyn was one of the Medical Officers of the Board, and Dr William Henry Wood was proposed in 1839.

The nephew was probably Fredrick S. Verity who was reported as having passed the examination of Apothecaries' Hall in the Cambrian, September 1837.

The son was Abraham John Verity who became a member of the College of Surgeons in 1840, and was Medical Officer of the Board. His deputy, Abraham Verity (Senior) must have been the Abraham Verity who performed the post mortem.

Photograph taken in 1985 of the north-east section of the Workhouse (foreground) connecting with the Workhouse Infirmary. These became St. David's Ward and Glanogwr Ward of Bridgend General Hospital, now demolished

Chapter 12

Medical Officers (1862-1886)

Vaccinations and Official Enquiry, Isolation facilities, Smallpox, Cholera, Diet of Inmates, Appointment of Nurse, Illness and Death of Drs. Allan, Jenkins, Bates and Verity.

The importance of Vaccination was recognized by the Government and led to the creation of an Inspectorate. In March 1864 Dr Seton, the Government Inspector of Vaccination, indicated that as vaccination in the Cowbridge and Maesteg area was largely carried out by deputies, Guardians should verify what medical qualification these 'gentlemen' had. Dr Maurice Jones of Maesteg, who had vaccinated for Dr Lewis was LRCP, LSA and was accepted, but Dr Bates was asked to rearrange his work so that he could do all the vaccinating himself.

In July of the same year the Poor Law Board informed the Guardians that when Cod-liver-oil or Quinine was prescribed by the Doctors it should be 'at their own expence', but the Guardians wrote back stating that their salary was too small for this and that all expensive drugs should be paid for by the Board of Guardians. The P.L.B. then relented and suggested that 'a quantity of Cod-liver-oil should be kept in the Workhouse and Quinine by a specified local Chemist'.

Dr J. W. Phillips (Western) resigned in March and Dr Michael Allan replaced him. He had obtained MRCS(Eng) and LRCP(Ed) in 1861 and was registered but he lived in Bridgend and not in the district concerned. Consequently the appointment was on a temporary basis and would remain so until he moved to the right address - which he did a year later. The appointment was then ratified although Dr Robert Abraham Verity was also a candidate.

Three cases of Smallpox and one of Typhus were seen that month.

In June 1866 it was commented that too few were being vaccinated by Dr Bates (Cowbridge) and the Guardians were asked to give an explanation. When they replied that many children were being vaccinated privately and that Dr Bates was 'not enthusiastic because of illhealth' they were told that the service of a deputy should be obtained. Dr D. J. Edwards, who had deputized previously, was sought by Dr Bates and he seemed to be suitable.

The following month a circular was received from the P.L.B. listing the duties contained in the Disease Prevention Act as issued by the Lords of her Majesty's Privy Council. The Clerk was asked to write to all doctors within the Union Area regarding the action to be taken if Cholera, or severe diarrhoea, returned. They then ordered a hundred gallons of Carbolic Acid from Messers Calvert, Bradford, and half a ton of chloride of lime from Thomas Jones, a local Chemist, and distributed both to suitable centres. Messrs Knight and Company (London) supplied 500 booklets in English and Welsh titled 'Plain Advice to all during the visitation of Cholera'. A fortnight later there was another communication from the Privy Council to the effect that the Board of Guardians had jurisdiction (among other authorities) over the Port of Cardiff. They replied that they were not aware of this but that they certainly had jurisdiction over the small ports of Porthcawl, Newton, Ogmore and Aberthaw. The P.L.B. explained that there was a Public Health Bill before Parliament which would delineate the responsibility of the nearest 'Nuisance Authority' for the ships then in Port.

Dr D. J. Edwards refused to deputize for Dr Bates because the local newspaper had queried his fitness to do so. The Clerk told him that the Guardians were in no way responsible for what appeared in the press.

By late September a four-bedded wooden isolation ward, thirty by sixteen feet, had been built behind the Workhouse with a partition separating the sexes. It is not clear how many patients with Cholera were admitted to it. Such cases were certainly being seen in the community because 'bedding clothing and bedclothes' of a household in Newcastle were destroyed following the death of four people from the disease. On the 29th two more cases were seen in Llangynwyd Lower and one in St Bride's Major. By the third of November a further eight cases had been recorded (six in Maesteg) giving a total of fifteen. None occurred after that date. In early January (1867) the Doctors were paid extra for the 'zeal' in dealing with the outbreak - Dr Lewis received £50, Dr Verity £20, Dr Allan (Western) £10 and Dr Bates (Cowbridge) £2. Dr John Pritchard and Dr W. H. Thomas (Maesteg), both private doctors, received £10 each. The Relieving Officers also received gratuities - Richard Leyshon £10, William John £5 and David Lloyd £2. The Guardians expressed their appreciation for all the good work. Dr Leahy of Aberkenfig thought that the money was unnecessary in his case and Dr Thomas Griffiths, late assistant of Dr Lewis, was refused a gratuity. He was the only one who applied for it!

Several cases of Typhoid and Typhus were seen in scattered communities throughout the year.

In May a circular was received from Dr Edward Smith MD, FRS. Medical Officer to the Poor Law Board, requesting that an effort be made by all Guardians to adopt 'uniform basic principles of diet' for inmates. This was followed by the observation that Medical Officers for the Workhouse should enter in a Book the details of Special Diets requested.

In October a letter arrived from the House Surgeon of Swansea Infirmary indicating that a patient of theirs in the Hospital had spinal disease and needed special support for his back. Would they pay for it or would they prefer to transfer the patient to a Metropolitan hospital such as the Royal Orthopaedic? The Clerk wrote to that hospital to find out their charges, but unfortunately the patient died before being transferred although a spinal support costing £4 had been supplied by friends.

In January 1868 Dr Verity commented on the P.L.B.'s suggestion that a paid Nurse be appointed (Chapter 7): "I have never had occasion to find fault with the present system of nursing the sick by employing a fit person from the House. I do **not** see the necessity of employing a paid nurse at present but should an epidemic break out it will then be time to have one. They all think it a great honour to aspire to the position of a nurse and are very careful in carrying out my instructions. Should we ever be visited with Cholera or Fever at any future time I shall take care to make an early application for the required assistance". The Guardians concurred with this view.

Later that year (24th August) the doctors were asked to report on the condition of the Workhouse from their point of view. In response they identified the need for 'cleansing the drains of the yard, cleansing and ventilating the water closet in the infirm men's ward, cleansing of the Itch garret and the fever hospital, cleansing of the privy in the women's yard and the water closet in the lying-in ward'. (The Itch garret was probably the ward they isolated children with infectious and other disorders of the skin in 1853 – Chapter 11). This report convinced the Guardians that the doctors could be useful in a general way and so they were asked 'to attend the Saturday Board meetings monthly when it was convenient for them to do so'.

Dr Verity asked for an increase in salary in March '69 pointing out that he had served the Board for 25 years and adding: "At first the Workhouse contained 25-30 inmates but at present the number is over 130 and the Workhouse has become mainly an Infirmary for the whole Union area. The district work has also increased and is now almost double what it was". When the matter was considered it was pointed out that his yearly earnings for vaccinating, visiting the pauper lunatics at home and carrying out extra recognized medical duties was upward of £110. Dr Leahy, as Board member proposed that the salary be increased to £65 per annum. Seven voted for the proposal and 7 against, but the casting vote of the Chairman was in favour. It was later agreed that £50 should be for district work and £15 for that of the Workhouse.

In November Dr Stevens, who was now the Vaccination Officer of the P.L.B., wrote to say that two vaccination centres for Bridgend were not acceptable. All the vaccinating centres for the town had to be in one centre. The difficulty had arisen because of the district boundary changes (Chapter 7). It was also important to include in the returns the number of parents who had refused to allow vaccination. Persistent refusal despite warnings would lead to legal procedings. There were 131 refusals in Bridgend and 188 in Maesteg over a six month period - they all consented later.

Dr Lewis (Northern) requested leave of absence over the winter months because of illness in his family and suggested that Dr John Davies MD,MRCS would be a suitable deputy. This was readily agreed to. [Dr. Lewis' only son, a student at Oxford, became ill and died.]

In February of the following year (1870) a coroner's jury found Dr Verity guilty of neglect in the care of an Elizabeth Randall. She was not a pauper and the verdict was therefore of no direct concern to the Guardians, nevertheless they expressed the view that 'he should take it as a warning'.

Non-resident paupers, living in England, sometimes needed hospital attention. For instance, Dr Steele of Guy's wrote to them that Jonah Jenkins, a pauper with cancer, had been an inpatient for 44 days and that they owed £28.4.0. There was a further bill soon afterwards and the P.L.B. questioned its need.

Dr Lewis resigned his Poor Law post in August and was thanked profusely for his 'hard work, diligence and wisdom'. He was unusually well-qualified for a provincial doctor having obtained the MRCS in 1841, the external LRCP (London) in 1843, the FRCS (England) in 1859 and the MRCP(London) in 1870. Apart from being a Poor Law Medical Officer and a private Doctor he was also a Medical Officer to the Maesteg Iron Works and to Brogden's Mines. One of his main interests was in the recovery of patients after illness or accident. In 1862 he acquired two cottages in New Road, Porthcawl, for convalescence and in 1878 replaced the cottages with a specially designed building near the coast - The Rest, Porthcawl. This was one of the earliest rehabilitation centres in the country and served not only Bridgend and district but also Cardiff and Swansea. Dr Lewis died in Penarth in 1890 at the age of 73 years. The Rest exists to this day.

There were two applicants for his post, Dr William Hopkin Thomas and the previously mentioned Dr John Davies; both were resident in Maesteg. The latter was appointed at a salary of £40 a year with extras (to include the costs of medicines apart from cod liver-oil, quinine, and trusses).

In March 1871 Dr Verity suggested that the Workhouse inmates should be re-vaccinated because of the prevalence of Smallpox. A week later there was a circular from the P.L.B. stating that there was a severe epidemic of the disease in London and Liverpool and that the local populace should be vaccinated or re-vaccinated if need be. Refusals should be indicated in the returns from the Relieving Officers who would be known as Vaccination Officers and paid a shilling per reported case. Dr Home, Medical Inspector for the Local Government Board - which had replaced the Poor Law Board - requested the Guardians to draw up new contracts with the doctors specifying a weekly attendance at a main station and a rotating 6 monthly attendance at substations. Bridgend needed five of these and Cowbridge, nine. The service in Maesteg needed complete reorganization.

In the middle of January 1872 Major Turberville brought a complaint against Dr Allan (Western). Apparently the Doctor had been asked to visit an ill patient on the 13th of December and had not done so until the 25th - despite three requests. There was an internal inquiry. It transpired that Dr Allan had visited the patient before the 25th and had been told by the patient's wife that he was progressing satisfactorily. The Board was satisfied by his explanation; but he had erroneously entered in his book that he had visited the patient on the 18th under the impression that his assistant had done so. This was a grievous 'sin' and he was told to take more care in the future.

On the 13th a Vagrant admitted to the 'Casual Ward' of the Workhouse from Maesteg was found to have Smallpox - to everyone's horror. The Cwmdu Board of Health was censured and asked to provide a building that could be used as a temporary Isolation Hospital. A similar request was sent to the Bridgend Board of Health and to the Overseers of the parishes. The Vestry of Llanmaes and that of Coity Higher thought such a precautionary move unnecessary, but Coychurch Lower, Ewenny, Llangan and St Mary Hill stated that they would take the appropriate steps. St Mary Church already had a spare cottage and Bridgend could use No 1, Llangewydd Street, Newcastle as a temporary hospital. St Bride's Major rented a house from Philip Llywelyn and his daughter Ellen for 2/0d per week. Lack of available property proved a difficulty in Maesteg but the Poor Law Board proposed that a 'Tramp Ward' be constructed near the Police Station which could serve as an Isolation Unit as needs dictated (Chapter 13). Later two small cottages by the hill-side were acquired for the purpose and arrangements made for the supply of free disinfectant to affected households.

The first batch of Smallpox cases were seen on the 13th of April - one in each of the following hamlets: Cwmfelin, Aberkenfig, Newcastle, with two in Llandyfodwg and later, one in Ynysawdre and two in Llandyfodwg.

The fee for vaccinating was 1/6 at the main centre, and 3/0 if more travelling was involved and re-vaccination at 2/0 and 1/0 respectively. In August, Dr Bates claimed payment for 36 at 3/0, 13 at 1/6, 36 re-vaccinations at 2/0 and 5 at 1/0.

All the Medical Officers now claimed more payment for district work with the result that Dr Verity's salary was increased to £60 and the others to £58 per annum.

Dr Allan (Western) was again criticized for supplying an incorrect weekly report. It seems that he had entered a visit as having been done on the Sunday – a day in advance of the actual date of the visit. It was stressed on him that the Medical Book had to be filled in by the employed Medical Officer and not by a deputy or assistant.

On the 31st of May another case of Smallpox occurred in Newcastle and was duly reported to the Bridgend Local Board of Health.

In October Typhoid was diagnosed in 7 patients, 5 in Maesteg and one each in Newcastle and Aberkenfig.

In August 1874 Dr Verity was admonished for being careless in filling in details of the special diets in the Workhouse Book. He had specified the type of special diet but had failed to record the days and month, and the reason for their prescription.

There was dissatisfaction with Dr Allan because 'he remained irregular in supplying his weekly reports' and had not attended Board Meetings despite personal invitations. Furthermore, he had not attended a year later despite repeated promises to do so. Mr Nicholl, the Chairman considered his obstinacy so insulting that he brought a 'charge of neglect of duty' against him. When it was discussed in May 1876 the Board, surprisingly, decided that he 'should have another chance'. It is likely that there were humanitarian reasons behind this leniency because he died on the 31st of October.

The vacant post was advertised twice in the Lancet and in the Central Glamorgan Gazette and on alternate days for a fortnight in the Western Mail. Three applied: Dr John Jenkins (Bridgend), Dr G I Llewelyn (Bridgend), and Dr Charles Broom (Crediton). The first two were shortlisted and Dr Jenkins appointed (February 1877). Unfortunately he did not live in the district concerned and the

Guardians were asked why this had been overlooked. They replied: "He lives within a few hundred yards of the most populated part of the district which is more convenient than if he lived in some remote part of the district". The appointment at a salary of £58 per annum was approved but the L.G.B. added that it was: 'Only till the end of December next when the post has to be re-advertised'.

The following July the House Surgeon of Swansea Hospital wrote to say that a boy they had accepted from the Bridgend Workhouse ostensibly with 'Scrofula' had in fact got Scabies. Dr Verity disagreed, so the Guardians queried the diagnosis only to be told that three of their doctors had seen the patient apart from the Resident Medical Officer, and that they were all of the same opinion. Dr Verity was away at the time but the information was conveyed to him.

The Rev. Stacey brought a complaint against Dr Bates concerning a patient with 'apoplexy', but as the patient was not a pauper the Guardians commented: "It is not our business".

The year 1878 started with a query from the L.G.B. to the Guardians: "Why are there 67 unvaccinated children in Dr Jenkins' district (Western)?" The explanation was: "Vaccination has been postponed because there is a great deal of illness among the children". Dr Verity was then asked to supply 'a full report on the children in the Workhouse'. It seems that Scabies was rife - probably contracted from the child who had returned from the Swansea Hospital. By April 'only 4 boys and 3 girls were affected and being treated'. He explained that the outbreak was due to overcrowding, lack of isolation facilities, and 'no Itch ward'- presumably the Itch garret had been considered unsuitable. He suggested that: "Such children should be farmed out in ones and twos as lodgers in the country to be attended by the local doctor". The problem was discussed by the Guardians and they concluded: "A separate block should be set apart for such exigencies". In the meantime the Clerk was to ascertain the practice in other Unions. Dr Verity joyfully announced in July that all the children were cured. He was given £10 in recognition of his care. Dr Jenkins was at last able to complete the vaccination of children in his district and in August was paid £52.10.0 for 350 at 3/0 each. (The total cost of the whole programme throughout the Union over 6 months was £113.6.3)

Early in 1879 all the doctors in the Union area were instructed to report all contagious diseases to the Clerk of the Sanitary Authority and to the Poor Law doctors in their capacity as Medical Officers of Health (Chapter 13). There was also a strange edict that: 'Either Medical or Surgical qualification entitles to a fee for amputation'.

In July a lady from Llanharan was reported to have died in child birth and had not been attended by either Dr Verity or his deputy, Dr Leahy. There was an inquest during which Dr Verity was severely censured. It was reported that both doctors had been too ill to attend the confinement. The Guardians perceived that they could not be blamed but felt strongly that there should be a deputy for the Workhouse and another in Llanharan so that such eventualities would be covered.

Dr Bates (Cowbridge) was granted sick leave in September with Dr Daniel Edwards deputizing. He was still away ill in November.

In January 1880 Mr Blandy Jenkins of Llanharan House, a prominent Guardian, complained that Dr Verity had not attended the vaccination station in Llanharan as he should have. Had he done so he would have been told about the sickness of a nearby pauper. Dr Verity's defence was that he was too ill to go there that day. This failure to attend had occurred previously and to avoid recurrence Dr D. W. Davies was invited to be Medical Officer for the Sub-district. He accepted the offer at a salary of £10 per annum.

Measles, Diphtheria and Scarlet Fever were rampant among the children in the community and, in March, Typhoid re-emerged.

Dr Bates (Cowbridge) was still ill, and in April resigned after 20 years in post. Dr Evan Thomas Davies of Llantwit Major was appointed as replacement, on a temporary basis, at a salary of £10 per annum. They explained to the L.G.B. that although not residing in the district concerned he was the only suitable Medical Officer available. This was palpably untrue because Dr J. W. Phillips took over a few months later having been appointed by local personnel. Dr Phillips was previously Medical Officer to the Western District and had resigned in 1865 probably because he was moving to Cowbridge. William Howells of Wick wondered about the legality of the appointment because: "No ballot has been taken by the Guardians". Nevertheless it was confirmed and a salary of £50 per annum allowed. Dr D. W. Davies of Llanharan nominated his son, Dr W. Naunton Davies, as deputy but Dr Phillips said that Dr Stannestreet would be available for him.

The question of superannuation for Dr Bates arose and it was proposed that he should receive £47 a year (two thirds of his salary) but an amendment against the proposal was carried (18:14). The Rev F W Edmondes tried to rescind the amendment a week later but his effort was heavily defeated (29 votes to 12). This meant that Dr Bates was leaving empty-handed!

At this time Dr Verity became Medical Officer to the Cottage Homes (Chapter 13) at a salary of £10 per annum. However, there then arose a question about his medical qualification and whether he could continue in post 'because he is not LSA or LRCP'. It was finally decided by the L.G.B. that: "As he has practised for so long it should be allowed". Dr Jenkins (Western) took 5 weeks holiday in mid-summer and the immediate question was: "Who takes over?". The reply was that Dr Verity would cover his district work and Dr Owen his other work.

Two weeks before Christmas the L.G.B. requested full information about a Michael Jordan who had committed suicide by drowning. He had become violent at home and Dr Leahy with Dr Jenkins' agreement had arranged admission to the Workhouse. Their intention was to request the Magistrates for an order to transfer him from there to the Asylum, but unfortunately he 'escaped' the next morning and drowned himself. The L.G.B. considered that he should have been kept in a locked room when in the Workhouse under the care of a Porter and a Nurse. The Guardians replied that Dr Verity considered him sane and that in any case they did not think a Porter and a Nurse necessary. The comments about the Porter is interesting since it was considered essential by them when the Workhouse first opened (Chapter 13).

The appointment of Dr D. W. Davies, Llanharan, was extended for another year in June 1881 and the salary of Dr John Davies of Maesteg increased by £10 to £50. Dr Stannestreet, deputy to Dr Phillips (Cowbridge) died in October, apparently killed by a train near Llanharry Station after attending an inquest. He was replaced by Dr George Gerald Reynolds.

A month later Mr Spear, the Inspector for Vaccinations, complained that the doctors were claiming for private vaccinations carried out by their deputies and in many instances were being paid twice. The alleged malpractice had to be investigated. Dr Davies (Northern) stated that this did not happen in his district though many vaccinations were not being recorded by the Vaccination Officer (Chapter 14). Dr Verity claimed: "All vaccinations are being done by me. Occasionally I give fresh lymph vaccine to private colleagues and they send me the vaccination papers". Dr Jenkins (Western) stated: "Dr Verity or Dr Leahy sometimes vaccinate for me. Is this wrong?". There the matter rested for the time being.

Information was received in December that the retired Dr Bates was in financial difficulties as all he had to survive on was £30 superannuation granted by the Cardiff Union for being the Medical Officer to Bonvilston. An effort was made to overturn the previous refusal and allow a smaller sum, perhaps £15, but again it was 'negatived'.

The L.G.B. informed the Guardians in February 1882 that they were asking Mr Bircham and Mr Spear, Inspectors for the Workhouse and Vaccination, to carry out a combined official inquiry into the Public Health Vaccinators - Dr Verity, Dr John Davies and Dr John Jenkins. A month later they reported that the three doctors were 'guilty of irregularities' and 'had received monies to which they were not entitled'. Dr Davies had even vaccinated in the Neath Union (This was Llangynwyd Higher - Chapter 8). He had kept all money for vaccinations done by Dr W. H. Thomas and had not carried out any at the Tondu station. None of the doctors, especially Dr Davies and Dr Jenkins, had attended their stations regularly. They wrote: "All could be proceeded against. Dr Jenkins and Dr Verity have been warned but can continue. Dr Davies on the other hand, should refund the money he has falsely claimed and do so within a month". They continued: "We greatly regret the lack of supervision by the Guardians and we suggest that a committee of the Board of Guardians be formed to supervise from now on".

In May the need for a paid Nurse for the Workhouse was again discussed and again it was decided that such a post was not necessary. The question of re-appointing Dr D. W. Davies (Llanharan) was also causing difficulty because he lived in Llantrisant which was outside the district. They decided to ignore this 'as no other suitable person was available'. The L.G.B. allowed them to do so provided the post was advertised annually.

Dr Verity was asked to nominate a deputy for the Workhouse and named Dr Wyndam Randall, whose appointment was later ratified. Dr J. W. Phillips (Cowbridge) caused considerable displeasure by going on leave without informing the Guardians. He had covered himself to an extent by informing William John, the Relieving Officer, that Dr Samuel Wallace would act as his deputy. Two weeks later an out-door pauper became seriously ill. The Relieving Officer requested an 'emergency visit' by Dr Wallace but he 'delayed going'. Dr Edwards was then asked to see him; he responded but charged 5/0. The Officer complained to the Board and they asked Dr Phillips for his version of events. This summarizes his response: "John called on Wallace dinner time and Wallace said – 'I'll see him after dinner' – John immediately left without giving the pauper's address. He could have called on me because I was home on Sunday. If you are dissatisfied I am prepared to resign". The offer of resignation was accepted!

Dr William Naunton Davies (deputy to his father in Llanharan) and Dr Evan Thomas Davies (Llantwit Major) applied for the post. The latter was appointed by a majority of one (24:25). Three months later Blandy Jenkins said that according to the L.G.B. Dr E. T. Davies was also the new Medical Officer for Bonvilston and asked:"Could not someone else do one of them?". The Guardians replied that: "Davies is the best for Cowbridge" (Note also that Dr Bates had covered the two districts).

On August 24th a Nurse was appointed but as a part-post with Assistant Matron (Chapter 10). According to the Consolidated Order of 1847 the only qualification required by a Workhouse Nurse was to be able to read written instructions on medicines. In 1865 there was an edict to all Guardians that only paid Nurses with practical experience should be employed. In Bridgend the first reference to the need for such a post was not until 1869. By then there was also the perceived need for Night Nurses to be employed in large institutions. Formalized Nurse training did not start until 1874. The use of paupers as Nurse Assistants continued until 1879. Tasks included the cleaning of wards, distribution of food (but not the feeding of patients) and to help the Nurse to change the clothes of 'a wet and dirty person'. According to the 1851 Census there was a Midwife aged 62 years in Angelton (Pen-y-Fai) and a Nurse who was a 'widow with child' living in Bridgend'. Ten years later records show that there were three Nurses in Bridgend, one age 36 years and the other two aged 15 and 16 years!

Contrary to popular opinion considerable attention was given to the diet of inmates. In 1836 the Commissioners had given three examples of variations in the choice of a weekly diet. The Bridgend Workhouse adopted a diet which was in use in the Carmarthen Workhouse (Chapter 13). The meals provided were probably more balanced and nutritious than the diet of poor people (as opposed to paupers) living in the community. Nevertheless, comparison with what would be accepted as a balanced diet today shows a deficiency of Calcium, Iron, Vitamin C and Folic Acid whilst total calorie intake was barely adequate. The diet was rich in fibre because 'one way flour' or 'seconds' was used in baking and this was less refined than that used by the affluent. In 1876 the L.G.B. devised a diet that would provide more meat and vegetables to the ordinary adult inmate and an extra pint of milk a day to breast-feeding mothers.

Alcoholism was a major problem, socially and medically, and was a significant cause of pauperism. In an effort to control the scourge there was an attempt to close public houses on Sundays (Chapter 9). In November 1883 there was a letter from Newcastle-on-Tyne Union advocating the development and use of 'Inebriate Retreats' in Workhouses, Asylums and elsewhere. 'Habitual drunkards' would be accommodated without 'restriction of duration' and the cost reclaimed when the person returned to work. This was discussed and supported, although the Medical Officers appeared not to have been consulted - perhaps their views were represented by Dr Leahy who was a member of the Board. No action appeared to have been taken despite their approval.

In March 1884 Dr Verity became ill and the Guardians thought that he should give up work but Dr Leahy impressed on them that such action was probably premature - he returned in July.

Dr John Jenkins (Western) died in early August and Dr Llewelyn undertook his duties on a temporary basis. Later on in the month Dr Verity resigned: "Because I am incapacitated by age and infirmity". He hoped that the Guardians would agree to superannuate him at the expected rate of two-thirds of his annual income (i.e. £52) but in October a resolution to that effect was defeated. Dr Verity then withdrew his resignation claiming that he was well enough to cope with his district duties so long as he could relinquish those of the Workhouse and Cottage Homes. Further consideration was then given to providing him with a superannuation of £30 but this was also 'negatived'. Dr Verity countered with a request to remain the Public Vaccinator for the District while relinquishing all other duties to Dr Randall who had been appointed as a temporary replacement. This was allowed for the time being. Sadly Dr Verity died the following year and Dr Randall was appointed to the permanent post. He was to receive £25 for the Workhouse duties and £10 for the Cottage Homes.

There were two applicants for the vacant Western post: Dr George Joseph Llewelyn (Park Street) and Dr Philip James. Dr Llewelyn was preferred, but as he was not resident in the district he knew that there would be opposition from the L.G.B., and so a month later, resigned. When re-advertised Dr Thomas Jones (Aberkenfig) and Dr Philip James applied. The latter was successful – at a salary of £35 a year. He lived in Porthcawl.

At around this time the Ogmore and Garw district was established (Chapter 9) and Dr D. John Thomas of Nantymoel became its Medical Officer.

In May there was another complaint of a financial nature. Dr John Davies (Maesteg) in the Guardians' opinion had overcharged for treating a female pauper with a fracture - particulary since doubt had been cast on the diagnosis by Dr W. H. Thomas, a colleague of Dr Davies. Dr William Pritchard and Dr Leahy were asked to arbitrate. They found that the 76 year old female had an inch of shortening of the right leg and was too feeble to get out of bed. They thought that the diagnosis had been correct and that the weekly visits by Dr Davies were fully justified.

Vaccination against Smallpox remained a major item and supervision of the innoculation programme was fastidious. It involved not only the recently formed Vaccination Committee of the Guardians but also the lay Vaccination Officers and the Vaccination Inspector of the L.G.B.. The slightest delay by the doctors in carrying out the procedure or in its reporting led to immediate and searching questions. For instance, in February 1886 it was apparent from the dates of birth that a large number of children in the Western district had not been vaccinated. Dr James was asked: "Why is this?" He explained that it was due to a severe outbreak of Measles in Porthcawl. Dr Randall was also interrogated': "Why did you visit the vaccination station in Wick on the wrong day?" His excuse was: "I did not have a supply of lymph on the notified day".

In May, John Deere, assistant Overseer of Llantwit Major, complained that Dr E. T. Davies had taken a long time to visit an ill old man who had died the following day. After an Inquiry the doctor was 'exonerated'.

It would appear that nearly everybody complained about the doctors at some stage but that rarely were the complaints upheld by the Board.

Despite the meticulous supervision of the Smallpox vaccination programme little concern was expressed about the death-rate from other infectious diseases. Mortality among children was high. For example, in 1886, 11 children died from measles, 9 of scarlet fever, 7 of diphtheria, 25 of the 'mysterious fever' and 50 of whooping cough in Bridgend and Maesteg alone.

Photograph taken in 1985 showing the partly-demolished bell tower (left) marking the site of the original schoolroom, later converted to a chapel.

Chapter 13

Education

Inmate as Porter, Porters with Wife as Schoolmistress, Schoolmistresses for Workhouse children (1854-1878), Report of School Inspector on the Teaching of Workhouse Children at the National School, Cottages and Industrial School (1876-1886), School Attendance Committee, Payment for Pauper Children in Board Schools.

In February 1839 the Workhouse was ready, but the Guardians thought that paupers should not be admitted until a Porter had been appointed. It was agreed that such a person should be bilingual and able to read and write. A resolution was passed that the appointment should be made the following month; an amendment that Thomas Davies (Senior) of Cowbridge be 'elected' at a salary of £12 per annum with maintenance was rejected. The matter was then postponed for further discussion in a fortnight. The issue was raised again in March. The Reverend Robert Knight proposed, and Richard Llewelyn seconded, that the previously mentioned Thomas Davies be forthwith appointed. No other person was suggested, but when it was put to the vote it was obvious that a large majority of the Guardians were firmly of the opinion that such an appointment was unnecessary. As a way out of the dilemma it was decided to send a copy of the discussion – with a copy of the protest – to the Assistant Commissioner for opinion. The reply was that a Porter was necessary but that there was no urgency about making such an appointment, and that there was certainly no need to delay admissions. The comment that a Porter was necessary was accepted, and the previously mentioned Thomas Davies (Senior) was appointed. Three months later he was dismissed for 'absenting himself without leave from Sunday last to Thursday' – and paid £2.15.5d. The Reverend Robert Knight's judgement of character had not been infallible!

The question of a replacement was deferred until 1844. In February of that year the Reverend Charles Ramsay Knight proposed, and the Reverend John Harding seconded, that an advertisement be placed in the Cambrian and the Merthyr Guardian for a married couple: 'Capable of undertaking the situation of Porter and Schoolmistress at £40 per annum without board but resident in the Workhouse and provided with coal, candles and washing'. The man had to be able to read and write and speak both Welsh and English. Applications had to be supported with testimonials.

In March William Williams and his wife Ann, from Llantwit Major, were appointed on a month's trial until the 5th of May – 'two weeks notice to be given by either party in the event of disagreement' but soon after taking up the post

William Williams was dismissed: 'As he had been caught with his ear at the keyhole listening to the proceedings'. Richard Franklen, supported by Popkin Traherne, then suggested that the difficulty might be overcome if an old soldier of good character could be found who was fluent in both Welsh and English. His salary would be £12 per annum 'with rations'. Evidently the idea of having a 'wife Schoolmistress' had been abandoned. Contact was made with a Lieutenant Hollingworth of the Horse Guards and he recommended someone by the name of George Jenkins. Unfortunately Jenkins could not read or write and was deemed totally unacceptable, and there was no-one else the Lieutenant could suggest.

The Guardians then returned to the original proposal: a double appointment of a husband and wife as Porter and Schoolmistress. There was no-one of sufficient ability in the Workhouse to become a permanent Porter, but Evan John, an old soldier inmate was asked to fill the post for the time being. Meanwhile they re-advertised for a married couple on the same terms as before.

In July it was proposed by Popkin Traherne, and seconded by Lord Adare, that William Blethyn and his wife of Loughor be appointed Porter and Schoolmistress, provided they 'did not allow their family to live within ten miles of the Workhouse'. In reply Mr. and Mrs. Blethyn stated that they could not accept the post because it meant separating from their two children. The Guardians insisted that the terms could not be altered. It was then decided to pay Evan John - the temporary Porter - two shillings a week and his keep. He was also given a blue coat to distinguish him from the other inmates. A special waistcoat, trousers and hat were supplied later.

Meanwhile the children attended the National School. This had been sanctioned by the Commissioners as a temporary measure 'provided the Establishment paid one penny per child per week to the Headmaster'. A branch of the National Society for the Education of the Poor was founded in Bridgend by Sir John Nicholl (father of John Nicholl MP) in 1812, and the school was established as an offshoot of Newcastle Church in 1822. The school year started in October and the pupils were taught reading, writing, arithmetic and Religious Knowledge, in English. The girls' schoolroom was in the Poorhouse, Nolton Road, rented from the Vestry of Coity Lower, and the boys were accommodated at the Town Hall by permission of Lord Adare. In 1824 a school was built in Nolton Road and had 82 boys and 131 girls on the register. This was the school the Workhouse children attended. (Its replacement – the school by the station – was not built until 1859).

In November a charge was brought against Evan John - temporary Porter - that he had misbehaved with a female inmate in the laundry. A woman claimed to have seen him do so, but Evan John vociferously denied that any impropriety had taken place. The Guardians were not convinced that the woman was speaking the truth and so the charge was dismissed, but some suspicion remained and they resumed their search for a husband and wife partnership. In December, 1844, David Phillips and his wife, Sarah, were appointed Porter and Schoolmistress - provided they 'found accommodation for their child outside the Union Workhouse'.

On the twenty-first of the month, sixteen shillings was paid to the National School for the children's education. They continued to attend the school despite the recent appointment of a Schoolmistress. Her duties were to look after them generally and 'to take them out daily for half an hour's exercise after 4 p.m.'. In February 1845 the husband accused the Master – another Mr Phillips – of being drunk on duty but failed to substantiate the accusation and was consequently dismissed – together with his wife, the Schoolmistress. They were paid £3.15.0d for their seven and a half week's service.

Mary Gavener, an in-door pauper, took the children to school, and Evan John resumed as Porter but in June the Commissioners issued an edict: 'To immediately appoint a Schoolmistress and Porter in place of David Phillips and wife'. The Guardians pointed out that at the time (June 1845) there were 47 inmates of whom only 17 were children with 4 above nine years of age and 13 below. Twelve of the 17 went to the National School (with the Commissioners' consent), while the remaining five, who were under six years of age, 'were prevented from doing so by regulation of the Establishment'. No action was taken despite the Commissioners edict.

In the voluminous reports based on the Education Survey of Schools in Wales 1846/47 there were comments about the teaching of Workhouse children, and reference was made to the school in Cardiff, Neath, Swansea, Llanelli, Carmarthen, Haverfordwest, Pembroke, Newcastle Emlyn, Narberth, Llandovery and Llandeilo. There was no mention of Bridgend and the report gives the impression of neglect in the education of the Workhouse children. A comment about the contribution of the National School would not have been amiss. It was stated that the teaching in the Church Sunday School - to which they also went - 'was conducted wholly in English'.

In November 1848 Mr Edward Hurst, the Poor Law Inspector for the district, attended a Board meeting and impressed on the Guardians the importance of starting a school for the education and the industrial training of the pauper children within the confines of the Workhouse itself. As an example he referred to Bridgenorth, Shropshire, where a small farm had been taken over and cultivated by the pauper children 'at a profit of £65 last year'. He was asked to put his views in writing and send them to the Board. When his letter arrived a special meeting was convened to discuss its contents. The general opinion was 'that they were most inconclusive', and the Reverend Robert Knight supported by James Reynolds carried a motion: 'That the Board declines to proceed'.

Mr Hurst visited Bridgend again the following March, and after noting that the boys' and women's bedrooms were offensive because of poor ventilation, wrote in the Visitors' Book: "I am happy that the Guardians are now disposed to take a small quantity of land for the industrial training of their children. Education of this description is the most effectual check to pauperism in the rising generation". A number of local land owners were approached in the effort to obtain this additional land. In June 1849 Sir Digby Mackworth's solicitor responded that Sir Digby was unwilling to sell the land they had desired because it was being used for pasture. Furthermore, if the Guardians at any time changed their plans and returned the land the value of it would have dropped. Similarly with land owned by Lord Dunraven. Mr. John Randall, the estate's agent, pointed out that the land in question was occupied and that 'possession of it would not be possible for a long time'. There was no other suitable land nearby and so the scheme was abandoned for the time being.

In April 1850 Mr Alfred Tutte, Headmaster of the National School, was paid 5/0d for the 'instruction of Workhouse children'; 4/8d in September, 9/3 in January '51; 16/8d in December and 5/1d in November '52.

There had been a new development the previous month. Mrs Dalton, the Matron, resigned and the Guardians thought they might be able to abolish her post and replace it with a combined post of Nurse and Schoolmistress – under the general supervision of the Master. A letter to this effect was sent to the Poor Law Board (which had replaced the Poor Law Commissioners in 1847) and a week later received the information that the Board did not approve of the 'union of the office of Nurse and Schoolmistress in the same person' but that they were prepared to 'sanction the appointment of both a Nurse and a Schoolmistress in addition to a Matron'. This was an unexpected turn of events, the impact of which was compounded when the Reverend John Harding informed them that the Management Committee of the National School Board had adopted a resolution that henceforth they would 'decline to admit children from the Workhouse to the school'.

In November John Graves, the Poor Law Inspector for the district, visited the Workhouse and advised them to advertise for a Schoolmistress who would be free from other duties. They accepted this advice and decided that she should have a thorough knowledge of Welsh, be able to teach reading, writing and arithmetic together with knitting and sewing to the girls, and general instruction to both sexes that would 'fit them for service'. The salary was to be £20 a year 'with rations' – or more if the Committee of the Council on Education so specified. The advertisement duly appeared and much to their surprise there was no applicant.

They then re-advertised the post, not only in the usual county papers, but also in the Ecclesiastical Gazette, omitting the need for knowledge of the Welsh language but insisting on a certificate of Competence from the Board of the Council on Education. Again there were no applicants.

In October '53 Mr David Jenkins, the Headmaster who had replaced Mr Tutte, received 19/0d for teaching seventeen children at four pence per week per head. A further £3.8.0d was paid him in May '54.

Her Majesty's Inspector of Schools, Jelinger Symmons (appointed in 1846) visited the Workhouse in July '54 and wrote in the Visitor's Book:

'I have examined the fourteen children who go to school. It is hardly credible how they can have managed to learn so little. They are all but perfectly ignorant. Two only can read intelligently. Of religious knowledge they understand nothing. As a specimen I asked: "What did Jesus Christ come into the world to do?" and the answer was: "To judge the quick and the dead". Fifteen pence they said was two shillings, and three multiplied by seven was twelve. Three only can write at all and one of them made a capital E backwards in trying to write his name. No industrial training is given to the girls and, in fact, the children are brought up in idleness, both mentally and bodily, excepting one who gardens.

I beg respectfully to recommend to the Board that a good, active, industrious Schoolmistress be appointed whose salary would be paid by the Government, provided a comfortable room was provided for her, and if the Guardians choose it I would be happy to look out for a fit person'.

A special meeting was convened to consider this shattering report and from the tone of the discussion that followed it was obvious that the Guardians were irritated by its contents. After all they had tried to find a Schoolmistress and it was not their fault that the teaching at the National School had been so ineffectual. When it was proposed that further efforts be made to obtain the service of a Schoolmistress the motion was defeated. Moreover, it was unanimously agreed that the children should continue to attend the day school as before. The School Managers' objection, previously voiced by the Reverend Harding was not mentioned, so presumably it had been withdrawn. It is perhaps surprising that no-one suggested that the poor results could have been due to the children being taught and examined in a language they did not understand!

By October the Guardians had regained their composure. A motion by the Reverend Blosse, seconded by the Reverend Harding, proposed that another effort be made to appoint a Schoolmistress who was preferably Welsh-speaking; none demurred. They also agreed that Mr Symmons should act on their behalf in identifying a suitable person, but as an amendment they reserved the right to appoint whomsoever they wished. They also decided that preference would be given to an applicant who had been trained in a Training College. (One had been opened in Brecon in 1846 and another in Carmarthen in 1848). A letter was sent to the Inspector asking him what salary he suggested, and what salary should be paid to insure repayment by the Government. Parliament, in 1846, had approved of a grant of £15,000 towards salaries, the amount allocated to a particular teacher to be proportional to the number of children being taught and the quality of the instructions given. The following month, November '54, Mrs Elizabeth Thomas of St. Mary Hill was appointed Schoolmistress and she was to receive 'free food and keep in the Workhouse'.

Identifying an area suitable as a Schoolroom had to be considered. The room originally earmarked for the purpose had been converted into a Chapel in December '38 (Chapter 3) and the only spare room that was available became a day room in April '53, so that now they were faced with building a separate room or dividing one of the larger rooms. They concluded that the latter was the easier solution and so they split off a section of the girls' bedroom for use as a Schoolroom, which therefore was upstairs as in the Narberth Workhouse. The stage was now set for the residential tuition of the children.

In February Mrs Thomas was granted two days' leave to visit the Cardiff Workhouse in order to study their method of teaching. Mr Symmons revisited in April, with the object of discussing her salary. The following month Mrs Thomas resigned – because her husband had returned from Australia!

Once more the Guardians were faced with a dilemma, but this time they had a safety valve in the person of Mr Symmons. He advised them that the post should be re-advertised at a salary of at least £30; but at a special meeting called to discuss this suggestion the Reverends John Jones and Lynch Blosse argued strongly that £20 was sufficient. Their view was accepted.

Mrs Jane Dunn of Coychurch was appointed in July '55. She was allowed three weeks holiday leave in December '57 – the first that she had had. In June 1858, the then Matron, Mrs Margaret Williams, resigned and Mrs Dunn was appointed in her place (Chapter 10) with the result that the post of Schoolmistress was again vacant.

It was advertised in the Bridgend Chronicle, the Swansea Herald, and Knight's Official Advertiser. The appointee had to be unmarried, or a widow with no encumbrances, and be the holder of a First Class Certificate of Education. The salary would be £25 per annum. No mention was made of the need to know Welsh.

No-one applied, but when it was re-advertised there were three applicants. Mrs. Marianne Griffiths of the Neath Workhouse was appointed on condition that she produced a Certificate of Competence from the Committee of the Council on Education. No such certificate was produced and so the post was re-advertised. This time there were two applicants – Agnes Cockburn of Penyfai and Anna Hawkesford, an employee of the Hackney Workhouse. In May '59 the latter was appointed at a salary of £30 per annum together with 'board and lodging'.

Mr Symmons revisited the Workhouse in June and recommended that certain books and articles be bought for the school. The Guardians complied. He approved of Mrs Hawkesford and promised to supply her with the necessary Certificate of Competence. The following month she requested the services of a woman 'to bath and comb' the boys and girls after school hours, and 'to accompany them to bed' if she was not available. Her request was granted.

In September, she wrote to the Guardians stating that she had been appointed Matron to the Caerleon Industrial School, and wished to resign immediately: "Because the important post is vacant". Her sudden departure after only four months in the post surprised the Poor Law Board and they wrote to the Guardians for an explanation. The Clerk supplied the necessary details and added that: 'she had discharged her duties satisfactorily' and that 'there was no slur on her character'.

The Guardians again had a problem. How were the children to be taught between her departure and the appointment of a new Schoolmistress? They decided that the only sensible solution was for the Matron to undertake teaching duties temporarily while still performing her own work. The Matron, Mrs Emma Mitchell, was a recent appointee, the previous one having resigned (Chapter 10). She agreed to co-operate if they paid her the additional salary. The Poor Law Board approved of this action and so the crisis passed.

The advertisement for a replacement appeared in November. It stated that in addition to teaching duties the post entailed 'superintending the industrial training of girls, the managing of younger children, the looking after of their clothes and the performing of any other duties that were necessary'. The salary would depend on the type of certificate the successful candidate possessed – 'if a Certificate of Permission the salary would be £25 per annum, if of Probation £30 and if of Competency, £36'.

There were two applicants. Mrs Ann Spencer, whom they preferred, withdrew and so they appointed the other, a Mrs Wilhelmina Jane Warnum who was 30 years of age and a widow. She accepted at a salary of £30 per annum with 'board and lodging' and arrived from Middlesex in January 1860. In December the Matron, Mrs Mitchell, resigned and for the month that the post was vacant the Master and the newly appointed Schoolmistress undertook the duties involved and were allowed to share the extra money between them.

The Bridgend-Cowbridge Union was not the only Union to have problems with the teaching of their Workhouse children. The previous year a letter was received from the Clerk of the Swansea Union stating that they were considering setting up a Union School and wanting to know whether the Bridgend-Cowbridge Union would join. The proposal was rejected.

The approach from Swansea may have been an effort to establish a District School. It had been suggested by the Commissioners in 1838 that several Unions could combine to form such a school in order to remove children from the Workhouse atmosphere. The practice had been authorized by Act of Parliament in 1844 and by 1849 six District Schools had been established – three in London and three elsewhere – despite resistance from Guardians. The concept was supported by the Poor Law Board until 1861, but over the next ten years or so the general view became antagonistic. The establishments became known as Barrack Schools reflecting perhaps the failure of the concept. The Board of Guardians at Bridgend may have been instrumental in preventing the setting up of such a school in Glamorgan.

Mr Ruddock, the new School Inspector, visited the Workhouse in July '61, and gave a certificate of Probation (3rd class) to Mrs Warnum which entitled the Guardians to a grant of £16 from the Paymaster General towards her salary of £30. He commented that the state of the school was unsatisfactory. Another School Inspector, Mr J. B. Browne, came in August '64 and agreed with the certification given to Mrs Warnum.

In April '65 there was a communication from the Cardiff Union to the effect that their Industrial School had many vacancies and that they were prepared to accept children from the Bridgend-Cowbridge Union at a charge of four shillings and three pence per person per week to cover food and clothing. The Guardians showed little interest in the offer.

In March 1866 Mrs Warnum was upgraded to 2nd class entitling the Guardians a moiety of twenty pounds from the Paymaster General toward her salary.

A year later she became ill. Dr Verity diagnosed 'partial paralysis' and indicated that she would have to go on leave for several months. Dr. Leahy agreed, and stated that a change of air and the use of an Electro-Magnetic

Apparatus and sea water baths would help. He thought admission to Guy's or Bart's Hospital should be considered and admission to the former was arranged. She was asked to forfeit seven shillings per week of her salary, and a young lady, Elisabeth Davies, was employed to undertake her duties. Mrs Warnum was given seven pounds toward the cost of the train journey with a companion. They also paid her salary for the two months subsequently spent in hospital. She then resumed duties but her health remained precarious and in January 1868 she resigned. Elisabeth Davies was re-employed at the same salary as before, and the post was advertised.

In March a Miss Hayden was appointed. In November she was allowed a month's leave because of illness, but on returning to duty she worked for only two weeks and then gave in her notice. Miss Louisa Ridewood, from St. Bride's Major, came in December at a salary of £16 pounds per annum 'to be increased to £30 should her grading be satisfactory'. Mr. Browne, the School Inspector, assessed her the following March (1869) and wrote in the Visitor's Book. "The state of the school remains unsatisfactory and the children are ignorant, disorderly and very deficient in arithmetic". He had found Miss Ridewood so ignorant in the subject that he was not prepared to classify her – "she tried to subtract the greater number from the smaller". In view of this indictment the Guardians could not continue to employ her. When she realized this she resigned but asked for a testimonial to allow her to seek a post as a Nurse in another Workhouse. Interestingly they complied stating that she had been 'hard working, kind, considerate and friendly'.

There were six applicants for the post from as far apart as Abingdon, Plaistow, Ross, Crickhowell and Carmarthen. All, apart for the applicant from Carmarthen, were certified Schoolmistresses and were shortlisted. Miss Ann Benallick from Chichester was appointed at a salary of thirty pounds. A month later she resigned. The Guardians then invited Miss Tregerthin from Crickhowell to fill the post. She agreed at the advertised salary . When assessed by the School Inspector in December she was granted a Certificate of Competence (2nd class) and the Guardians were told that this would qualify them for a Government Grant of twenty-nine pounds and eighteen shillings.

A ten-day leave of absence was granted her the following July and again in December over the Christmas period. Mr T. B. Browne visited the Workhouse that month and was disturbed to find that the girls were: "Nursing babies to allow the mothers to attend at a place of worship although in many instances they only go out". He continued: "These mothers are often vicious and contact with them is harmful to the girls. All this would be avoided if the children went to church with their teacher". The practice was discontinued and the Clerk wrote to the Poor Law Board a fortnight later: "Only two do not now go to church with the teacher – one of these goes with the mother and the other accompanies a sick pauper".

In August 1871 Miss Tregerthin left having been appointed to a similar post with the Bedwellty Union. The Clerk gave her a good testimonial stating that the Guardians regretted losing her and that she was leaving of her own free will.

Several Workhouse Schoolmistresses applied for the vacant post – from Pontypridd, Derby, Bristol and Cardiff. A Miss C. Spear was appointed. She came from Westbury Workhouse School near Bristol and already had a Certificate of Competence.

In July '72 the Clerk received a copy of a petition from the Salford Union requesting support. They objected to a section of the Poor Law Amendment Act of 1866 which allowed Guardians to remove children from the Workhouse school and send them to schools 'of a religious background' with the Union paying. The Board agreed with the tenets of the petition but felt it was too soon to discuss it because it had not yet reached the House of Commons.

In August they received a circular from the Local Government Board referring to their role in the terms laid down by the Elementary Education Act of 1870. The gist of it was: 'Although School Boards can enforce the attendance of children and to remit or pay school fees when parents are too poor to do so, it is within the discretion of the Guardians whether or not to supply moneys when the parents are receiving out-door relief'.

There was a request in October for a testimonial from the Stow in the Wold Union. Mrs. Wilhelmina Jane Warnum, who had left because of illhealth, had been appointed there as Schoolmistress. The Clerk replied that the Board had a high opinion of her skills, but wisely refrained from mentioning the illness.

An important development occurred in November. The Board decided to co-operate with the Swansea and Neath Unions in their desire to establish a conveniently situated Industrial District School. Mr Doyle, who was then the Government Workhouse Inspector, suggested that representatives of the three Unions should meet to discuss the project, but that while the school was being built the Bridgend and Cowbridge Union could use the facilities of the Ely Industrial School 'if need be'.

In August '73 Miss Spear resigned. There was considerable regret at her going because she had proved to be pleasant and highly efficient. There were three applicants for the post – a Miss Swaffield (Clifton), a Miss Anne Dale (Barnsley), and Miss Peters (Holloway, London). They chose Miss Anne Dale and she started work in September receiving a Certificate of Competence, 3rd class in December, which justified a Parliamentary grant of twenty-eight pounds.

The Union had already started to pay the school fees of children with pauper parents (i.e. the out-door poor). In December fees totalling one pound fifteen shillings and six pence were paid to the 'Managers' of the Bryndu School, Kenfig Hill, and one pound one shilling and ten pence to the 'Manager' of the Cornelly School for three months' tuition. Mrs Barlow of The Home, Bridgend received twelve pounds and one shilling for two pauper children who had been resident there for six months.

In January '74 the payment of such fees became more formalized. At the request of the Local Government Board each Relieving Officer (Chapter 14) was supplied with tickets on which were entered the name of the child, the school and the number of attendances per week. The first two were entered by the Officer and the last two by the Schoolmaster (or Mistress). Each school was given a weekly ticket for each child. A separate record was kept by the Relieving Officer and the accuracy of each school's half yearly account certified. The fee was then to be paid directly by the Guardians to the Schoolmaster. Interestingly, parental preference was to be a priority in the choice of school. In February this procedure was adopted by the Guardians after verifying that the same procedure also applied to other Unions.

In March the Guardians were asked by the Local Government Board to ascertain the number of children who had reached third standard because they could then leave school. In May they were reminded by the Newhaven Union that under the terms of the Elementary Education Act; 'Children need not go to school in agricultural communities after reaching the age of eleven years'. The Guardians thought it premature to discuss the document.

Miss Dale resigned in June. There were two applicants for her post – Miss Ellen Hills from Farnham and Miss Sarah Morgan from Mountain Ash. The latter was appointed on the condition of a satisfactory testimonial. This was not supplied, and Miss Hills of Hartley Wintley School was offered the post. She took up duties in August pending a satisfactory testimonial. It duly arrived.

The Head Master of Llanharan school was paid £1.15.2 for three months' tuition of pauper children and the Roman Catholic school 15/2d for a similar period. (The paying for the education of out-door pauper children had been fully accepted).

The following December it was decided that a meeting of the Swansea, Neath and Bridgend-Cowbridge Union would be held in January (1875) to finalize arrangements for the Industrial School and then seek permission to proceed from the L.G.B. They heard at the meeting that Swansea had decided 'not to concur'. During the subsequent discussion it became apparent that the Swansea Union was 'indisposed to join the Neath Union'. Mr Doyle, the Government Inspector, suggested the establishment of an Industrial School based on the Cottage System at Bridgend.

A committee was formed to consider the feasibility of this and the following Guardians were appointed members of it: Mr J. C. Nicholl and Rev. C.Ll. Llewelyn (Chairman and Vice-Chairman of the Board), Reverends Blosse and Knight, Stephen Nicholls, James Barrow, Hugh Bevan, John Garsed, Lewis Jenkins, John Lewis, (Llansannor), R.W. Llewelyn and Thomas Loveluck.

In the meantime Miss Hill, the Workhouse School Mistress, resigned (March '75). Advertisement of the vacancy produced no response.

In December, Dr Clutterbuck, the School Inspector, observed that the Workhouse children had not been educated for five months. He wrote: "It is a good idea to have a Cottage School but what about the education of the children meantime?" The Guardians replied that a pupil teacher, Mary Morgan, "will attend to them daily and on Sundays for the sum of 8/0d a week". However, the post of Schoolmistress was then re-advertised. There were two applicants, a Mary Jane Vanstone (Axminster) and Sarah Jane Holden (Usk). The former was appointed at thirty-five pounds a year.

A second committee was established to consider the development of the

Industrial School. Its membership differed slightly from the 'feasibility' committee and included Rev H.T. Nicholl and Major Turberville. They decided that there should be a central administration block with six separate cottages accommodating up to ten children per block. The appointed architect, Mr. Harris, thought that the Schoolroom could be reduced a little but otherwise the general plan was feasible and would cost about five thousand pounds. If accepted by the L.G.B. then the Chairman, Mr Nicholl, was prepared to offer a suitable site of about eight acres at a minimal rent.

The children were still being educated in the Workhouse by Miss Vanstone, but the teaching must have been chaotic because she 'hit a boy severely on the head with a knife' and was immediately dismissed. Miss Mary Morgan took charge as before and the post was advertised. Two applied – Miss Mary Vincent, a Schoolmistress in Wallington Union Workhouse and Miss Margaret B. Laing who was teaching at the South East Shropshire District School. They appointed Miss Laing after verifying that she was not leaving because of some indiscretion!

A tender of £4,940 from William David, Newcastle Hill, for building the cottages was accepted and £5,500 borrowed from the Metropolitan Life Assurance at 4½ interest to be paid over 30 years – £3,000 of which was placed with the London and Provincial Bank. Mr Nicholl gave the land on a 99-year lease at a rental of 2/6 per year.

There was still some difficulty with the Workhouse children and Miss Laing wrote to the Clerk complaining about the conduct and attitude of some of the inmates. The doors between the boys' and girls' yards were locked and a Timothy David – probably an inmate was asked to take charge of the boys (Chapter 10).

The School Attendance Committee, formed in May 1877, requested the appointment of a School Attendance Officer in August at a salary of 8/0d a day with expenses (excluding transport). John Williams was appointed.

Miss Laing was given a good testimonial in support of an application for the Matronship of the Chadwick Orphanage, Bolton, but her efforts to leave failed. It is ironic that the Inspector who visited the school at this time wrote in the Visitors' Book: "The Workhouse School is now efficient".

The L.G.B. informed them in January '78, that although they could pay for the attendance of pauper children at the Board Schools, the money was a loan to parents and was recoverable. At the same time it was suggested that a register of the children in the Workhouse School should be compiled.

The building of the Cottages was progressing apace and the inside was being attended to in April. In June Mr David was asked to design the entrance and to design and construct the connection with Merthyr Mawr road.

Soon afterwards they decided that a married couple should be appointed as Schoolteachers and Industrial Trainers at seventy pounds a year with 'accommodation, coal and rations'. They also decided to advertise for six respectable females between thirty-five and fifty years of age to take charge of the Cottages. Each would be a 'Mother and Trainer' at a salary of twelve pounds per annum with keep. Notice was given to Miss Laing that her services would not be required beyond the quarter as the children would be in the Cottage Homes [She later became Schoolmistress to the Wigan Union]. Mr and Mrs Thornton from Birkenhead were appointed at the end of the month at a salary of forty-five and twenty-five pounds respectively. He was to be Schoolmaster and Administrative Officer and his wife Matron and Industrial Trainer.

The balance of four hundred and forty pounds was paid to Mr David in September and ninety-six pounds one shilling and sixpence for the road and entrance. A sum of forty pounds was allocated provisionally for the furniture. Mr Harris, the architect, received fifty pounds.

Mrs Moore from Swansea and Mrs Thomas from Cardiff came as Mothers and also Miss Dean from Birkenhead who was later replaced by Mrs Davies from Caerleon. The Committee appointed to supervise the development of the Cottages suggested that parents and friends could visit the children on the first Monday of the month between 1 and 2 pm provided they received prior permission from the Guardians via the Clerk. In the event of an emergency such as illness: "The Master of the Workhouse can give permission with the concurrence of the Superintendent of the Homes".

The Catholic inmate children attended the Catholic Day School and the Catholic Sunday School. When it became apparent that on transfer to the Cottages their education would be the same as that of the other children the Rev. R. Green the Catholic priest said that he had been requested by the Mother Superior of St Michael's House, Treforest, to ask for the seven Catholic children to be transferred there. The Guardians asked: "Why?" and a fortnight later, 23rd November, 1878, declined the request.

In January '79 Mr David was paid the final eighty pounds for additional work at the Cottages. It was decided that on the fourth of the month fit children, as judged by the doctor, could be moved from the Workhouse to the Cottage Homes. Another mother, Mrs Cecilia Howard, had been appointed but there was still one vacancy. By April the children had settled in their new environment.

The School Attendance Committee reported that there was difficulty in many Board Schools because of the poverty of parents. Seldom would the parents apply for help to the Guardians because of the 'similarity to paupers'. It is interesting to note that apparently shoes and clothing were not covered in contrast to previous practices: records show that in 1877 the Guardians had paid four pounds to enable a child from Neath to attend school.

A Management Committee was now formed consisting of Mr Nicholl (Chairman), Blandy Jenkins (Vice-Chairman), Rev F. W. Edmondes, Rev H. F. Nicholl, Mr. Garsed, A. B. Price, D. A.Thomas, Thomas Rees (Pyle), Hugh Bevan, Lewis Jenkins, Evan Preece, Mr Ferrier and Morgan Williams. Books worth Six pounds fifteen shillings and four pence were bought from Joseph Yorwerth.

The Mothers in June were: Mrs. Elisabeth Moore (Ffynnon St. Swansea), Mrs Elisabeth Thomas (Sophia Street, Cardiff), Celia Howard (Llynfi Street, Bridgend), Mrs Ann Berry (Llandovery), Mary John (Ogmore) and Mrs Emma Bale, who had been allowed to keep her eleven year old daughter with her provided she attended another school. The salary had been increased to fifteen pounds a year. In July, a child's mother by the name of Catherine Austin had her next visit to the Home cancelled because of 'misbehaviour on the last visit'. The mothers of all the children were told that this restriction would be imposed should any of them misbehave when 'meeting their children out of church'.

In November there was a 'letter of complaint' to the Guardians signed by five of the Workhouse inmates regarding the treatment of children in the Homes. They enquired: "Is it permissible to cut the hair of a girl of fifteen years close to the head when there are no sores ?" and: "Is it allowed for others to be beaten around the head until they are black and blue?" The Rev. F. W. Edmondes investigated the complaint and decided that it was groundless'. He wrote :"There is no girl aged fifteen in the Homes – the oldest being thirteen and the hair is not cut too close".

The expense of the School Attendance Committee for the year was fifty pounds. The District Auditor, Mr A.W. Roberts, was allowed to use the Board Room of the Workhouse for auditing the Board Schools of Bridgend, Coity Higher, Coychurch Higher, Pencoed, Llandyfodwg, Llangan and St. Mary Hill. Dr. Verity became Medical Officer for the Homes at ten pounds a year (Chapter 12).

Early in 1880 a further fifteen children were admitted to the Homes.

Later in the year Mrs Elisabeth Thomas, one of the Mothers, was dismissed. No reason was given and she was replaced by a Mrs Ann Preece from Cardiff. About the same time Cornelius Murphy, one of the boys in the Home was sent to the Magistrates' Court for insubordination. The Clerk, Mr Stockwood, wished to know whether the Home would pay for the boy's weekly upkeep if he were sent to a penal Industrial Unit. The payment was agreed to as long as the sum did not exceed seven shillings. The boy was sent for training to an Industrial ship, the Havannah, stationed in Cardiff.

A strange petition was received in July from the Newton Abbot Union. In the opinion of their Guardians subjects such as Latin, French, German and Botany 'might be excluded from teacher's training for young children in elementary schools'. The Bridgend-Cowbridge Guardians gave tentative support – provided that reference to Training Colleges was omitted.

Mrs Bale resigned in December. Finding a replacement proved difficult. The post was advertised twice with but one applicant, a Mrs Janet Lloyd. She was a pauper whose husband had deserted her and was thought to have subsequently died. Some members of the panel wanted to appoint her, others expressed reservations and so they compromised by appointing her pro tem while advertising for the third time. There were four applicants including Mrs Lloyd. Although the latter seemed the best candidate they again prevaricated and decided to re-advertise with Mrs Lloyd continuing in the post. Three candidates applied, again including Mrs Lloyd. Support for her this time was overwhelming and she was appointed. One of her sisters promised to look after her seven year old child and the committee agreed that the other could stay with her provided she paid two shillings and six pence a week for the child's keep. Mrs Thornton later refused to allow the child to attend the Cottage School because the mother was no longer a pauper. This action was supported by the L.G.B.

The role of Dame Schools was considered by the Attendance Committee in March 1881. They commented that pauper children should not attend such schools because: 'They are poorly built, keep no records and the Justices will not grant school attendance allowance even when children are properly taught'.

The Census returns for the year showed that there were sixty-six children in the Homes, thirty-nine of whom were boys. The age range was from four to thirteen years. One, a girl of thirteen was considered to be an 'imbecile' and a boy of twelve and a girl of six 'idiots'. The Cottages were now fully occupied. Most of the children were from the Union area but eight were from elsewhere including Cardiff (2), Birmingham, Chepstow, Neath, Portsmouth, Bridgewater and Manchester.

Dr. Clutterbuck, the School Inspector, visited the School in September and reported that they were all doing well. He tested forty-eight in reading, writing, arithmetic and they all passed. It was decided that when the children left the Homes they could take the clothes that they wore with them. As mentioned elsewhere (Chapter 9) the clothes were supplied during the week they spent in the Workhouse awaiting admission.

A new Attendance Officer, Robert Burnell, replaced John Williams in March '82 at a salary of 2 guineas a week. The School Attendance Committee reported that during the previous year fifty-seven warnings has been sent to parents regarding non-attendance of children. Thirty-one Magistrates' Orders and five summonses had been issued leading to four convictions with fines. There were two convictions against outsiders for the illegal employment of children and the total cost of the proceedings amounted to forty-nine pounds eighteen shillings and six pence.

A request came from a Vicar in Maesteg that the School fees of poor children be paid by the Guardians, but they informed him that they could not do so unless the parents applied directly to them.

It was recognized at this time (April 1882) that the population of the Garw Valley had so increased that arrangements had to be made to educate 135 additional children from Pontyrhyl. The Attendance Committee decided that Bettws should provide the facilities rather than Llangeinor.

John Scott, the gardener at the Cottages, resigned in July and Evan Thomas, from Bridgend, replaced him at the same salary of eighteen shillings per week. Meanwhile the salary of the Mothers had been increased to sixteen pounds a year – two pounds eight shillings being paid by the Government because it was accepted that the Mothers had a role in training.

Mr and Mrs Thornton were requested to visit the children who had gone out to service in order to verify that their performance was satisfactory. Two months later, in October, Mrs Thornton stopped a mother from seeing a child in the Homes 'because he was having medical treatment'. The Guardians stressed: "no undue obstruction is to be placed on parents seeing their child".

In April 1883 there were 555 warnings to parents for their children's absence from school, and twenty-two summonses were served followed by seventeen convictions. One person was fined thirty shillings for illegally employing a child.

During this period, Schools in Llanharry, Llanharan and Llangan were closed following an outbreak of Measles. Bettws had been unable to provide places for the 135 additional children and so a School Board was formed – which removed the problem from the purview of the Attendance Committee of the Guardians.

There was a request the following month from the Pyle School for the Guardians to pay three pence a week for the education of each pauper child instead of a farthing per visit and one and a half pence for books. They explained that their fee for a child under seven years was 3 pence per week, and five pence per child beyond that age, adding that no family paid more than one shilling. The Guardians complied and henceforth paid three pence per child per week with one and a half pence for books. Dr Clutterbuck continued to be satisfied with the teaching as all the children had reached the expected standard.

Mrs Ann Preece left in August to become a nurse in Swansea and Miss Mary Jenkins, Oldcastle, Bridgend replaced her. Ann Berry, another Mother, also resigned and Ellen Meredith was appointed. She had a child who was allowed to stay with her as long as she contributed 2/6d per week. The Parliamentary grant for Mr Thornton was £53.8.0d and for Mrs Thorton £33.13.0d. The school fees for pauper children over six months amounted to £57.11.6d, and the cost of the Homes was £535.9.6d – each child costing 5.2½d per week with 1.9½d for loan repayment. In the Workhouse it had been 4.9d.

There was a letter in January 1884 from Mr. John Stockwood, Magistrates' Clerk, enquiring whether they would maintain the children of a Mr Joseph in an Industrial School. He had been convicted a number of times of 'non-compliance' with the Attendance Officer's orders and had even been sent to jail. The answer was: "Yes".

Educating pauper children in the various schools was expensive and intricate: for three months' tuition, fourteen shillings and six pence was paid to Pontrhydycyff, one pound and sixteen shillings and five pence to Porthcawl, one pound seven shillings and three pence to Maesteg Merthyr Colliery School, two pounds four shillings and ten pence to Bridgend Board School (one pound fifteen shillings and four pence for girls and nine shillings and six pence for infants), one pound six shillings and four pence to Newton Nottage, one pound fifteen shillings and ten pence to Bryncethin National School, one pound nineteen shillings to Llandyfodog Board School and five pounds to Bryndu School.

The Mothers at the Home in March 1884 were: Mrs Moore, Mrs Howard, Mrs John, Mrs Lloyd, Mrs Meredith and Miss Jenkins. A niece of Mrs Thornton, the Matron and Schoolmistress, came to live with her in October at a charge of twelve shillings a year provided she attended another school. In the same year Mrs Janet Lloyd resigned and her replacement was Mrs Ann Berry who had been with them before.

The children in the Homes had to be fed 'according to a special dietary' devised by the L.G.B. and in April 1885 it was decided that cocoa would be given once a day on three days a week – those under nine years to receive three-quarters of a pint and those over that age to receive half a pint. Later they were allowed to choose between cocoa or milk on its own before breakfast and supper every day of the week – the milk to contain on average ten percent cream! It was claimed that the general health of the children improved as a result.

During this period the number of children in the Homes was decreasing and the Management Committee suggested that one of the Homes could be closed but the Board thought such action premature. (The reduction was probably maintained because the Census returns of 1891 showed that there were only fifty-five children there).

Nine hundred and forty warnings were issued to parents by the Attendance Committee the previous year; seventy-three were summoned and sixty-six fined a total of fourteen pounds four shillings. Two adults were convicted of illegally employing children and were fined forty shillings and twenty shillings respectively.

Mrs Ellen Meredith resigned in May 1886 and was replaced by Ellen Connor. More school accommodation was necessary for Bryncethin and Tondu although attendance was being disrupted by an epidemic of Measles (Eleven children died of Measles in Bridgend and Maesteg – Chapter 12).

In August a boy, James Ryan, was referred from the Homes to the Magistrates' Court because of 'incorrigible behaviour'. He claimed that there was 'indecency at the Homes' but the Authorities concluded: "He is the only culprit". The sentence was that "he be taken to the Havanah Training School and stay there until he is sixteen years of age". The Guardians undertook the payment for his keep 'up to seven shillings a week'. Whether James Ryan was treated justly must remain a question. Perhaps a full enquiry would have been more appropriate?

Chapter 14

Relieving Officers

*District Officers, Registrars of Births and Marriages and Deaths,
Enquiry into Account of David Davies, Attempt to Reduce Salaries,
Enquiry into the Account of Mr Arnott, Assistant Officers for
Vagrants, Resignations and Appointments, Requirements in
Education, Vaccination Officers, Residency Neath and Maesteg.*

Relieving Officers were forerunners of Social Workers. Their task was to
alleviate distress due to poverty by dispensing 'out-door' relief in money and
kind. No other official help was available. Each Officer worked unaided and was
responsible for the welfare of the poor in a defined district. The poor had to
approach him if they could not cope. Urgent cases were dealt with according to
the Relieving Officer's initiative. Elective or non-urgent problems were referred
to the Guardians for consideration.

When money was granted by the Board the Officer had to be sure that the
paupers received it. In the past paupers too old or disabled to collect money from
the Parish Vestry had had to ask others to collect their due at a cost of about three
pence a week! The Officers were to guard against this practice by delivering the
money in person either at the home of the client or at a pre-arranged suitable
location.

When the Workhouse became operational there were instances when paupers
were admitted against their wishes. Old age and ill health were frequent reasons,
as were destitution, desertion and alcoholism. The 'lunatic poor' and the
'impotent old' were also difficult to support at home, as were unmarried mothers
– particularly when pregnant. Personal information had to be entered in a special
book and the reason for the admission amplified.

The amount of money handled was considerable and so careful accounts had
to be kept by each Officer and checked weekly. The Chairman then signed the
appropriate page or pages. This was called 'authentication'. A sum of money
approximately equal to that spent the previous week was then given to deal with
the following week's requirements. Each Relieving Officer was bilingual and his
suitability for the post guaranteed by two persons acceptable to the Board, and a
surety of sixty pounds.

The first Relieving Officers were William Jenkins for the Cowbridge district,
Edward Jenkins for the Bridgend district and David Davies for the Maesteg district.
A month after appointment Edward Jenkins resigned, David Davies was transferred
to Bridgend and William Preece was appointed for the Maesteg district.

In December 1836 they became also Registrars of Births, Marriages and Deaths for their respective district. William Edmondes, the Clerk to the Board, was appointed Superintendent Registrar. This required the approval of the Registrar General in London.

The money distributed each week amounted to about £34 for Cowbridge, £26 for Bridgend and, in the early years, about £13 for Maesteg. Farthings were sometimes specified, as in August '38, when the respective sums were £34.11.0½ d, £28.7.2d and £18.17.9¼d. Their salary of fifty-two pounds a year was received quarterly and to this was added the payment for Registrar duties. In June, '38 this amounted to £3.15.0d for David Davies, £4.8.0d for David Jenkins and £2.17.0d for William Preece – for three months' work.

In October of that year in order to ascertain 'where allowance could be discontinued', they revised the list of those paupers who had their rent paid and the list of pauper children who were placed 'in service' with a weekly allowance.

From time to time the Relieving Officers communicated with their counterparts elsewhere. An instance of this was in November '39. One of the Relieving Officers of Merthyr Tydfil wrote to complain that a widow with three children, who had been living in Newton Nottage when her husband died, had been allowed six shillings a week by the parish officers but since coming to his district had not received any money. The Board desired information about her circumstances before deciding to continue the payments. They commented: "The parishioners of Newton Nottage have exceeded their authority."

Another problem, indirectly concerning Merthyr Tydfil, occurred about the same time. A lady from Merthyr residing in St. Bride's Major wished to return and a nephew from Merthyr Tydfil had come over to accompany her on the journey. He, an able-bodied person, applied for 'financial assistance to fulfil his intentions'. The Relieving Officer offered him five shillings in money and a shilling for bread as a 'temporary relief'. These he declined because acceptance would mean that they would have to travel on a Sunday – and they were not willing to do so. The Board deliberated over the problem and then directed the Relieving Officer: "To give relief in kind this day, tomorrow and breakfast Monday. If he afterwards neglects to return to Merthyr Tydfil apply for a warrant".

There was an instance in February '42 when relief was given as a loan and David Jenkins, the Relieving Officer concerned, was asked to make that fact clear to the recipient who was living in Newcastle Lower.

Later in the year William Preece(Northern) was replaced by William John. In June '43 David Davies resigned and was replaced by Thomas Arnott. The Board had become dissatisfied with the record of accounts in Davies' Book despite the fact that they had been authenticated weekly. A committee was set up 'to investigate possible irregularities'. It reported that the entries had been irregular and that they were unhappy on five counts:

The relief ordered by the Board had not always been paid or charged.
Sometimes the relief had been given but not charged.
Occasionally relief had been charged but not given.

Relief had been charged and probably given but not at the request of the Board. Relief in kind, that had been ordered by the Board and probably given, had not been charged.

'Furthermore, bills were being received for debts in goods – STATED to have been supplied and STATED to have been advanced to Davies and via him to paupers'. Moreover, 'Davies had for a long time been giving tickets to shopkeepers for goods when relief in money had been ordered'.

The committee stressed that a similar system should NOT be followed by other Relieving Officers.

The Clerk was asked to prepare a short statement of the accounts. There was no evidence of misappropriation of funds and therefore it is reasonable to assume that Davies had been inefficient rather than dishonest. It is astonishing though that he had tried to introduce a sort of Truck system into relief work when it had been illegal since 1831.

Early in 1845 Mr John Garsed complained to the Board that 'a pauper and his wife in Llantwit Major, both bedridden, had not been visited by the Relieving Officer for a month'. David Jenkins, the Relieving Officer concerned, was 'reprimanded and cautioned'. Depite this admonishment it is interesting to note that in January 1850 he and his wife were appointed Master and Matron of the Workhouse. David Lloyd, a publican in Cowbridge, was appointed to the vacated post. The bond of surety of £60 was guaranteed by William Lewis, a Gent, of Llwyncelyn, Llanbleddian and Thomas Lewis, an innkeeper. Acquisition of the post of Registrar of Births, Marriages and Deaths was confirmed by the Commissioners in April.

Around this time the Guardians thought that the salaries of the Relieving Officers should be reduced because 'farm produce was at a low rate'. The Commissioners did not consider such action to be justified but the Guardians persisted in their view pointing out that the Relieving Officers were also paid for being Registrars of Births, Marriages and Deaths. Mr. R.C. Nichol Carne, Esquire, a member of the Board, was asked 'to draw up a petition as indicated for presentation to the House of Commons and the House of Lords'. In August the Clerk wrote to the Duke of Beaufort and C.R.M. Talbot, M.P., asking them 'had they presented the petition'. (The Duke was written to because the second Marquess of Bute, whom they usually contacted, had died in 1848). It transpired that Mr. Talbot was ill, but he assured them that he had done as they had requested. His Grace, the Duke of Beaufort, maintained that he had not received it, but added that he had received petitions in the past from Bridgend, Swansea and other parts of Glamorgan and had always presented them to the House of Lords. The Guardians went further and expressed the view that 'the salary of all Officers connected with administration of the Poor Law should be proportionally reduced'.

Their effort was unsuccessful as evidenced by the fact that the salary of all concerned remained as before.

Amusing complaints were sometimes heard by the Board as when the Relieving

Officers indicated that the doctors sometimes wrote to them 'on small scraps of paper'. The Officers were asked to include the scraps in their weekly reports!

Paupers receiving out-door relief were now being divided into two groups of 'settled and non-settled poor'. In July 1850 the Treasurer of the Cardiff Union was paid £10.14.6d for 'relief of non-settled poor on account of this Union during quarter'. The Bridgend Union received £41.2.0d from the Cardiff Union for the same reason. The books of the Relieving Officers also showed this division. In August, David Lloyd gave £37.17.10d to the settled poor and 14/6d to the non-settled, William John gave £25.15.0d and a farthing to the settled and Thomas Arnott £29.8.10d to the settled and 7/0d to the non-settled. The division continued throughout the succeeding years.

Overseers of the Poor and the Wardens did not always know what was being given to the paupers in their parish, and so in December '50 the Clerk was asked to devise a method whereby they would be kept informed. As a result the amount of relief, in money and/or in kind, was entered on a card and kept by the paupers for showing to the Officers of the parish 'every six months for inspection'.

Able-bodied people who became ill, or indisposed for any reason, were given 'temporary relief' by the Relieving Officers. In January '52 a person with Epilepsy received 5/0 a week, another with 'Eruptive Fever' 6/0 a week, and a third a similar sum following 'amputation of finger'.

When a pauper moved from one area to another, either from choice or from compulsion, the Board then responsible was informed. One such instance was in April '52 when an application was received from the Swansea Union Board that 'a pauper widow with four children, a native of Swansea, living in Newcastle Higher be granted 4/6 weekly'. Thomas Arnott was asked to arrange it.

There then followed an odd sequence of events. Thomas Arnott accepted the post of Constable for Coity Lower, intending to occupy it while still working as Relieving Officer. The reason he gave for doing so was that he would then be allowed to 'search the Casual Poor' when they applied for relief. He maintained that this would make him more useful to the Board of Guardians. They took the opposite view, and informed him that if he accepted the post of Parish Constable he would no longer be an 'Officer of the Board'. Under the circumstances Arnott decided 'not to attend to be sworn in'.

In 1853 the weekly amount of out-door relief granted was approximately equal in the three districts: £36.1.10d, £33.9.1d and £34.1.9d (December records). This was the year that 'Nuisances' were being removed following the Health Act of 1848. 'Notices' were served on landlords who were not anxious to co-operate, indicating what improvements had to be carried out. These 'Notices' were signed by Mr. Sadler, the Chief Officer, and by both Relieving Officer and Medical Officer of the locality. William John and David Lloyd refused to do so, as did Dr. James Lewis. (Chapter 12). The Poor Law Board decided that 'it was not obligatory for them to sign.'

The vaccination of children against Smallpox had been recently introduced (Chapter 10) and the Relieving Officers were paid three pence for every successful case that they registered. In March '54 David Lloyd, for instance, received 5/9 for registering 23 cases of vaccination successfully performed 'on children born since August '53'.

Members of the public sometimes complained direct to the Poor Law Board, and they in turn referred the complaint back to the Board of Guardians. Evidence of this was when a letter was received from them indicating that a pregnant lady in Coity Lower maintained that she had been refused both in-door and out-door relief. It transpired that Dr. Verity had examined her and had concluded that she was only seven months pregnant and that therefore there was no need to admit her to the Workhouse for the confinement. Mr Arnott, against whom the complaint had been made, explained that the woman concerned had not approached him again after finding that she had two months to go to term. Consequently, no out-door relief had been deemed necessary. The Board accepted his point of view but thought that the best action to take under the circumstances was to admit her forthwith to the Workhouse.

Mr Arnott was not a tranquil sort of person. In May '54, he resigned and then withdrew his resignation saying that he had 'sent it in anger'. The Clerk told him, on behalf of the Board, to be 'less hasty in future'.

The money paid to paupers as out-door relief had increased. David Lloyd paid out £78 the week preceding the twenty seventh of May, William John £66 and Thomas Arnott £76.

Mr. Arnott resigned again in October after being criticised for admitting a pauper to the Workhouse without issuing a written order beforehand (Chapter 7). It now became apparent that many paupers in his district had not received 'the relief they should have for several weeks past'. Mr Arnott was asked to attend the next Board meeting to explain this omission but he failed to appear 'owing to a severe bout of diarrhoea'. His resignation was accepted and the other Relieving Officers were asked to attend to his duties 'for the time being' and to supply the Board with 'the names of paupers in arrears and by how much'.

An ad hoc committee was set up composed of the Reverend John Harding, the Reverend Blosse, Thomas Preece and Hesekiah David to investigate his affairs and to recommend who should replace him.

Arnott was paid the £9.17.0d that was due to him as Registrar of Births. Marriages and Deaths for the months of April to September inclusive. But the Auditor calculated that he owed the Board £24.16.1d. This was paid and no legal action was taken. Some paupers had received relief without it being entered in the books (i.e. 'charged for'), while others had not received any despite its being 'charged' in the accounts. According to Thomas Phillips, victualler of Bridgend, a nearby pauper had not received any relief for months.

There were six applicants for Arnott's vacated post. Three were referred to the Board for a final decision and Richard Leyshon chosen. Surety of £100 was guaranteed by William Leyshon, stationer, Bridgend and Robert Leyshon of Island Farm, Laleston.

Liaison between the Relieving Officers and the Medical Officers was close. They were expected to receive the doctor in the pauper's house when a visit by him was necessary and to accompany him if the journey was arduous or complicated. It was not always possible to make mutually suitable arrangements and when difficulty arose with a visit in Llantwit Major, Dr. Llewelyn, the Medical Officer for Cowbridge, was able to get the rule relaxed. Henceforth there was no compulsion for the Relieving Officer to be present during the doctor's visit but he was expected to collect medicine from the surgery if there was no-one else in the house or vicinity to do so.

Another of the Relieving Officer's duties was to take paupers when necessary to the Assizes, the Workhouse, the Asylum or to another parish. Transport of the 'lunatic poor' was often troublesome and time-consuming. Most of them were taken to Vernon House, Briton Ferry (Chapter 11), but occasionally longer journeys were necessary, as in January '55 when David Lloyd had to go to Prestwick Lunatic Asylum, Lancaster to convey a 'dangerous pauper' from there to Vernon House.

When Cholera returned to Bridgend in the later months of '54 and blankets and cotton sheets were requested for the depots that were set up, it was the local Relieving Officer who ordered them.

In March '58, the three Relieving Officers sent a signed 'memorial' to the Board requesting a rise in salary. They pointed out that it had not changed since 1836 despite the known increase in population and the complexity of the Act relating to the Irremovable Poor. At the discussion that followed Dr. Leahy (then a Guardian) proposed that their salary be raised from £52 a year to £60 a year, and despite an objection from Leyshon Morgan and William Yorath, who moved an amendment that it was inexpedient to do so, the proposal was carried.

The non-resident poor were visited periodically to verify their need for out-door relief. David Lloyd and Richard Leyshon each received £5.3.6 in May 1863 for visiting the Union's paupers in Llansamlet, Port Talbot, Swansea, Ystalyfera, Cwmgwrach, Cardiff, Newport, Blaina, Brynmawr, Dowlais, Merthyr, Taffs Well, and Treforest. A special room was processed in Maesteg for the paying of relief – allowance of £4 per year being paid.

In April '66 William Powell, Assistant Overseer at Maesteg, was appointed as deputy to William John the Registrar of Births Marriages and Deaths; similarly Morgan Richards to Richard Leyshon.

There were very few complaints against the Overseers and indeed until 1867 there had been no official complaint for a number of years. In March, however, the Poor Law Board sent the Guardians a copy of a letter they had received from the Reverend James Ramsay, Rector of St Mary Church, alleging that the Assistant Overseer, Robert Howe, had refused relief to a seventeen year old boy with a fractured leg. The employer, J. Spencer, had referred the matter to the Magistrates in Cowbridge, but when the Guardians investigated all the circumstances they found no fault with the Officer.

Later in the year the question of supplying clothes to the out-door paupers arose and it was agreed that the best method was to rely on Tender and Contract as in the Cardiff Workhouse.

In March '68 William Powell, deputy Registrar for Births, Marriages and Deaths, was appointed Assistant Relieving Officer to deal with Vagrants in the district. He was also to be a Collector of money for the Board at a salary of 5/0 'for every day spent doing so' together with expenses. His surety was £100. It was also suggested that he be a Removal Officer. This entailed taking people to varying types of establishments as needs dictated or to another Parish if 'settlement' had not been legalised. This did not please the P.L.B. who were adamant that the removal of paupers remained the responsibility of the Clerk: 'Because he has the power to arrange such journeys and the money to pay for them'. Moreover they thought that Mr Powell should be paid a fixed sum of £5 a year in his role as Relieving Officer for the Vagrants, and as Collector should receive a separate fixed sum or 'a poundage based on the sum collected'.

An example of his role as Collector occurred in August '69 when he took proceedings before the Magistrates to obtain money from a father in Sarn as contribution to the maintenace of the man's son in the Asylum.

In October '69 the P.L.B. wanted to know why the Relieving Officers did not indicate which children had not been vaccinated. 'Changes in the boundaries of the district' was offered as an explanation: "If the P.L.B. approved of the changes fuller records will be sent".

In December Richard Leyshon became ill and requested the temporary services of a deputy. The Reverend Blosse thought that Josiah Lewis, Assistant Overseer of Coity Lower and Newcastle Lower, could be asked to help at £1 weekly. This was accepted but payment was later reduced to 12/6 a week.

The P.L.B. continued to be extremely vigilant. In January '71 they wanted to know why a pauper in Aberkenfig had received out-door relief for three weeks and then been admitted. The reason was that he had been offered suitable work which he had refused. Had he accepted 'he could have supported himself and his wife'. In June Richard Leyshon was granted a month's 'sick leave' with Josiah Lewis deputising as Relieving Officer and Robert Leyshon, Island Farm, acting as Registrar for Births, Marriages and Deaths. Six weeks later, on the 19th of August, he died. The Clerk wrote to his widow conveying sympathy and expressing appreciation for the way he had performed his duties.

The Vacant post was advertised at a rate of £60 per annum with residency in Bridgend. There had to be two sureties and guarantees of £100. Fluency in Welsh was essential. The appointee would be expected to take on the duties of Registrar of Births, Marriages and Deaths; Robert Leyshon would cover duties until the end of the year.

There were thirty applicants including a chemist, a schoolmaster, an accountant, a surveyor, an insurance agent, the master of Aberystwyth workhouse, an assistant clerk to an Union and Caleb Scott, Secretary to the Mechanics Institute in Bridgend. Six were shortlisted and Thomas Jenkins, Assistant Overseer of Llangan, was appointed. His sureties were local farmers, John Jenkins and Rees Jenkins.

The District Auditor reported in December that the late Richard Leyshon's accounts indicated that a sum of £104.0.7d was owed to the Union. Later, a local butcher, Edwin Williams, claimed £5.7.7 for meat supplied 'on the order' of the late Officer. The claim was dismissed in the County Court; the Guardians were represented by Mr Ensor, a solicitor in Cardiff.

David Lloyd, the Relieving Officer for Cowbridge, requested permission to employ James Turner, attorney's clerk as deputy to cover illness. The request was granted.

The following month, February '72, the Assistant Relieving Officer, William Powell resigned and was replaced by Police Constable Loyns (see Chapter 17).

In March the Rev H. Morgan brought a series of complaints against David Lloyd citing slowness in distributing relief to out-door paupers. These complaints were verified and Lloyd was severly censured.

Towards the end of the year William John requested an increase in salary 'as it had not changed for thirty years despite increase in work'. He was granted an increase of £10 per annum: £5 for increased workload and £5 for long service.

In August '73 the Rev. H Morgan again complained that David Lloyd was 'slow and irregular' in paying relief. The Board thought that 'more than censure' might be necessary since he was also not submitting his Record Book regularly to the Clerk and Auditor. Following investigation it transpired that 'he had failing eyesight and other infirmities' and he was asked to resign. The District Auditor reported the following July that he owed the Union £67.8.8 ½ d.

There were four applicants for the post – all from the locality and William John from Cowbridge was appointed. He had the same name as the Relieving Officer for Maesteg and this caused consternation. It was decided that he would be called William Hopkins John – as there was someone by the name of Hopkins in his family. His salary was £60 pounds per annum and his sureties were Peter John – a sawyer in Porthcawl and Thomas Hopkins- a miller in Ewenny. A month later he became Registrar of Births, Marriages and Deaths with Thomas John, Cowbridge, acting as his deputy as required.

In June William John, the Relieving Officer of Maesteg, resigned because of illhealth and the post was advertised specifying that fluency in Welsh was essential. There were ten applicants – the furthest was from Swansea. John Davies a Police Officer in Bridgend, William Rees a Police Sergeant in Penarth and William Leyshon from Merthyr Mawr, were shortlisted. The latter was appointed with Robert Leyshon. Island Farm, and John Williams, Merthyr Mawr as sureties – both were farmers. As part of his contract a month's notice of resignation or forfeiture of a month's wages was stipulated.

The question of superannuation for the departing William John was then discussed. His emoluments for the last full year of employment had been £137 which justified a grant of £52 per year. This was approved by the Guardians and ratified by the P.L.B.. Their treatment of retiring Medical Officers was far less generous (Chapter 12).

In August William Hopkins John's salary was increased to £114.7.0 – this included £14.7.0 for being the Registrar of Births, Marriages and Deaths . The following January (1875) the LGB requested that 'Hopkins' be removed from his name 'because his namesake in Maesteg has resigned'! The Guardians concurred.

In September William John visited non-resident paupers in Cardiff and

Pontypridd and decided that relief could be reduced in one instance and discontinued in another because the elderly pauper concerned lived with his son who was a station-master earning 30/0 a week. In November he was asked to investigate the circumstances of a Matilda Turpin of St. Athan. She was a native of Swansea and the Guardians had heard from the Justices that she was neglecting her children. John reported: "She is a violent person, not thrifty, and the children are dirty. She threatens their life if no relief is forthcoming, and one day they were taken to the police station for protection". He did not think that the giving of out-door relief was the answer and thought that the Clerk should prosecute her in the petty session for neglecting her children. This was done and she was found guilty and sentenced to fourteen days imprisonment. The children were taken to Swansea Workhouse.

In December the L.G.B. wrote to the Guardians asking: 'Is William Leyshon living in Maesteg as required by the terms of his employment?' The Clerk replied that he was living in Tondu which was the most convenient location and added: "Part of his garden is in Maesteg"! In July the following year records show that he admitted two' lunatic paupers' from the district to the Lunatic Asylum in Bridgend.

Checking school attendances was now an accepted part of the Relieving Officers' duties and in 1877 William Leyshon and Thomas Jenkins were paid an extra £8 a year for the additional work as outlined in the Education Act (Chapter 13).

There was close supervision by the L.G.B. of the roles of the Officers appointed by the Guardians. As an example, Assistant Relieving Officers had been appointed to deal with Vagrants (Chapter 17) but the L.G.B. was careful to define their limitation: 'The presence of these Officers does not in any way diminish the responsibilty of the Relieving Officers if the Vagrants are destitute'. The intention of the Guardians to extend William John's role to be their Collector was challenged by the L.G.B.: 'Is it the intention to make other Relieving Officers Collectors in their own District?' The Guardians replied that in their opinion he could certainly cope with the additional work. It is of interest that later he became Collector for the whole district apart from Cwmdu. The L.G.B. appeared to accept this: 'Providing that he be paid 6 per cent of the sum he collects'. William Powell remained the Collector of the Poor Rates in Cwmdu and his salary was increased from £75 to £95 per annum in June '78.

The L.G.B. Board, in August, ordered William Leyshon, the Relieving Officer of Maesteg, to live in the Town. This was despite a previous appeal by the Guardians explaining that to live in Tondu was 'more convenient'. He complied and moved house.

The total out-door relief for resident paupers for six months ending May '79 was £4,483 and for non-resident paupers, £133.3.11. William John's annual salary was increased from £100 to £104 in April 1880 and that of Mr Leyshon and Mr Jenkins from £60 to £70.

It was learned in August that Jenkins was a member of the Bridgend School Board despite being fully employed as Relieving Officer. The Guardians had no objection to this but wondered about the reaction of the L.G.B. to the information. Somewhat against expectation they did not comment!

In September, William John in his role as Collector took proceedings against the Oddfellows Lodge, Llantwit Major for the recovery of sick pay given to George Thomas, a pauper. Thomas Stockwood was employed as solicitor. The claim was later withdrawn.

It is clear that all three Relieving Officers had many and varied tasks. In addition to the distribution of out-door relief they also checked, within reason, the claims of those who were non-residents. They were Registrars of Births, Marriages and Deaths, and coped with the requirements of the Education Act and the Compulsory Vaccination Act. The complexity of their role is illustrated in the record of payment to William Leyshon in February 1881. He received £13 as Registrar of Birth, Marriages and Death for the quarter ending the previous December; £1.5.6 for copying the entries of Births for vaccination (2p each); 12/3 for delivering 149 notices of vaccination at 1p each and 3/0 for copying 18 entries of Deaths. Records also show that the fee for registering successful vaccination had risen to 10p each. Their work in pursuance of the Education Act is recorded in Chapter 13.

In October three females claimed that William Leyshon's conduct had been 'improper' towards them and apparently there had also been several irregularities in the payment of out-door relief. Mr Bircham, the L.G.B. Inspector, was asked to hold an inquiry. A month later Mr Leyshon resigned – on the grounds of illhealth. Forty applied for the vacant post – two from England and the remainder from Wales. There was a signalman, an overseer, a carpenter and a porter in the six shortlisted. Mr William Punter, a signalman from Aberdare, was appointed and his two sureties accepted.

Mr Leyshon continued to be the Vaccination Officer, but in February the L.G.B. dismissed him stating that if he was too ill to be a Relieving Officer then he was too ill to be the Vaccination Officer. Mr Leyshon questioned this adding that his health had improved and that there had been no complaints against him as Vaccination Officer. "Can I not continue?" he asked. "No" was the reply. Mr Punter took over his duties in March.

William John (Cowbridge) collected £39.9.8d in August and a month later complained to the Guardians that Dr Wallace, Dr Phillips' deputy, had not seen a pauper as requested (Chapter 12).

In February '83 the L.G.B. asked the Guardians whether they thought that 'extras' or 'relief in kind' should be given direct to deserving paupers in preference to the allocation of money. The question was referred to the Medical Officers and they decided that relief in kind was preferable. It was also agreed that money could not be given to a child unless the child was 'having responsible care' which usually meant an adult deemed to be a suitable custodian by the Guardians.

Out-door relief in December was £3,146.14.1d for settled paupers over the previous six months and £131.0.0 for the non-settled.

In February '84 William Punter residing in 17 Alfred Street, Maesteg applied for an increase in salary for the following reasons: "My railway fare alone is 8/0 a week and out-door relief has diminished over the past two years. In 1880 it was £3,705 and in 1881 £3,498, but in 1882 it was £3,054 and in 1883 £2,483." The Guardians decided that an increase to £90 a year was justified and this was ratified by the L.G.B..

The original archway connecting the Tramp Ward (left) with the Men's excercise yard.

Chapter 15

'Nuisances'

G. T. Clark's report on Bridgend's sanitation; Mr. Sadler's reports on
that of the parishes; Notices, Summonses and Prosecutions;
Cowbridge's objection; Inspector of Nuisances;
Formation of Sanitary Authorities; Medical Officers of Health.

On the fourth of November 1848 the following entry was made in the minutes:
'By virtue of the Nuisances Removal and Diseases Prevention Act of 1848 the
Guardians have received several Notices to operate the Act. Permanent
committees have been appointed and also Inspectors.' As a result it was resolved:
'That Thomas Thomas, Sergeant of Police, be appointed for Bridgend, and that
John Cox be Inspector for Cowbridge – reporting to a committee appointed for
that district'.

   This Act, the first Public Health Act, was passed in an effort to prevent further
recurrences of Cholera. There had been a severe epidemic in 1831-32. It was first
recognised in Sunderland, then it spread to adjacent areas and soon appeared in
the ports and industrial areas of South Wales. A second epidemic began in
Scotland in 1848 and again involved districts further afield. A large institution of
pauper children in Tooting was affected, and of the 300 who became ill 180 died.
By June '49 it was rampant in pockets throughout the country, and had reached
Cardiff, Swansea and Merthyr Tydfil. In August it was diagnosed in Maesteg and
Bridgend (Chapter 11). A General Board of Health was formed centrally with
power to create Local Boards if petitioned or if the general mortality rate there
exceeded 23 per 1000.

   The cause of Cholera was not known and the Miasmic approach to the
causation of infectious disease still prevailed. This belief, or theory, postulated
that excreta or refuse, gave off 'miasma' into the atmosphere which produced
disease that could automatically change from one to another. This was the belief
held by members of the General Board of Health whose Chief Adminstrator,
Edwin Chadwick, had previously been an Assistant Commissioner of the Poor
Law. In 1842 he wrote a General Report on the Sanitary Condition of the
Labouring Population of Great Britain. Mr Farr was compiler of Abstracts at the
General Register Office from 1839 to 1874, and John Simon (later Sir John)
became the first Medical Officer of Health to the City of London in 1847.
Together they pursued the removal of Nuisances throughout the country and
noted the effect it had on the prevalence of infectious diseases. Dr. John Snow's

view that Cholera was spread by water contamination with the excreta of Cholera patients had not yet been accepted. This was the reason why as much attention was being given to the presence of dung-heaps and ash-heaps as to unsafe cesspools and poor sanitation. They were considered to be equally dangerous. Inadequate ventilation was thought to compound their effect.

George Thomas Clark, Superintending Inspector, visited Bridgend in August '49 and wrote a report on the hamlets of Coity Lower and Newcastle Lower, in which he acknowledged the assistance of the Reverend John Harding, the Reverend Robert Knight, the Reverend Lynch Blosse, Captain C. F. Napier, (Chief Constable for Glamorgan), William Llewelyn Esq, Mr Thomas Stockwood (Clerk to the Magistrates), Mr Lewis, Mr Price, Mr Edwards and others who were not named. He included comments and descriptions from Dr Abraham Verity and C.F. Napier. They both emphasised overcrowding, poor ventilation, absence of privies and drainage, close proximity of pigsties, and a lack of water supply in most of the houses they had visited. Lodging houses harboured a number of tramps and Irish paupers who went around begging. In one room of 10 feet square slept 12 or 14 navvies, in beds that were never cool since by day they were occupied by women and at night by men. In Oldcastle, where the Irish principally lodged, there was only one privy for nine houses. Number 5 Phillips Court: "Consists of three rooms. There are seven beds in which 25 persons sleep, the ground floor is damp, the house is in a filthy state, the walls are streaming with water. When entered the stench is unbearable. They have no privy or drainage": "The windows are kept permanently closed and pasted all round": "They keep a large pan within the door (having no privy) and when night comes they deposit the whole upon the dung-hill near the entrance, the effluvia from which is abominable and the appearance disgusting": "The inhabitants depend mainly on the river for water. Many privies open into it and garbage from private slaughter houses": "Pigsties are a great nuisance being built close to the front doors, or in small ill-ventilated back yards and kept in a dirty state": "Women carry water from the river in pails for which they are paid ½d a pail": "Many persons get water from the adjacent cattle pools." These were some of the observations included in his report.

A Sanitary Committee already existed in Bridgend. It had issued hundreds of summonses and much filth had been removed, but it had no power to prevent repetition. In view of this inadequacy he proposed that a responsible local governing body be formed under the name of a Local Board which would be responsible for the highways, sewers and water supply of the town. Following this petition a Local Board of Health was formed in 1851. On it were the following:- The Reverend Blosse, the Reverend Harding, C. F. Napier, William Lewis (Solicitor), Randall (Agent of the Dunraven Estate) and four tradesmen from Bridgend. Members had to own £800 or be paying rates on a property with a rateable value of at least £20 per annum. The Guardians did not concern themselves directly with the clearing of 'Nuisances' in Bridgend. That was left to the Local Board. Their attention was focused almost exclusively on the remaining parishes of the Union.

The General Board of Health directed them in September '53 to divide the Union area into four districts and to appoint a local committee for each, members of which would be resident in the district concerned.

It was decided that DISTRICT ONE would consist of Bettws, Cwmdu, Llangeinor, Llangynwyd Middle and Lower and also Ynysawdre. John Traherne (Coytrahen), Charles Hampton (Maesteg), Morgan P Smith (Newhouse) and William Major (Gadlys) were asked to serve on it.

DISTRICT TWO would cover St. Bride's Minor, Coychurch Higher and Lower, Llandyfodwg, Llanilid, Pencoed and Peterston and the committee would consist of the Reverend John Harding (Bridgend), the Reverend Thomas Morgan Davies (Llanilid), the Reverend Samuel Jones (Coychurch), George Hamilton Verity (Sarn Fawr, St Bride's Minor), and Evan Bevan (Trebryn, Pencoed).

DISTRICT THREE was to include St. Bride's Major, Coity Higher and Lower, Ewenny, Kenfig, Laleston, Merthyr Mawr, Newcastle Higher and Lower, and Wick. The nominated committee members were: William Llewelyn (Court Colman), the Reverend John Harding, the Reverend H. L. Blosse, and the Reverend Charles R. Knight.

DISTRICT FOUR would consist of: St. Athan, Colwinston, St. Donat's, Eglwysbrewis, Flemingston, Gileston, St. Hilary, Llanbleddian, Llandough, Llandow, Llangan, Llanharry, Llanmaes, Llanmihangel, Llansannor, Llantwit Major, Llysworney, Marcross, St. Mary Church, St. Mary Hill, Monknash, Penlline and Ystradowen (Cowbridge was omitted). Members of the Committee would be: The Reverend Thomas Edmondes (Cowbridge), the Reverend John Griffiths (Llansannor), W. R. Jenner (Llanbleddian) and John Garsed (Llantwit Major).

Mr Richard Sadler, Superintendent of Police at Bridgend, was appointed their Inspector of Nuisances.

He reported on Mynydd Kenfig and Tythegston in October: "I visited them on the 4th and 5th. Many houses were dirty, damp, badly ventilated and without drainage. Only a few had backdoors or privies. Females answered call of nature in the house and threw into an open gutter in the morning. There were only 22 privies for the use of 848 souls and 13 of the 22 were unfit for use, several of them running into gutters on the side of the road. Many offensive pigsties draining into open gutters. Roads filthy. In 1849, 57 died of Cholera in these two hamlets. Number of houses visited (129), number of occupiers (285), lodgers (748). Total adults (433), children (415), offensive privies (12), other privies (10), total privies (22), houses without privies (107). Occupied offensive pigsties (66), offensive stagnant pools (15), manure and ash heaps (75), total number of souls (848)".

Mr Sadler's first appointment had been for areas adjacent to Bridgend, but after the Guardians had read his report (15th October) they appointed him Inspector for the whole Union area for an initial period of three months, at a 'gratuity' of £15.

He soon looked further afield and on the 22nd produced another report: 'Llanbleddian – several privies in a dirty state and Overseers promised to attend to them. Many offensive pigsties in the parish road – some promised to remove them, others not. Suggest Notices against them.' 'Llandough (juxta Cowbridge) – Offensive pigsty of miller: no attention to your Notice to remove. Apply for summons against him.' 'Llantwit-Major – Several foul and offensive pigsties running into parish road. People refuse to pay attention to your Notices. Stagnant gutters which Surveyor promised to remove.' 'Mynydd Kenfig – Visited with Mr Llewelyn agent to Mr Talbot (the principal landowner). Mr Llewelyn will compel tenants to build privies for occupiers and every pigsty will be removed from roadside.' 'Maesteg – So many Nuisances that I'll visit again. One instance needs immediate attention – underground room used for keeping pigs in, and the drainage oozes through the wall into the dwelling house of Catherine Williams, who has so severe an attack of Cholera that the floor is in a continued state of ferment in consequence of the drainage of the pig-sty. I have prepared a Notice.' 'There are 8 Notices existing at Llantwit, 1 at Cwmdu, and a Notice has been sent to a farmer in the Lower hamlet of Tythegston. The premises will be examined by a Court of Guardians 24 hours after receipt of the Notice.' Evidently, the first Notice was just a warning, the second was followed by a visit from two or three members of the local Nuisances Removal Committee, and if then there was no improvement the person or persons concerned were summoned and proceeded against before the Magistrates.

Over the next seven days Mr Sadler revisited Maesteg, Llanbleddian, St Bride's Major, Mynydd Kenfig and Aberkenfig.

More data was given about Maesteg: "Great quantity of ash heaps and manure to be removed. Vast numbers of offensive pigsties, privies and straight pools. Houses much over-crowded and badly ventilated. Row of 8 houses built without windows or backdoors – earth drainage. That from a row of houses in rear runs through living room of the occupiers and empties by front street door. Stench complained of. I caused one of the drains to be opened – it was very offensive and full of black mud. In one of the houses an Irishman was very ill. Mr Thomas says he will fill up the gutters and provide drains. I visited an underground room measuring 12 feet by 12 feet that had no backdoor, or window, or any ventilation. It contained 1 man, 2 females and 7 children. Stench terrible. They had money to pay for a better residence, but couldn't get one. Several similar cases where poor people are forced to live underground. One said that 2 children had died of Fever five months ago – mother thinks the cause was 'closeness' of house. Also offensive underground room used as a slaughter house, occupier living directly over it – promises to discontinue slaughtering there. Great many stagnant pools and ash heaps on Maesteg Iron Company property. Mr Buckland promises to have them removed."

"Mynydd Kenfig: Improved. The three persons you summoned appeared before the Magistrates on the 22nd and were ordered to comply and pay costs. They have now done so."

"Aberkenfig, Llanbleddian, St. Bride's Major: They are removing many Nuisances. Others I've allowed another 7-14 days to do so."

He reviewed the situation on the 19th of November:- Mynydd Kenfig still had many Nuisances 'though a month had been allowed' Cornelly was satisfactory, Cefn Cribbwr was 'just starting to remove Nuisances'; Llantwit Major, St. Bride's Major, Aberkenfig and Coychurch were 'removing satisfactorily.' He added: "Apply summonses against Mynydd Kenfig failures." Five Notices existed in Maesteg. The saga was continued on the 3rd December: 'Cowbridge – several Nuisances: 'Maesteg, Nuisances still existing despite Notices – would like to summons: 'Llanbleddian – Notices to a few. Six Notices already in Llanbleddian and 11 in Maesteg – if not attended to, summons."

A fortnight later the Town Clerk of Cowbridge insisted that, as Cowbridge was a Borough with its own independent authority, the Board of Guardians had no jurisdiction over it. The Clerk was asked to write to the Poor Law Board for their guidance. The same week a letter was received from Dr. H.I. Payne – the newly appointed Medical Officer of Health for Cardiff – informing the Guardians that there had been a Ball in Cowbridge around the middle of November, and that: "Gastric fever in a Typhoid form has visited many of the families that were present: Forty cases in all – some fatal – attributable to offensive drains and privy by the basement of the Ball Room." It has been suggested that the Ball was held at the Bear Inn, but the site was not mentioned in Dr. Payne's letter – it may have been at the Town Hall.

On the day Dr. Payne's letter was considered by the Board, namely the seventeenth of December, the following information was received from Mr Sadler: "Since my last report I have visited Coychurch, Treoes, Llangan, Coity, Llansannor, Penylan and Aberthin. There are many Nuisances in each of them and Notices have been given in all without improvement. What steps should be taken to compel? Summonses obtained against 3 in Maesteg. One removed the Nuisances before the hearing. The other two have two days to go. One has about fifty cartloads of refuse from pigsty and slaughter house to remove. Further Notices are necessary but the Relieving Officers (William John and David Lloyd) refuse to sign. Also Dr. James Lewis. What further steps should be taken?'

[The Poor Law Board pointed out that it was not obligatory for them to sign. Notices could still be served – Chapter 9.]

The decision of the Poor Law Board on the objection from Cowbridge arrived on the 24th. It was straightforward: "Although Cowbridge be a Borough the Guardians are still charged with the duty of superintending and seeing to the execution of the regulations and directions of the Board, and they may direct the Inspector of Nuisances to visit any part within the Borough when they think any necessity will arise. Furthermore the Board will be much obliged for any information on the recent outbreak of Fever."

Two days earlier, on the 22nd, Mr Sadler had been asked to appear before the Town Council of Cowbridge when, in their wisdom, they had appointed him Inspector of Nuisances for the Borough. The position was thus regularised. What had happened to Mr Cox is not stated.

Mr Sadler promptly took advantage of the appointment and presented his report. The Town Clerk agreed to have as many Nuisances removed as possible and to prepare Notices on others. An Engineer was also appointed to survey the town. There were thirty-nine Nuisances – mainly offensive privies. They are summarised as follows: 'Very offensive open gutter – known as Town Ditch – extending from back of Bear Inn to the Old Workhouse and then at side of garden of Thomas Lewis, Horse and Groom Inn, and under premises of John Thomas and John Morgan. Stench horrible in these premises. Twenty-four privies open into gutter. Offensive privy used by occupiers of Town Hall and persons using market also open into it, as well as an offensive pigsty owned by the Reverend M.A. Farrar. Fourteen pigsties open into it near Bear Inn and two at the back – they drain on the surface through the Stock yard. The Malthouse yard has dirty and stagnant pools. There is also an offensive privy, pigsty and dung heap at the side of the sheep market.' "The Town Drain opposite the Bear Inn is offensive. It passes over Church Street where it opens into an open gutter. Several privies empty into it." He recommended "that the Town Ditch be removed and replaced with a barrel drain extending from the Bear Inn to the river. A nearby well could be diverted into it for flushing purposes. The Town Drain should be cleansed and reconstructed."

The reluctance of the Officers of Cowbridge to accept the right of the Guardians to investigate the 'state of affairs' is understandable since one of their duties was to safeguard cleanliness. It was written into the laws and ordinances of the Borough: "Butchers must not throw heades, feate nor noe other garbage in the highe street to the annoyance of neighbours, pigs not allowed within town wall, nor cows milked in street". One wonders what it was like on market day!

On the 8th of January the Guardians were told that Magistrates had ordered three persons in Mynydd Kenfig 'to abate Nuisances and pay expenses.' There was a similar order against two in Maesteg. One of them had to pay 10/0d a day while the Nuisances persisted, and the other was given some latitude because "husband had been injured falling off a horse." He added: "I am being delayed in my progress because some poor people need time to clear pigs, and sometimes ashes are husbanded for potato growing". The £15 owed him for the period 8th October '53 to 8th January '54 was paid and his contract extended. In February further Notices of Nuisances were issued – 7 for Tythegston, 9 for Pyle, 17 for Llangynwyd, 1 for Llandough juxta Cowbridge and 10 for Llanbleddian. They were prepared by the Clerk. A month later a second Notice was sent to John Bennet of Laleston. He was a Gent and had been a Guardian. It stressed: 'This is a Notice for the abatement of an offensive pool opposite the Mackworth Arms Inn which is injurious to people living in the neighbourhood. If it is not forthwith abated proceedings will be taken against you.' The Guardians, certainly, did not pay attention to the importance of individuals and it is also clear that they believed in the Miasmic Theory.

Mynydd Kenfig was still troublesome and there was Fever in the houses. Mr Sadler suggested that proceedings be taken against the local Royal British Bank as owners of the properties, and a Notice to that effect was sent. He was paid a further £15 for the work he had carried out the previous three months.

In September the never-ending faults continued to be described:- MAESTEG: 'Still filthy. Many insist on keeping hogsheads full of pigwash close to doors and dwellings. Those who have refused to remove Nuisances should be prosecuted – names appended. On the Tram-road side leading from the Crown Inn to the Post Office there is a foul and offensive stagnant gutter. It is on the Llynfi Railway property but is caused by houses adjoining the Tram-road. A covered drain will be made'. PONTRADDU: 'Twelve houses filthy though whitewashed. Tondu company will attend to drainage.' ABERKENFIG: 'Several Nuisances removed. There is a gutter running through living room of one house from nearby 3 houses.' COYCHURCH: 'The whole of the premises of Evan Watkins is filthy with drainage to gutter in Turnpike Road. Proceed against.' TREOES: 'Several Nuisances removed. One stagnant pool, 1 offensive privy, and 2 offensive pigsties remaining. Prosecute.' FOUNTAIN: (near Aberkenfig) 'Two houses occupied by Irish Labourers – filthy. In them are 26 lodgers, apart from occupiers, 36 souls in all. Several lodgers removed and houses cleansed.' It was agreed that proceedings would be taken against 3 people in Aberkenfig, 1 in Coychurch, 4 in Treoes, 2 in Fountain and 13 in Maesteg. Sadler was asked to conduct the prosecutions in person.

By October many more Nuisances had been dealt with but there was still resistance by individuals, particularly in Maesteg, though Sadler now saw a glimmer of hope: "The proprietors of the works there have placed a labourer's time and a horse and cart at my disposal." He continued: "I intend to visit every house in Maesteg and cleanse and remove all existing Nuisances on the spot." He was authorised to complain to the Magistrates about 20 persons in Maesteg, 12 in St Athan, 1 in Gileston and 1 in Mynydd Kenfig.

On the 11th of November he reported that he was going to institute proceedings against 18 in Mynydd Kenfig, 6 in Cefn Cribbwr, 3 in Aberkenfig and 6 in Pontraddu. Bridgend was also going to be checked.

He was re-appointed for three months on 9th December and in April '55 stated that progress was satisfactory but that he would continue 'to inspect.' At long last he could relax having performed a Herculean task. He had been born in Chelsea and was only 31 years of age when the Census was taken in 1851.

How do we explain the extent of the filth that he met? Undoubtedly rapid industrialisation accounted for the lack of drainage, poor housing and overcrowding in Maesteg, Mynydd Kenfig (Kenfig Hill), Cefn Cribbwr and Aberkenfig but what of the other parishes and hamlets? It would be myopic and incorrect to postulate the same reason for them. Have we not to remember the ignorance of the age? People were unaware of the dangers of pollution and were almost totally ignorant of the basic principles of hygiene. But did this explain the resistance to change that so many of them showed? Did they not, perhaps, object to the fact that the instructions came from the Guardians, who were responsible for the Workhouse, and who were members of the upper class? Or were they objecting to interference from an English member of the relatively new Police Force? After all, in 1842 three thousand people registered their objection to the Constables because they were ineffective, but in 1847 most of them desired the Force to be increased.

The rearing of pigs close to Housing was a common practice throughout the Union area and enlightened people must have wondered whether another animal, cleaner in its habits, might not sometimes have been kept. The idea was hinted at in a letter that appeared in the Merthyr Guardian on the twenty-fourth of August 1839: "The common goat might be rendered infinitely more useful than it now is. Where is the Welsh cottager too poor to keep an animal which, like the ass, will pick up its food anywhere, and costing nothing to its owner, will yet cheerfully supply him with much nutritious food?" Had the observation been heeded perhaps Mr Sadler's task would have been a little easier.

In March '58 a letter was received from the General Board of Health enclosing copies of a report written by Mr. Ranger, the Superintending Inspector who had been appointed to inquire into the sanitation of Cwmdu. As a result the Cwmdu Local Board of Health was formed the following June. The Reverend Pendril Llewellyn was its first Chairman and Dr. James Lewis one of its twelve members. W. H. Buckland became its elected Chairman.

There were no further developments between then and February 1864 when the Reverend E. P. Nicholl proposed that an Inspector of Nuisances be appointed for all the parishes and hamlets of the Union apart from Cwmdu, Cowbridge, Coity Lower and Newcastle Lower. The proposal was not accepted at the time but it was agreed that the Medical Officers should report on the 'sanitary condition of the parishes in their respective district'. These reports were duly received and it was evident that an Inspector was necessary. John Garsed felt that Laleston, Llangynwyd Lower, Llantwit Major, Newcastle Higher, Pyle, Tythegston Higher and Ynysawdre needed special attention. Mr Sadler was approached and he consented to be their Officer for a year while continuing as Superindentent of Police. His salary was to be £10 per annum 'apportioned among the above parishes at a rate depending on the number of inhabited houses in them at the last Census'. The Bridgend portion of Dr Verity's report was referred to the Local Board of Health.

In April Mr Sadler reported that many houses in Newcastle Higher were filthy and that thirty-one had no privy, but that those in Laleston, Pyle and Tythegston Higher were reasonably satisfactory. Llantwit Major had a few offensive drains.

He commented next in January '65. Smallpox had been diagnosed at the Navy's barracks in Porthcawl and a man nearby: 'Is slaughtering sheep and pigs on the same premises where 58 people - including women and children - reside'. In order to enable him to take immediate measures to cope with the problem he was appointed Inspector of Nuisances for Newton Nottage for three months and paid £1. At the end of that period his total salary was regularised at £12 per annum for which he was to continue checking on the afore-mentioned parishes as well as Newton Nottage. He was re-appointed a year later and in July of that year (1866) became Inspector over the whole Union apart from Bridgend, Cwmdu and Cowbridge. The area was then divided administratively into ten sections with the Guardians in each section forming a committee to send Notices and to summon when necessary much as in 1853. There were already fifteen complaints in Kenfig Hill regarding offensive privies and proceedings were taken against two in Llantwit Major 'for refusing to abate Nuisances'.

Four hundred and fifty Notices had been issued by August but the sixteen they were going to proceed against complied before the hearing. There were still thirty-one without privies in Newcastle Higher – and thirty in Tythegston Higher. In Aberkenfig and Kenfig Hill night utensils continued to be emptied on the road 'where the contents remain till it rains'. The doctors claimed in September that the sanitation was slowly improving. This was the year that the fourth epidemic of Cholera occurred (Chapter 12).

In April '67 Mr Sadler was paid an additional £20 a year 'to be obtained from the appropriate parishes'. There was a suggestion that he be paid £38 instead of the accepted £32 and that this should be apportioned among all the parishes, but this was not approved. In the same month a circular was received from the Medical Department of the Privy Council stating that Sir Thomas Lloyd, Member of Parliament for Cardigan, believed that the Nuisance Removal Act was being imperfectly applied in Wales – particularly with regard to drainage and water supply. He thought that a Permanent Inspector of Nuisances should be appointed by all authorities. The Guardians convened a meeting to consider this suggestion and decided by an overwhelming majority (25:10) not to accept it.

A year later Mr Sadler became Inspector of Nuisances for the whole Union area, but again the appointment was a temporary one. Overcrowding was still present in Tythegston Higher and Newcastle. He was re-appointed for a further year in April 1870 at a reduced salary of £15, and again in March '71. The following August he reported: 'Scarlet Fever has been prevalent at Bridgend and some rural parishes. The Nuisances have abated apart from the enclosed list. The worst places are Aberkenfig and Tythegston Higher though improved. I am requesting an order to enforce Notices if required and I beg to apply for a Nuisance Book. There is an offensive privy near a brook in Aberkenfig, an offensive gutter on the parish road by Penyfai and an offensive water closet and cesspool in Maesteg'. The book was supplied and he was given permission to continue as he saw fit.

The Cowbridge section of the Union had not recently been referred to, but in March 1872 the Rev. Hamer Morgan (St Athan) requested the Guardians to permit the Inspector to investigate conditions in St Athan, Eglwysbrewis, Flemingston and Gileston. A committee was formed specifically for that purpose and the Rev. T. T. Edwards was an ex-officio member of it. Mr Sadler's findings were not discussed by the Board but they re-appointed him in April.

There was now a major development. Mr Doyle, the Poor Law Inspector, informed them that by the Public Health Act recently passed the Board was to be the sole Rural Sanitary Authority for the Union area, and in consequence of this they held their first meeting as a Sanitary Authority on August 3rd 1872. There were eleven members present under the Chairmanship of Mr J. C. Nicholl. and they decided that for the current year responsibility would devolve on twelve Guardians, namely, the Chairman; Rev. Lynch Blosse, Rev. C. R.Knight, Rev. John Evans, Major Turberville, Robert Leyshon, Mr Morley, William Thomas, John Lewis, Mr Preece, David Jenkins and Morgan Williams. Thereafter the activities of the Sanitary Authority remained separate from those of the Board although they had the same Clerk and Medical Officers. When Harmar Cox became Clerk in 1883 he was paid £130 by the Board and £50 by the Sanitary Authority (Chapter 9). The five Poor Law Medical Officers became Medical Officers of Health for their Union district and Mr Robert Leyshon, one-time Vice-Chairman of the Board, the sole Inspector of Nuisances and Surveyor for the Rural Sanitary Authority. Dr Randall was paid £30 per annum for being M.O.H. for Bridgend, Dr David W. Davies £10 for Llanharan, Dr E. T. Davies £30 for Cowbridge, Dr Philip James £30 for the Western district and Dr John Davies £5 for Maesteg. The Authority met fortnightly after receiving the report of the Inspector of Nuisances who attended personally, but the Medical Officers' participation was limited to sending quarterly reports often irregularly.

Bridgend, Cowbridge and Maesteg each had its own Urban Sanitary Authority which was separate from the Rural Sanitary Authority of the Board. In 1887 the Northern division of the Rural district was much curtailed by the formation of the Ogmore and Garw Local Board District, and the Cwmdu Board of Health took in part of Llangynwyd Higher to become the Maesteg Board.

By 1889 Dr W. H. Thomas was M.O.H. for Maesteg and Dr C. B. Mellor for Cowbridge. This was the year that Mr John Spear, in a comprehensive report on the Union's Sanitary Administration, suggested that one full-time Medical Officer of Health might be more effective than the five they then had. He did not question their value as Poor Law doctors.

Chapter 16

'Lunatics'

Lunatic Poor, Vernon House, County Asylum.

The public's attitude toward 'lunatics' was emotive. Institutionalization was favoured by the community and often by family and friends. Those wishing to care for relatives at home were disadvantaged by the absence of statutory help, and the invariable result was their referral to an Asylum, incarceration for life.

An example of such an institution was Bethlem in London. It was functioning in 1786 when an insane female who tried to stab George III was sent there. Thackeray wrote of a visit to a similar London Asylum in 1845 and thought the place appalling. Hydrosudopathy was popular as treatment: it involved sweating the patient in blankets and then dousing with ice-cold water two or three times a day.

There was no Asylum in South Wales, but the Secretary of State had requested a survey in 1837 with the intention of establishing one in the County of Glamorgan and the Bridgend Guardians clearly favoured 'institutionalisation' of the mentally ill. This resulted in hardship to relatives and patients as little thought was given to the 'placement', and no consideration was given to the proximity of relatives or friends. When Mabel Morgan from Penlline was removed to 'Bailbrook House Lunatic Asylum, Bath' in March 1840 no consideration was given to her being a monoglot Welshwoman, or to the arduous journey that would face the relatives if they wished to visit her – provided such visiting was allowed. Other 'lunatics' were often sent further afield.

Those less mentally disturbed were sometimes admitted to the Workhouse. In May 1840 Dr. Pritchard, the Medical Officer, was asked to procure two 'strait-waistcoats for the use of the Establishment'. These were for 'restraining purposes'.

Board members were anxious to avoid too many such admissions and so in December 1843 a sub-committee was set up to inquire into the state of affairs. The Reverend H. L. Blosse was its Chairman and the members were: William Thomas, Edward Thomas, Richard Jenkins, and Morgan P. Smith. It was to study 'the relief list of paupers' in order to ascertain: 'How many lunatics or idiots (not dangerous) are in the various parishes, and to consider the expediency of admitting them to the Union Workhouse'. They concluded that there were '26 lunatics or idiot paupers, most of whom required daily or almost hourly attendance'. Reports were obtained from all the Union Medical Officers and also 'the Medical Officer of another Union that had many insane persons'. They advised against admitting them: "If they are admitted, two separate wards – one male and one female – must be allotted, as well as additional servants as there are few pauper inmates who can be entrusted with their charge - even when not dangerous. Should the House become filled with inmates (some for a time) the subject should be reconsidered. At present it would not be prudent in point of expenditure, or beneficial to the sick, that they be removed from their friends and admitted to the Union Workhouse".

While the committee was sitting fate intervened. Evan Thomas, an inmate, became 'deranged and dangerous. He attempted to burn himself and threatened violence to others'. The son was prepared to look after him at home. In view of this he was discharged and allocated out-door relief of five shillings a week. The District Medical Officer was expected to 'keep an eye' on him. Their report, strengthened by this case, convinced the Board that they had to be careful. Never again did the Guardians knowingly admit a 'lunatic' into the House.

Members of the public were quick to voice their disquiet at what sometimes occurred in the community. In July 1844 William Lewis, a Solicitor in Bridgend, informed the Board that: "A brother and sister, aged 28 years and 26 years, are sleeping together". They were both idiots and 'the brother was violent'. They lived in Llanilid with their mother and step-father. The Guardians applied to a Justice of the Peace for an order for their removal to Bailbrook Lunatic Asylum, Bath. The Commissioners approved. Information was then received from the Asylum that 'the Magistrates there' would be almost certain to discharge them 'on their first visit'. They then applied to Vernon House, Briton Ferry. This was the first time the institution was mentioned. They were both accepted. The following week a letter was received from the Reverend D. Griffiths, Rector of Llanilid, agreeing with their decision: "Because parish support is too expensive".

In December an inmate became 'insane and dangerous'. There was no equivocating this time. He was promptly transferred to the Lunatic Asylum, Briton Ferry.

In March 1845 the first bill from Mr. Robert Valentine Leach, manager of that institution was received. It amounted to £21.3.2 'for the quarter ending Lady Day last':-

David and Elizabeth Hussey (Llanilid) = £10.3.6 (Brother and sister: 12 weeks 5 days at 8/0 per week)

Rachel Williams (St. Bride's Major) = £5.9.10 (12 weeks 6 days at 8/0 per week) (Clothing 7/0)

Margaret Gibbon (St. Bride's Major) = £5.9.10 (ditto)

He stated that the three had improved; one considerably so.

In March 1846 Mr. Leach was referred to as the proprietor of the Briton Ferry Lunatic Asylum. At that time it had three pauper lunatics from the Union and the bill came to £16.9.6, the weekly charge being still 8/0d.

In May 1846 Mr. Leach, now referred to as proprietor and manager of the Asylum, informed them that the charge had been increased to 10/0 per week, and in December '48 the cost was £92.11.0. There were thirteen lunatic inmates from the Bridgend and Cowbridge Union, and the bill covered their cost as well as that of a funeral at £2.12.6.

Discharge of the patients was always difficult because of unsuitable home circumstances and their tardy response to treatment. The usual approach was for the Clerk of the Board to write to Mr. Leach requesting that the patient be discharged if a close relative was prepared to take full responsibility without claiming out-door relief. The giving of money was the main concern. An example of this occurred in March, 1849, when they requested that: "a female pauper be discharged to the care of her brother, who will look after her without charging the Union". Mr Leach replied a week later: "The above pauper has been discharged but she should be visited occasionally because she has terror and fear of her relatives". The Board requested Mr Arnott, the Relieving Officer, to 'check that she is being kindly treated'.

The authorities in the Asylum did not always comply. On the 24th of the same month there was a letter from Dr. Hopkin Pritchard, Medical Officer to the Asylum, stating: "The two lunatics you have mentioned are not on the Visitors' list at present for discharge".

A certificate was issued by a Magistrate before a 'lunatic' pauper could be admitted to an Asylum. Thomas Stockwood, the Clerk to the Magistrates, Bridgend, was paid £1.6.0d in April 1849 'being fees due for the proceedings taken to remove Nuisances, and the certificates supplied for the admission of pauper lunatics to the Asylum at Briton Ferry' (The 'Nuisances' were unconnected and concerned public health – Chapter 15).

The Medical Officers were paid extra for examining 'lunatic paupers' as it did not come within the purview of their official Union work. In September 1849 Dr. Leahy was paid 10/0 for the examination and certification of a 'lunatic' in Llangeinor.

Mr. Leach was granted a further three years' lease on the Asylum in December, and wrote to inform them that the weekly charge was being increased to 12/0. The cost to the Union was now considerable. In June 1850 it amounted to £101.8.0d for the care and treatment of thirteen patients for thirteen weeks at 12/0 per week.

It is not surprising that the Board tried to reduce it. Unfortunately, they sometimes chose the wrong patient for discharge as shown by a letter from Mr. Leach in August, 1850: "The relatives cannot be aware of her mental state. She is suicidal and occasionally very violent (recently viciously attacked the Surgeon). She has paroxysms of acute mania, wanders in the nude and makes indelicate overtures to men. Mr. Nicholl, your Chairman, and our Visitors saw her recently. They all agreed that it would be unwise to discharge her". The Board requested that the Visitors' report be received 'as soon as possible'. A month later another bill came. This was for £98.7.9 (twelve shillings per week for thirteen 'lunatics' for thirteen weeks plus £2.12.6 for a funeral). There were also 'lunatics' in other Asylums as they were not always transferred to the Asylum at Briton Ferry. The same week as the above bill was received there was another from

Hanwell Lunatic Asylum, Middlesex, for £12.2.8. It concerned a patient from Cowbridge and was therefore debited to that parish.

In December '51 Mr. Leach sought an agreement with the Union - charging 10/0 per week and foregoing the £2.2.0 paid for clothing – on the understanding that the patients would remain under his care until the contemplated County Lunatic Asylum was completed and fit for patients. The terms were accepted, but 'a specific period was declined'. The following March, £91.16.0 was due for fifteen 'lunatics' at 10/0 per week for thirteen weeks, and £6.1.4 to Hanwell Asylum.

The fee for examining 'lunatics not in the Workhouse' had hitherto varied from 10/0 to £1.1.0 depending on the circumstances. In no instance had the amount been specified centrally. But in October 1853 the Poor Law Board issued a directive, under the terms of a new Act relating to Lunatic Asylums (Section 66) that henceforth: 'A fee of 2/6 shall be paid to the Medical Officer for each quarterly visit to a lunatic pauper not in the Workhouse'.

The 'lunatic' in Hanwell Asylum died in December and Thomas Barnard Chappell, its Vestry Clerk, was paid £2.18.3. The weekly charge had been 8/9, and the funeral costs, 17/0. They were both less than what would have been charged by Mr. Leach at Vernon House. He was paid £91 the same month for the care of fourteen 'lunatics' (at 10/0 per week). Two of them were from Cowbridge, two from St. Bride's Major, and the others from Llangan, Ystradowen, Pencoed, Coity Lower, Laleston, Merthyr Mawr, Newcastle Lower and Newton Nottage. The remaining two were from the Workhouse and had not been 'settled' in a parish, so the cost of their treatment was paid from the 'common fund' while that of the others was debited to the appropriate parish.

In February 1854 Mr. Leach informed the Board that the charge had gone up to 12/0 per week because 'of the increased cost of maintenance'. The Asylum's Visitors considered it justified and the Swansea Union had accepted. There was no way the Board could disagree.

The number of 'lunatics' seen by the Medical Officers in the community was appreciable. Despite being paid only 2/6 for each examination, Dr. Abraham Verity received £1.5.0 for the quarter ending March 1854. The bill from Mr. Leach in December was £128.15.0 (for seventeen 'lunatics' at 12/0 per week). Prestwick Lunatic Asylum, Lancaster, was more expensive. It cost 14/0 a week to keep a patient there, as shown by a bill of £8.4.0 for the 'care and maintenance of a 'lunatic' from Monknash for eighty two days'. It is not surprising that they transferred her to Vernon House. The Relieving Officer fetched her at a cost of £6 to the parish of Monknash. By then another £3 was due. Compared with this the bills from Mr. Leach of £117 for April and also June for seventeen of the Unions 'lunatics' seemed reasonable. The charge went up to 13/0 a week in October 1857 with the intention that it would remain at that level until the County Asylum was erected.

The Visiting Committee of Vernon House was now reconstituted in order to have a wider base and be more authoritative. The Board was represented by the Reverend H. L. Blosse, William Llewelyn, Richard Franklen and John Cole

Nicholl. The other members were: Admiral Warde, Henry Vivian M.P., Llewelyn Dillwyn M.P., Howell Gwyn, Hopkin LL. Pritchard and John Dillwyn Llewelyn. The Clerk was Thomas Dalton.

The following November the Guardians received a copy of their 'inspection report'. They had been impressed with the 'cleanliness and the ventilation of the wards, the various amusements and comforts that had been organised, the state of the yard and the cheerfulness and general health of the patients'.

However, in January 1858 Isaac Harry, a pauper 'lunatic' referred by the Guardians, committed suicide in tragic circumstances and an inquest was held following which there was an inquiry by the Commissioners in Lunacy. It transpired that 'an attendant, Langabeer, neglected to reckon the knives after dinner and permitted Isaac Harry to absent himself from the ward after dusk. An opportunity was consequently afforded for him to destroy himself'. Mr. Leach was asked by the Guardians to 'give a pledge' that a similar incident would not recur as otherwise their confidence would not be 'secured'. The attendant was sacked and a promise made 'that in future all knives would be collected after each meal and locked in a secure place'. The following August Evan James a 'lunatic' from Pyle 'escaped on the eighth of the month and was not recaptured until the twenty-third'. This did not enhance their opinion of the Asylum.

By April 1859 Dr. C. Pigge had become Medical Superintendent of Vernon House, and on the ninth of that month he wrote to say that John Howell, chargeable to Merthyr Mawr, and Martha Smith, chargeable to Penlline, were being discharged. He had also decided to allow Anne Richards to go home 'on two months' trial'. This was a new and interesting innovation. Mr. Leach was paid a six months account of £316.10.3 in November. £176.7.8, in December and £162.5.11 in May 1860. The quarterly accounts had become fairly stable.

An occasional 'pauper lunatic' was still being cared for in Asylums other than the one in Briton Ferry because in September, 1860, Captain Giles the Treasurer of the Somerset County Lunatic Asylum, was paid £8.6.10 for the care of William Edwards, 'chargeable to Llanharry'.

The Asylums were sometimes registered as 'Licensed Houses', like the one owned by Edward Byas, Bow, Middlesex. The Overseers of the Poor of Saint Margaret and Saint John the Evangelist, who were responsible for it, sent a bill to the Officers of Cowbridge 'for the care of Elizabeth Griffiths – who had been duly adjudged to be from that parish'.

Vernon House had been the home of the M.P. for Glamorgan in the 1780's. Robert Valentine Leach, a businessman from Devizes converted the house into an Asylum for 92 inmates in 1844. He reduced his commitment around 1865 and Dr. Charles Pigge, his son-in-law, took over. The Asylum closed in 1905. The last Visitors' report in 1895 records that there were only four inmates.

The prospect of an Asylum in the Bridgend area was viewed by the Guardians with considerable enthusiasm.

On December 12th 1863 the Board received a copy of the following letter that had been sent by Mr Leach to Griffiths Llewellyn, Baglan Hall, which read: "The County Committee and I agree that they (the Guardians) shall be at liberty to remove all or any portion of the Lunatics belonging to the Unions in this County to the County Asylum by giving me 3 months notice at Christmas or any subsequent day, or if preferred by the County Committee that they shall be at liberty to remove them on giving 1 month's notice at Lady Day 1864 or any subsequent day. If your committee approves will you be so good as to inform me at your convenience". The Board decided that a month's notice on Lady Day would be the most appropriate date for them. Despite this Mr Sadler (Assistant Relieving Officer for Vagrants) was paid £1.7.6 in April '65 for taking a 'wandering lunatic' to Vernon House, but in May they transferred a patient from Middlesex to the County Asylum. She had been there for ten months at a cost of £9. By September a female and two males had been transferred from Briton Ferry. But others remained in Vernon House for the time being, because in October a bill of £32.6.2 was received from Dr Charles Pegge (previously Pigge – the new proprietor) for the maintenance and treatment of eleven patients who had been there since June. Nevertheless, most of the Union's 'lunatics' by now were in the nearby County Asylum. Mr T. G. Smith, Manager of the National Provincial Bank, Bridgend, was its Treasurer. The cost was 12/0 a week. Thirty-two lunatics from the Union were in-patients there in October, and the charge of £206.6.3 was divided between Ystradowen, Llandow, Wick (£31), Llangynwyd, Llanilid, Bettws, St Bride's Minor, Merthyr Mawr, Cowbridge (£48), St Mary's Church and St Bride's Major (£56.10.0d).

Unusual admissions to the County Asylum sometimes occurred as when Thomas Evans, of Penlline, who had been committed to jail in August 1865 for assaulting a local female became insane eight months later and was removed to the Asylum by order of the right Honourable George Grey, Secretary of State, and made chargeable to the Union. They credited it to Penlline.

In April '66 the Board received a copy of a memorial that had been sent by the Sudbury Union to the P.L.B. requesting the House of Commons to consider in greater detail how pauper 'idiots' should be cared for and treated. The Union had thirty-two adult 'lunatics' in the Asylum at the time and six-monthly progress reports were being received. The number was the same in November. The following February a Visiting Committee was formed consisting of Robert Leyshon, Williams Williams and James Clark (Chapter 7) with the purpose of checking on the Union's Asylum in-patients and of reporting to the Board.

The weekly charge was reduced to 11/0 in January 1868 when there were forty-nine of their 'lunatics' in the Asylum – twenty-eight of whom were females. A further reduction to 10/6 a week was introduced in May '69, but the number of their 'lunatic inmates' had increased to fifty-four and the cost over three months was £330.2.6. Relatives paid their share as when David Griffiths in April 1870 subscribed £2.12.0 for the upkeep of his wife. In August the weekly charge was further reduced to 9/6. There were now fifty-five Union inpatients and the cost over three months was £311.6.8.

Continuous efforts were being made to discharge patients. This was controlled by the Court of Visitors which had been established on the 14th of October 1856 by Magistrates in the Quarter Sessions, but it did not prevent the

Board from having its own Visiting Committee. Dr Yellowlees was the Asylum's Medical Superintendent. An example of the difficulties encountered occurred in January '71. A female from Kenfig Hill wished to be discharged, but when she had gone home on an earlier occasion she had relapsed and 'had become immoral' within three months. It was therefore decided that she should remain in the Asylum: "Unless her father is prepared to take charge of her".

In May '72 the weekly charge was reduced to 9/0, but a year later - April '73 – it was returned to 10/0 'because of the increased price of coal and food'. There were 235 men and 222 women in the Asylum at the time, of whom sixteen males and thirty-nine females were chargeable to the Bridgend and Cowbridge Union.

In May '74 the Board's Visiting Committee went to the wards and workshops. They also visited the farm 'with its sixty-nine pigs of the best Berkshire breed' and reported that: "A pig weighing 8 – 10 score is killed every week throughout the year for use of the Asylum". The charge had returned to 10/6 a week and the Union was financially responsible for sixty-three 'lunatic pauper inpatients'.

In February '75 a letter came to the Chairman of the Guardians from the Clerk of the Peace enquiring whether 'idiots' and harmless 'lunatics' could be accommodated in the Workhouse rather than in the Asylum. The reply of the Board was: "We have no proper accommodation for them".

A year later £641 was received from the Paymaster General as reimbursement for the maintenance of their 'lunatics' in the County Asylum. The following month they reviewed their visiting arrangements for both Workhouse (Chapter 8) and Asylum and decided that four groups of three members would visit the latter 'with a change-over every three months'. In the first group would be the Rev John Jones, Evan Lewis and John Lewis; in the second, the Rev F. W. Edmondes, Williams Thomas and D. H. Davies; in the third, the Rev Nicholl, M. Spencer and Hugh Bevan, while the fourth would consist of J. W. Phillips, Illtyd Morgan and Edward Wilde. The cost over six months for the inpatient was £882.19.7d but the weekly charge per person had been reduced to 9/3d.

Overcrowding had become a problem in the Asylum by October and a memorial was received from the Swansea Union requesting an 'urgent increase of pauper lunatic accommodation by extending the present building', but the Board decided that it was 'inexpedient to do so at present'. Discharge of patients remained difficult as evidenced by the fact that the following December the husband of one of the patients refused to have his wife home, and when pressed to do so, disappeared. There was no alternative but to transfer her to the Workhouse. The position became so acute that in March '77 the order was given: "No more female idiots, imbeciles and epileptics to be accepted for the present". The Superintendent tried to ease the situation by drawing up a list of females who, in his opinion, were fit enough to be transferred to the Workhouse, but the Guardians would not co-operate, though they were prepared 'to check their state'. Dr Pringle, the new Medical Superintendent, thought they were going too far. "You have no right" he wrote in June '77 "to check on your patients as Visitors have already been appointed – but in any case prior warning of visits would help". Nevertheless, when the Workhouse trio arrived he welcomed them graciously and took them around. They agreed that the female wards were overcrowded and that the six females he had nominated could be looked after satisfactorily in the Workhouse. A report to this effect was sent to the Board and signed by F. W. Edmondes, Rees Thomas (St Athan) and Edward Wilde (St Donat's). The Board's response was to reiterate: "There is no accommodation in the Workhouse for lunatic patients". Furthermore, they objected to Dr Pringle's criticism and the Clerk informed him that they had 'every right by law to visit the Asylum'.

Dr Pringle informed them in January that he had sent a few patients to Vernon House and that urgent cases could now be accommodated. Soon afterwards the Relieving Officer, William Leyshon, received £2.16.6 for 'certifying and removing Gwenllian Davies to the County Asylum'. But by August '79 the crisis had recurred. The Board had seventy-eight patients in the Asylum and there was gross overcrowding which made them suggest to Dr Pringle that he should again contact Dr Pegge to see whether he could help. This was done with a satisfactory outcome, but in November Dr Pringle brought up another matter: "Patients with money come here taking up beds of paupers. Will you please consider. Are there any from the Bridgend-Cowbridge Union?". They did not think that they had any such persons in their area. By July 1880 seventy-six were chargeable to the Union – sixty-nine of whom were fully mobile – and six had been boarded out to other Asylums. One inpatient was suspected of having money in the Bank!

An interesting letter was received from the Commissioners of Lunacy in April 1882 worded thus: 'A Parliamentary Grant of 4/0 per week has been paid for each Lunatic Pauper in an Asylum since 1874. Do you think that this has crowded Asylums with patients who need not have been admitted there?' (signed by the secretary, Charles Spencer Percival). The reply was that they did not think the grant had caused crowding nor encouraged the admission of patients to the Asylum rather than to the Workhouse. They supported their conclusion with the following figures:-

Year	Lunatics	Imbeciles	Year	Lunatics	Imbeciles
1867	42	6	1874	52	6
1868	43	5	1875	58	6
1869	44	5	1876	59	8
1870	46	4	1877	61	9
1871	56	6	1878	64	8
1872	53	5	1879	62	10
1873	49	6	1880 1881	67 77	10 4

There was a new development in June 1883. The Union's Visiting Committee conveyed the exciting news that: "A contract has just been signed for a new Asylum at Parc Gwyllt, Bridgend." There were twenty-four males and forty-five females in the County Asylum with four 'boarded out' to Vernon House (at 10/6 a week), seven to Carmarthen (at 8/9 per week) and two to Abergavenny (at 9/9 per week). The cost of the 'lunatics' in the County Asylum over six months was £975.17.11, and £755 was received from the Paymaster General for the previous year. The Visiting Committee remarked: "The walls in the Asylum are decorated and this is better than the bare walls of the Workhouse."

Dr Pringle sent the Board's Chairman an unsolicitated letter in October '85 the purpose of which is not clear unless it was to praise his own establishment while simultaneously emphasising the difficulties he had to cope with. Its main points were: "In Abergavenny Mental Hospital the water supply and sewerage are dealt with by gravitation while in Bridgend there are pumps and tanks which necessitate payment to a private company. They have four times the land that we have and it's more fertile – ours is light gravel. Their patients number 800 to our 650 but the staffing is the same. Despite all this our weekly charge is 9/0 while the average for the County Asylums is 9/3. I have been Superintendent for 11 years and when I came the cost was 10/6 a week. The interest of ratepayers is certainly not overlooked!" One can, perhaps, conclude that the Chairman, the Rev F W Edmondes, had been overcritical of the cost when discussing the matter with someone who had informed Dr Pringle!

The L.G.B. wrote in December: "There should be accommodation in the Workhouse for mildly disturbed patients though this is not imperative". The Guardians were adamant: "We have no suitable facilities".

In February 1886 there were sixty-four Union paupers in the Asylum with four in Vernon House, and five each in Carmarthen and Abergavenny Asylums. There was a slight change by August – sixty-seven in the County Asylum and three in Vernon House with the remainder as before.

Certainly the presence of the Asylum simplified the management of the Workhouse but it increased immensely the work of the Guardians.

Modern photograph of Tramp Ward. Lower entrance of Bridgend General Hospital (left).

Photograph taken in 1985 inside the Tramp Ward showing an individual cell. Note the peep-hole which was used to confirm that the tramp had carried out necessary work such as bone crushing in lieu of his keep.

Chapter 17

Removals and Vagrants

A parish's responsibility did not extend to people who were not 'settled' in its area. Settlement was governed by the place of birth. In previous times attempts by parish authorities to restrict the expansion of its dependent population resulted in the undignified and occasionally brutal treatment of the poor. Pregnant females who were 'living away' were 'returned' to their parish of birth before the baby was born, to ensure that the child was 'settled' in the same parish as the mother. As a result pregnancies were hidden and babies abandoned and sometimes destroyed. Strategies were adopted to prevent people moving into a parish by making the person leasing them a house responsible for the cost of their removal should they claim parish relief. They even went so far as to fine a person if he hired a labourer from away for more than a year at a time.

The period of the establishment of the Bridgend–Cowbridge Union heralded a less draconian approach in the attempt to balance the financial constraints of the parish budget with the humanitarian needs of the poor. The Union's responsibility was more tempered in that support was not withheld from a pauper born elsewhere if he had lived independently for over a year in one of the Union's parishes – and could prove that it was so, or had been a servant to a parishioner for five years.

Application for 'removal' would be made to the Justices at the Quarter Sessions by Parish Officers and, if successful, an 'Order for removal' would be issued. It would then be acted upon, often at considerable expense. The fees of lawyers had also to be paid, particularly when the 'receiving' parish objected. Indeed, the legal wranglings that sometimes occurred were a fruitful source of income to solicitors and led to an increasing role of the Clerks in negotiations between Unions (Chapter 8).

Occasionally the 'Order of removal' was suspended as with Mary Griffiths, pauper of St. Bride's Major, who had been sent to that parish under 'a suspended order of removal'. The Parish Officers were permitted to discharge a bill of £3.12.6 'incurred in maintaining her'. The Relieving Officer paid and entered her name in the application book for out-door relief. That was in January 1838. Two years later the Parish Officers of Bettws were asked to apply to the Magistrates for the removal of Mary Griffiths (single) and her 'base child' to her last place of 'legal settlement'. No detail was given but as the name was the same in both instances it could be that they referred to the same pauper.

An 'Order of removal' was overturned in June 1840 when £19.11.8 was paid to William Lewis, solicitor, for successfully appealing against the removal of Mr and Mrs John Lewis from Bedwellty to Pencoed – 'The order was quashed'. Four months later 'the Parish Officers of Colwinston were authorized to appeal against an order for the removal of Thomas Llewelyn from the parish of Llandaff to the said parish of Colwinston'.

In October 1844 Mary Barret, an Irish able-bodied woman and Peter, her son, aged five years, described as being 'in the House and chargeable to Colwinston' were ordered 'to remain in the House while steps were forthwith taken for their removal to Ireland'. Clearly, the Board endeavoured to prevent paupers coming into their parishes, while at the same time taking whatever legitimate steps they could to get non-parishioners who were resident 'removed'.

There were also disputes between parishes within the Union, and paupers were moved back to the parish they had come from before out-door relief was allowed, but the practice was less clear-cut than when separate Unions were concerned. An example was a parishioner from Laleston who had become destitute in the neighbouring parish of Coity Lower. The Guardians wrote to the Commissioners for guidance. Their reply was: 'If the pauper was settled without dispute on the part of the Overseers in the parish of Laleston, his relief may be charged to them: if that is not the case then charge Coity Lower.'

The procedure was not whole-heartedly supported by the Commissioners because in April 1845 they presented a Bill to Parliament 'for the substitution of settlements by the New Union Boundaries rather than the old Parish limits'. This would make life easier for many paupers, and would, presumably, simplify the work of the Board. But, members took the opposite view – and they had reasons for doing so. They maintained that such a Bill would: "Augment hardships because it does not open the labour market wide enough, and will deprive the poor of local interest, and lessen the amount of employment produced. In a district that is partially agricultural and partially industrial and therefore fluctuating, the fixing of the rating for ever on the average of the payments by the parishes over the last seven years would be most unfair, and this Board protests against its adoption". A petition was organized and copies forwarded to Lord Adare, John Nicholl MP, John Henry Vivian MP, the Lord Lieutenant of the County, for presentation to both Houses of Parliament. A long, earnest document was composed, the gist of which was: 'The argument that it would increase the circle of employment of the poor is false. Even if it were slightly increased the disadvantages of the loss of effort by intimates would be far greater'. A fortnight later a letter was received from Lord Adare saying that he had 'presented the petition when the Bill was brought to the Commons by James Graham'. The Marquess of Bute wrote to say that he would support the Board if it came to the House of Lords. What transpired is not clear, but the law was not materially changed.

Many of the 'non-settled poor' were from Ireland and their journey home was expensive, but that did not deter the Board. In February 1849 Margaret Daisy, a widow with two children; 'previously settled in that part of the United Kingdom called England, and who had resided in Cwmdu for less than five years, to be sent back to Bollingcrock, Cork'. 'Also Thomas Williams, his wife and four children, residing in the same parish, to be returned to Ireland'. The order was signed by the Chairman, sealed with the Guardians' seal, and countersigned by the Clerk. The Officers of Cwmdu were 'ordered to take the necessary steps'.

By 1850, the recipients of out-door relief were being divided into 'settled' and 'non-settled' poor. In August of that year David Lloyd, one of the Relieving Officers, paid £37.17.10 to the 'settled' poor and 14/6 to the 'non-settled'. No mention was made of sending them back to their place of 'legal settlement'. Forty-one pounds two shillings was paid to Cardiff for the non-settled poor from the Union, £3.7.6 to Clifton, and £8.15.6 to Swansea. Similar sums were received by the Union to cover the cost of maintaining non-settled poor from elsewhere.

Nevertheless, paupers were still being 'removed'. An example was the husband and wife from St. Athan 'who became chargeable on the ninth of October, and remained so'. The Parish Officers were asked on the nineteenth of the same month to 'take steps to have them removed to their place of legal settlement'.

'Orders of removal' continued to be fought in the courts. In December 1850 the Overseers of Llanelly, 'in the County of Carmarthen', were paid £14.17.0d to 'cover the expenses incurred by the suspension of an order for the removal of a pauper and his wife from the said parish to Llangynwyd Lower'. In July 1851 an Order was given for the removal of two families who had been chargeable for two weeks. One was against a family from Wick (husband, wife and four children, aged ten years, five years, two years and seven weeks) and the other, a husband and wife, from Pyle.

A similar decision was taken in June 1852 with a husband, wife and three children, aged five years, three years and one year from Newton Nottage – who had requested relief a fortnight earlier – and again, a week later, with another pauper from the same parish.

The documentation and frequency of these 'removals' gives the impression that the Guardians were inhuman in their attitude towards these unfortunate paupers. They were certainly persistent, and even energetic, in their pursuit of the law – but were they inhuman? The answer became evident on the sixteenth of April, 1853, when the Reverend John Harding proposed, and R.C. Nicholl Carne seconded: "That this Board highly approves the principle of the Bill introduced into the House of Lords by Lord Berners for the Abolition of the Removal of the poor; and also the need for a more equitable system of assessment". It was unanimously accepted and Nicholl Carne was requested to draw up a supportive petition for presentation to both Houses of Parliament. This he did, but the Board was informed the following week that the Bill had been withdrawn. There was no pleasure in the Guardians' minuted comment:

"No further steps can be taken" and the 'removals' continued in the spirit of conformance to legislation.

In March 1858, the Officers of Laleston were instructed 'to take the necessary steps to remove Miss Ann Jenkins and her two-month old baby to their place of legal settlement'. Several other paupers, such as John Barry of Coity Lower were also 'removed'. (He was returned to Ireland).

In spite of the 'removals', a more humane policy was emerging. For example; when a person moved to a new parish and claimed relief, the immediacy of his return before it could be granted, was gradually being relaxed and there was a growing understanding that the person or persons might stay if the 'settlement parish' was prepared to reimburse the cost of relief. This is reflected in a letter from the Clerk to Swansea Union and dated 1859 enquiring whether they (Bridgend) would provide 'relief' to paupers originating from Bridgend. The answer was: 'Yes, we are quite prepared for you to do so, provided we are allowed to do the same with yours'.

There was a category of 'non-settled paupers' known as 'the irremovable poor'. In February 1861 a circular letter was received from the Clerk of the Bangor and Beaumaris Union enclosing a copy of a memorial they had sent to the Poor Law Board on resolutions that were being considered by a select committee of the House of Commons dealing with this category. They hoped the Guardians would send a similar memorial in support, but members of the Board thought that 'careful consideration' was necessary before such action was taken. The following month they received copies of a similar petition from the Clerk of the Merthyr Tydfil Union. The Guardians there were opposing two Bills – one dealing with the amendment of the law relating to the removal of poor persons to Scotland and Ireland; and the other with Parochial Assessment in England. They were 'praying that the clause reducing the term of irremovability from five years to three years would be deleted'. The Board thought this 'a reasonable request' and, unhesitatingly, 'adopted the petition'. The Clerk wrote to Mr. Talbot, Mr. Bruce, Mr. Dillwyn and Colonel Stuart asking them to 'support its prayer'.

In July 1863 a mother referred to as Ann and her daughter, aged $3\frac{1}{2}$ y from Newcastle Higher were 'removed' to Ireland because they had been 'chargeable' for two weeks. Ten days later another, a Mr John Lewis, was returned to his place of 'settlement'. He had been resident for only ten days.

In April 1868 the Board appointed a Removal Officer by the name of William Powell, but the appointment was rejected by the Poor Law Board (Chapter 14). They did however approve his appointment as Assistant Relieving Officer for Vagrants – referred to later.

The endless stream of 'removals' and associated bureaucratic demands continued as illustrated by the records of 1870 and referring to a Margaret Jones and her child. The Guardians wished to 'remove' her to Llandeilo Fawr but the Union concerned objected and went to appeal. This was lost and arrangements were made to 'remove her at once'. Occasionally the Bridgend and Cowbridge Union had to give way as illustrated in February 1878 when the Swansea Union wanted to 'remove a pauper to Newcastle Higher'. Following advice from the Clerk, the initial objection was withdrawn because: "There is no good case for rejecting her".

Vagrants:

The charities distributed by monks and, after dissolution of the monasteries by aristocrats, excluded a large proportion of the needy. As a result they formed bands and roamed the countryside looking for sustenance. These beggars comprised the unemployed, the unemployable, discharged soldiers, those dismissed from work, and the ever present tramps. Their primary object was to survive. In periods of depression the number and size of these gangs increased and desperation often led to an increase in lawlessness, particularly in isolated communities. Membership of these gangs was viewed by society as proof of criminal intent.

As a result Constables constantly pursued them and, if arrested, they were summarily sentenced to whippings and sojourns in stocks and at one period in history were branded. Houses of Correction, in which they could be trained, were built but these soon became indistinguishable from jails. There was one in Cowbridge until 1829, and near it the stocks. Magistrates passed sentences on them in the local Petty Sessions in accordance with the terms of the various Vagrancy Acts with little distinction made between them and petty criminals. In the eighteenth century Methodist Exhorters, who encouraged religious dissent, were sometimes given similar sentences. Occasionally society adopted the view that some of these Vagrants were 'unfortunates' and were granted 'the right to beg'. They were usually adult men and many were inexperienced Irish immigrants fleeing from famine.

The characteristics of Vagrancy were dire poverty, unemployment and the absence of a fixed abode. The various Enclosure Acts, combined with deforestation, accentuated the difficulties. They had to be distinguished from travellers who moved temporarily to other areas for a specific purpose – such as harvesting in the Vale of Glamorgan.

When the Poor Law Act of 1834 became law it was hoped that the Vagrants as an itinerant group would disappear. Dole money, as 'out-door' relief, would be given to the needy and work would be found for the able-bodied by the Overseers in the parishes. This view proved too optimistic, and the Magistrates, the Constables, the later Police Officers, and the Guardians continued to be troubled by the Vagrants – though their number had markedly diminished.

In December 1836, the Guardians ordered that the usual relief in kind should be given to paupers passing through Cowbridge, and in April 1838, they agreed to reimburse them for the 9 pence they had given as a 'pass' to George Williams. In February '42 the Clerk wrote to the Overseer of Cowbridge pointing out that his parish was the only one in the Union where 'travellers' were systematically 'relieved as a state of urgency'. The Guardians wondered whether he was exercising discretion in doing so because: "Relief of tramps encourages vagrancy and begging. We have paupers to look after and we should be careful how we dip our hands into other people's pockets to relieve strangers and very frequently impostors. We have no objection to you giving away your own money but there is great objection to you giving away that which is a tax on industrious and hard working contributors".

Vagrants, or wayfaring poor as they were sometimes called, found shelter not only in the Cowbridge Workhouse (which had been the House of Correction) but also in the Union Workhouse in Bridgend, where separate wards and a yard were allocated to them.

In January 1844 the Board considered their diet requirements and what work they should perform as payment for their shelter in the Workhouse. It was agreed that their diet should be limited to 1lb. of potatoes and 1 ½ ounces of cheese night and morning, and that the Master should set every adult 'not suffering temperature or permanent disability' the following task of work': "To crush to half an inch 28 pounds of bones or break a quarter yard of stones, provided no such person is detained against his will for more than four hours from breakfast the following morning". It was further stated that: "Such amount of work shall not be required from any person whose age, strength or capacity shall appear not to be suited". Three additional bone crushers and six large stampers were bought for £7.10 in order to ensure a sufficiency of equipment for the purpose. A wall was built to enclose and allow the womens' workroom to be used by Vagrants and Casual poor, and a privy was built therein at a cost of £10.15.0. The Master was to sell the crushed bones at the highest advertised price he could get.

Oakum picking was introduced a few years later (Chapter 10). The task given to Vagrants was the same as that given to the able-bodied paupers admitted to the Workhouse. Women were treated differently. They were not expected to undertake manual labour but they helped in the laundry, cleaned the floors, and performed sundry menial tasks.

In the following month, February '44, a letter was received from the Parish Officers and inhabitants of Cowbridge which delineated a new problem: "There has been a great influx of travelling paupers claiming relief in food and lodging which causes a serious increase in the Poor Rate of this parish – and lodging cannot be obtained under three pence a night. Parishioners get no compensation by putting them to any productive labour. The Corporation have commodious chambers attached to their Town Hall, the use of which they are willing to grant for the lodging of some portion of the Casual poor. The cost of fitting two rooms for such a purpose is estimated at £2.0.0. They request the Board to authorize the Parish Officers to provide what is necessary to convert these chambers into sleeping rooms – and diminish the Overseer's weekly expenditure, while providing suitable accommodation to the generality of the class of paupers who are passing from parish to parish". It was signed by M. Thomas and David Rees (Overseers), Thomas Edmondes (Mayor), John Bevan and Thomas Edmondes (Bailiffs), Mr. Ballard (Justice of the Peace), Morgan Griffiths, Richard Fellen, Edward Davies (Surgeon) and George Morgan; with James Reynolds and Thomas Lewis as Guardians. Cowbridge had had a Corporation since 1681 consisting of a Mayor, 2 Bailiffs, 10 Aldermen and 12 Burgesses which was not abolished until 1886. It had its own seal and a right to own property. It is interesting that paid overnight lodging, presumably in houses, had been granted by the Overseer six years after the Union Workhouse had become available in Bridgend. Needless to say, permission for the desired conversion was granted by the Board and ratified centrally.

The Visiting Committee of the House reported in December 1849: "The Vagrant Ward is disgraceful – filthiness on the floor, beds without blankets, tables covered with litter and ashes from the stove not cleaned out for a long time". There was an average of fifty paupers in the House and it could be that the staff of Master, Matron and her assistant had been unable to cope. This was despite supposed help from female inmates. There was evidently a fault in the internal organization. The Master and Matron felt that they had forfeited the Board's confidence and promptly resigned giving a month's notice. No effort was made to dissuade them (Chapter 10).

Proceedings were taken by the Board against the occasional Vagrant, but as this cost money they were loth to do so unless it was unavoidable. Misconduct, refusal to perform the allotted 'task of work', or persistent Vagrancy were the usual reasons. In December, '58, Thomas Stockwood, Clerk to the Magistrates at Bridgend, was paid 8/6d for one such case.

The treatment of Vagrants within the Workhouse was usually fair and it was very unusual for Vagrants to complain officially about their treatment – and even more unusual for anyone of note to have sufficient interest to refer their complaints to the authorities! There were exceptions however, as illustrated by an instance in January '59. Mr. Sadler, the Police Sergeant at Bridgend who did such stirling work in clearing 'Nuisances', sent three wayfarers, who were 'not professional tramps' along to the Workhouse for food and lodging. They were apparently refused food and taken to an unlit and unheated dirty room where they were supposed to sleep. The night was cold and frosty and not unnaturally they refused to co-operate and returned to the Police Station where they were given food and shelter 'at the expense of charity'. Mr. Sadler visited the House to see for himself the state of affairs and concluded that the accommodation offered was 'not fit for a human'. He told Thomas Stockwood what had happened, and he wrote an official letter to the Board detailing the complaints as outlined.

The Master was interviewed, and, as often happens in such cases, his version of events was entirely different. It appears that the five Vagrants were admitted by Lloyd – the pauper who acted as Porter – and there was no problem with two of them. They all came between 7 and 8 p.m. He took them to the 'Vagrant Ward' where two remained. The other three were dissatisfied and climbed over the wall and left. They returned a short time afterwards accompanied by Mr. Sadler. The two who had remained were in bed by then and had eaten their supper. They told Mr. Sadler that this was so. He listened to what was said and then left taking the three men with him. These had not been refused food – in fact two of the five had eaten their meal without complaint. The reason why the room was cold was that the grate had been moved to the infirm women's ward as requested. Had it been present a fire would have been lit. The Master had not himself seen the Vagrants but he was satisfied that Mr. Lloyd was speaking the truth. The result of the inquiry was sent to Mr Stockwood and it was stressed that the Master and the acting Porter were free from blame. The only action was an 'order' for the grate to be replaced.

In December, Mr. Graves, the Poor Law Board Inspector, reported that one of the Vagrant Wards was 'damp and unsatisfactory'. An attempt was made to improve its ventilation.

There is no information on how many Vagrants were accommodated over the years, but as there were two small wards set aside for their sleeping quarters their number must have been appreciable – though the five admitted on the same night in January '59 were probably exceptional.

Mr Graves, the Inspector, recommended in January '65 that wooden bedsteads and straw be obtained for the 'Vagrant Wards' and in July of the following year suggested that oakum picking would be appropriate as the main task.

The whole approach to the problem of Vagrancy appeared haphazard. This was highlighted in a document from the P.L.B. to the Guardians in November '67 stressing the need for 'uniformity of treatment as accepted by the Wrexham Union'. This was probably the reason why William Powell was appointed Assistant Relieving Officer for Vagrants in March '68 (as referred to in Chapter 14). The general management, nevertheless, remained inadequate. This was illustrated in a complaint from the Clerk of the Neath Union the following May. Apparently a Thomas Jackson had been 'poorly treated for exhaustion' in Pyle. The Rev. John Evans and the Overseer Jenkin John had assisted him to board the train for Neath, where he had been fed and sheltered for the night in the Workhouse. He was then given money to go to Swansea. The Bridgend Guardians thought that 'the treatment had been satisfactory' and emphasized in their reply that Jenkin John was not the Overseer. This last comment was of fundamental importance because it distanced them from any responsibility in the management of Mr Jackson!

A resolution was received from the Merthyr Union in September '69 that 'Police Officers should refuse relief to professional tramps and prosecute them under the Vagrancy Act'. The Guardians of the Bridgend and Cowbridge Union did not support this perspective but suggested to the local Police Force that they should distinguish as much as possible between such people and the 'destitute and deserving Casuals'.

There was a letter from Mr Tolfree, the Chairman of the Cwmdu Local Board of Health, in November '71, stating that there was insufficient accommodation for tramps in Maesteg and that this was causing overcrowding in lodging houses and that they had decided to build a Vagrant Ward. This would serve both sexes and would be located on Mr Talbot's land near the Police Station. The cost would be sixty pounds 'all of which could be recouped in about three years, and the running costs would be no more than ten or twenty pounds a year'. This was perceived as a local matter: the Board expressed no objection.

The Visiting Committee of the Workhouse indicated in January '72 that the tasks of the male Casuals should be more varied, because by the Regulation Act of 1871, Casuals who stayed for one night only should not be expected to do more than three hours' work. They thought that pumping water, flushing toilets, or digging the garden would be suitable, If they stayed more than one night then the hours of work could be extended.

The following month a Vagrant from Maesteg was admitted to the Casual Ward of the Workhouse and was found to have Smallpox (Chapter 12).

William Powell, the Assistant Relieving Officer for Vagrants, Cwmdu, was replaced in February '72 by PC Loyns with permission from the Chief Constable. It was agreed that the Casual Wards needed improving and that the wisest approach was to ask the L.G.B. for advice before embarking on any plan. Consultation was obviously important because a proposal by the Guardians to direct Vagrants to take on the task of toilet flushing had been rejected by the L.G.B. because: "It would allow the Casuals to enter the Workhouse premises" – this was not permissible.

In November '74 Sergeant Sadler became the Assistant Relieving Officer serving the Union area apart from Cowbridge, where Sergeant Henry Chalk was the appointee. The £5 paid to Sergeant Sadler and the £3 to Sergeant Chalk probably reflected the relative demands of their roles.

It was reported in February '75 that there was 'a great increase of Vagrants in Maesteg' and that there was still 'no proper provision for their accommodation in the district'. The Cwmdu Board of Health was asked to consider the matter as soon as possible.

The Guardians were sometimes critical of how Casuals were treated in the community. In May '75 Mr Sadler was asked: "Why is it that a Vagrant with a broken leg found in town on Saturday was taken to the Police Station and kept there until Sunday without seeing a doctor? When admitted to the Workhouse a fracture was diagnosed". The reply was: "He had been drunk, noisy and incapable when seen, and could use his leg then".

In January '77 Richard Sadler resigned and Superintendent Thomas became the Assistant Relieving Officer for Vagrants. The following month the Chief Constable instructed Police Officers to refuse tickets for a night's lodgings in the Workhouse to all professional tramps. He did this without consulting the Guardians and it left the Relieving Officers in a quandary, because they did not know what action to take should they be approached for advice and help by this sub-group of Vagrants. The L.G.B. informed them that assistance had to be given and shelter provided if such a person was destitute (Chapter 14).

Sergeant Henry Chalk left Cowbridge in March and was replaced by Sergeant Jennings who accepted the post of District Relieving Officer for Vagrants at £2 a year – which was soon increased to £4.

In December '79 a copy of a memorial sent by the Bristol Union to the Local Government Board was received. Its main premise was the adoption of Police Officers as Assistant Relieving Officers and for them to help 'legitimate Vagrants' by issuing 'work tickets'. It is no surprise that the Guardians supported the suggestion: they already had Police Officers as Assistant Relieving Officers and these were doing their utmost to recognize 'deserving Casuals'.

Sergeant Loyns left Maesteg in November 1880 and a letter of gratitude was sent him. He was replaced as Assistant Relieving Officer by Inspector Jennings from Cowbridge who had moved to the District; and Sergeant Martin filled the post in Cowbridge.

It was observed in November '81 that the total number of Vagrants in the Union was diminishing but the same accommodation was being maintained for them in the Workhouse. In 1885 it was recorded that there were two wards containing eight beds for males and six for females but unfortunately the occupancy rate was not mentioned. They left before the midday meal – if fit to travel – and so it is not surprising that none was mentioned in the Censuses of 1841 to 1891 (inclusive).

Although the management of Vagrancy was a side issue to the Guardians – as was the removal of non-settled paupers – both had an important part to play in the smooth running of the Union's affairs, because the law of the land had to be obeyed, and it was strict.

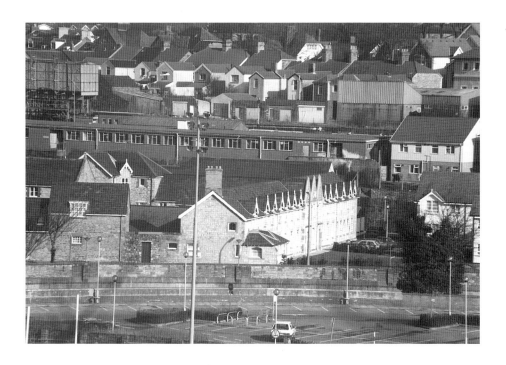

The finely refurbished Workhouses today.